The investor's guide to
UNITED STATES COINS

---

*Everything you need to know
about the No. 1 emerging
growth area for the '90s!*

Now! For the first time ever—
*the complete price history
of U.S. Type Coins!*
Your guide to spectacular
profits in the coming years.

By
Neil S. Berman
with
Hans M. F. Schulman

Published by
The Coin & Currency Institute, Inc.

Library of Congress Catalog Card Number: 86–072133
ISBN 0–87184–400–1
Printed in the United States of America

This edition published by The Coin & Currency Institute, Inc., by arrangement with Neil S. Berman, Inc., 250 West 57 Street, New York, New York 10107.

CONTRIBUTORS

Charles Anastasio
Silvano DiGenova
Martin E. Haber

Thomas Noe
Stephen York Rappaport
Joseph A. Saccento

ACKNOWLEDGEMENTS

The writer of this book would like to express his sincere appreciation to Marc Kristal for his tireless, unending efforts which greatly contributed to the writing and editing of this book, and to Arthur S. Goldenberg for his writing, research, and editing, without which this book could not have been written.

The following people also assisted: Edward Albert, writing and research; Vicki Rosen, endless typing and editing; Joseph A. Saccento, editing; James Simek, coin photography; Michael Wayne, cover photography; Richard Bagg; Paul V. Battaglia; Michael Dady; Charles DeStefano; Richard Doty; Leslie Elam; Arthur Friedberg; Beth Goff; Rita Hirsh; Robert Koppelman; Dennis Loring; William Mele; Linda Melton; Paul Nugget; Earl Stout; Anthony Terranova; the late Herb Melnick.

To Susan Ann Kerner, to whom all things seem possible.

CONTENTS

LIST OF CHARTS

"Once you have eliminated the impossible, whatever remains, however improbable, must be the truth."

—Sherlock Holmes

INTRODUCTION

This is a book about investing in rare, top-quality, gold, silver and copper United States coins. We would like to think it is the only book you will ever need on the subject. By the time you have finished, you will know what makes coins a good investment, how to buy and sell them, where they fit into your overall investment portfolio, and much, much more. You will be able to plunge into the market confidently, and with success.

The question you are probably asking right now is: Why coins? If you are like most people, you are more familiar with stocks, bonds, bullion, real estate, and a host of other common and popular investment options. Chances are you have never thought about putting your money into coins. Why, then, should you read this book? What is the point of learning what you need to know about an asset you might never have even heard of?

The answer is simple: Rare coins are one of the best investments to be found anywhere in the world today! They have consistently outperformed virtually all other, better-known assets, including all those mentioned above. They remain one of the best means of diversification within a complete investment portfolio. And they are a superb defense against all kinds of economic uncertainty.

The fact is, all rare coins have been lacking is someone to spread the word. The absence of hard information remains the single most important reason why many Financial Planners—and investors—exclude rare coins from otherwise well-rounded portfolios. This circumstance is virtually unique among major investments. Stocks, bonds, bullion, etc., have never lacked for spokesmen. Countless experts have devoted millions of pages to them, in books, magazines and newsletters. And there have been hundreds of books written to guide the lay person—as well as the professional—through the ins and outs of financial planning and investment strategy. Yet an informed, complete guide to rare coin investment has never materialized. While for years the stock market has issued tables that track the price movements up and down on each of the stocks on the Exchange, there has been no similar way to compare the long-term relative performance of one coin versus another.

Until now.

For with the publication of this book, we present, for the first time ever, the investment record of every type of coin issued by the United States mint. With this guide, every investor will now be able to look over the complete menu of coin issues, study their past performances, and, according to his tastes and available funds, acquire a portfolio of rare coins that should appreciate competitively with other types of investments in the years to come.

The timing of the book's publication is fortunate, as the rare coin market is now positioned for yet another period of unprecedented gains and record profits; indeed, the boom is already underway. Now more than ever, with all the exceptional investment opportunities rare coins offer for the future, investors, financial planners and other professionals need all the information they can get.

That is where this book comes in.

What will you find in these pages? In the chapters that follow, we are going to show you how to invest in rare coins. We will demonstrate why the rare coins you purchase not only belong in a well-rounded investment portfolio, but why they actually may be the most dependable portion of that portfolio.

You will see how, through good times and bad, U.S. coins have outperformed all other forms of investment and how their future was never as bright as it is today. Since we do not want you just to take our word for it, the first chapter presents the outcome of a recent Salomon Brothers survey, which looks at the compounded rates of return of 14 common and popular financial and tangible assets and investments for the past year, as well as their performance records over longer periods.

The results? The Salomon report for 1985 revealed that, viewed across a ten-year period, rare coins ranked first among investments, with an annual gain of 20.4%; and, across a 15-year span, second only to oil, at 17.7%. You will see, moreover, that, had Salomon Brothers based their research strictly upon investment-grade coins, instead of mixing ordinary and rare, circulated and uncirculated specimens, the average gain for the preceding decade would have surpassed, not just 20 percent, but fully 40 percent per annum compounded—independent proof of the strength and solidity of top-quality rare coins. Proof that coins are your best hedge against inflation and your best chance for growth of capital.

Building upon the Salomon Brothers data, Chapter Two presents the complete universe of choice-quality U.S. type coins, and their investment records over a period of 30 years, from 1955 through 1985. Every type coin issued by the U.S. from 1793 to date is listed, illustrated and annotated with dates issued, metal content, size, weight, designer's name, investment comments and price appreciation record in 30-, 20-, and 10-year intervals.

You will discover that the extraordinary value of choice uncirculated rare coins as an investment vehicle can be matched by few other assets. The top ten performance leaders all show gains ranging from 10,000% to 15,000%

for the 30-year period, with an original investment of $1,000 in 1955 growing to over one million dollars in 1985. For the 20-year period, the top ten performance leaders showed gains ranging from 2,075% to 4,611%. For the ten-year period, the top ten showed gains ranging from 226% to 759%. The gains for numerous other coins, you will see, are almost as impressive— and suggest that, though prices have risen enormously across three decades, the best is yet to come.

At the outset, let us make it clear that rare coins bear little relation to bullion coins, such as the Maple Leaf, Krugerrand or Mexican 50 Pesos, except perhaps that they are all round. In 1985, while the price of gold and silver bullion went south, prices for many rare coins advanced 25 to 50 percent. In addition, there is a dire shortage of top quality coins in today's hot market, which will only serve to drive prices even higher.

But nothing exists in a vacuum, and you can't hide a good thing forever. So, the smart money at some pension funds and large institutions has been quietly moving into rare coins. These sophisticated professionals, faced with falling interest rates, and seeking to diversify into a proven investment area with solid long-term gains, have taken positions in rare coins, which has helped to fuel the hefty price gains in the rare coin market.

In Chapter Two, you will see how every type of United States coin has performed over the past 30 years. Based on these results, you will be able to select the coin or coins that will satisfy your investment goals. And you will not have to lose sleep over how they will do in the short term because all coins should be purchased and put away for the long haul.

The job of selecting the coin or coins for your initial investment does not have to be an imposing one. In fact, it can be quite simple. The reason for this is that the coins are known as "type" coins, or the most common date coins of every type issued. Rather than being *rare* coins, these type coins have one thing in common: they are the most frequently found coins of their type, and have been selected only on the basis of their condition rather than their rarity. All of the coins listed are *choice uncirculated,* the highest grade coins available. No expert numismatic knowledge is required to select any of them so long as they are in pristine condition. One can almost select them by throwing darts at a random list of coins.

And what kind of results can you expect from these nondescript specimens? Herewith are a few examples:

—A $1,000 investment in Peace Type U.S. silver dollars in MS-65 condition in 1955 would be worth $230,000 if sold today!

—If you had bought $1,000 worth of ordinary Barber dimes 30 years ago and the coins were in choice uncirculated condition, you would have seen your investment grow to $616,666 today!

—If you happened to pick *any* date of MS-65 Liberty Seated half dollars minted between 1866 to 1891, which were easy to obtain in 1955, your $1,000 grubstake would be worth a grand $1,020,000 this year!

—And, if your preference runs to rare gold coins, and you bought $1,000 worth of MS-65 Type II Gold Dollars, your 1955 investment would have grown to a glorious $1,300,000 today!

Results like these will surprise even sophisticated coin investors who have been led to believe that only the high-priced coin rarities make the best investments.

In the third chapter, we will look into some of the things that make rare coins such a solid and profitable investment: supply, demand and quality; historical significance; their status as collectibles; bullion content; low cost and easy management; and high liquidity. Chapter Three also reviews the five major advantages of rare coin investment, including:

—Investments in rare coins are blessed with favorable tax treatment from the government, since they are tax-deferred: No taxes are paid until they are sold, and then they are taxed at the current low capital gains rate.

—They are extremely liquid. Thousands of coin dealers, private collectors and auction houses throughout the world trade in coins on a daily basis.

—There are no government registration requirements for rare coins as there are for the purchase and sale of bullion coins, as well as for stocks, bonds and other forms of regulated investments. Rare coin purchasers are thus assured of anonymity of ownership.

—There is a rapidly increasing demand for rare coins coupled with an ever-decreasing supply, two elements which almost guarantee the future price appreciation of rare coins over the long term.

—Coins are easily transportable and can be stored inexpensively and safely in a safe deposit box.

Add them all up and you can begin to see the many advantages inherent in rare coin ownership.

Chapter Three also provides an analysis of market cycles and delves at length into the single most important aspect of rare coin investment—*quality.* For those who can not resist the allure of precious metals, Chapter Three also includes a look at the pros and cons of bullion investment, as it relates to coins.

Chapter Four shows how to go about the actual process of investment. Here you will find the ten commandments of rare coin investment:

1. buy the best quality you can afford
2. diversify
3. buy coins that you can sell
4. seek professional help
5. make your purchases from a reputable dealer
6. do not overpay
7. become as knowledgeable as you can about your investments
8. take delivery of your merchandise
9. carefully store and insure your portfolio
10. buy and hold.

Chapter Four will also fill you in on the tax laws pertaining to rare coins, and it concludes with some of the means and methods of buying and selling rare coins, among them limited partnerships, coin shows and auctions.

Chapter Five goes into detail about the grading of coins, how it is done, how it evolved, and how it affects value.

In Chapter Six, we will look at some basic investment strategies, based on your financial position, and we will include a number of sample coin portfolios, and examine the role of the financial planner and the numismatist in constructing a sound investment program.

Next, after devoting all these pages to coins as an investment, Chapter Seven presents a concise history of coins and coinage, from primitive times to the present.

You will discover something else as well—something vitally important to you as an investor. While coins have traditionally done well primarily during periods of inflation, they now post strong gains no matter the economic picture. This is unprecedented; but there is a reason. As you will see in the next Chapter, signs of impending disaster are all around us. Bank failures are running rampant; the budget deficit is out of control; and, despite government forecasts to the contrary, the truth is, nobody really knows where the economy is headed.

In Chapter Eight, we will look at the economic waters in which *all* your investments will have to sink or swim, including such possible future market conditions as a devalued dollar, higher interest rates, and a crushing inflation. This way, you will be able to position, not just your rare coins, but your entire investment portfolio within a realistic, reasonably accurate context.

Are we forecasting the end of the world? No, but at times like these, investors need something on which they can depend; an investment that has almost always improved, or held its own; an asset with a strong, solid, realistic market, and ever-increasing opportunities for growth.

That is why, at this point in time, as in the past, nothing can stop rare, top-quality, gold and silver United States coins: *they are the only investment that fills the bill.*

But, as we said, you do not have to take our word for it. Before getting into the ABCs of rare coin investment, let us look at the *facts* . . .

Pre-Colonial Standard of Exchange

"PILLAR DOLLAR" OR 8 REALES, 1732–1772

One of the world's most famous coins, the Spanish Milled Dollar, the legendary "piece of eight," was one of the main coins of the American colonists and was the forerunner of our own silver dollars.

It was called a Pillar Dollar because of the twin pillars of Hercules that appear on the obverse. The coins were minted in Bolivia, Chile, Colombia, Guatemala, Mexico and Peru. The expression, piece of eight, stems from the practice of splitting the coin into pieces or "bits" as a way of making change; hence the derivation of "two bits" for a quarter dollar.

Readers of "Treasure Island" will remember Captain Flint's parrot shouting, "Pieces of eight, pieces of eight."

8 ESCUDOS GOLD, 1716
Lima Mint, COB Type

In the early 18th century, there was a considerable flow of gold and silver from Central and South America to Spain, and gold pieces like the Cob type 8 Escudos shown here were of the type buccaneers plundered from European-bound galleons on the high seas.

The name, cob, derives from the fact that to make the coins, gold bullion bars were cut into planchets—CABO (Cob) DE BARRA means cut from a bar. The two vertical columns represent the pillars of Hercules. On the reverse is a large cross of Jerusalem, with the crowned arms of Spain, the lion and castle of Aragon and Castile.

Chapter One
SALOMON BROTHERS' STUDY

No investment, viewed across the long haul, has performed as well, or as consistently, as American rare coins. No other financial asset commonly found in a diversified portfolio has returned as much, or has so successfully resisted the assaults of economic fluctuation. Nor are we required to rely on our own statistics to bear this out. Too often, champions of many types of investments are forced to present selectively edited figures and information to back up their claims. This is not so for the numismatist. Almost all independent analysts, looking at whatever facts and figures they choose, come to the same conclusion:

Rare coins have outperformed virtually all other more available and better known investment options.

We offer as proof a recent Salomon Brothers survey of financial assets, presented here in chart form. The survey looks at the compounded rates of return of 14 common and popular financial and tangible investments for a given year, as well as performance records over longer periods, in this case 10 and 15 years. The consumer price index is also included, as a representative gauge of inflation.

Why is the Salomon Brothers report important? First and foremost, the annual study represents a fair analysis of the track records of most significant financial and tangible assets, and thus offers a consistently reliable market overview. The study acts as a broad measure of market shifts, enabling an investor to determine the true value of a financial asset, rather than having to rely upon limited information from possibly biased sources. Moreover, the research of Salomon Brothers, one of the world's largest and most respected investment banking houses (and *NOT* a dealer in coins), carries a good deal of weight. Their research is studied and taken seriously by savvy, successful investors worldwide.

The Salomon Brothers report for the year 1985 revealed the following:

CHART 1   SALOMON BROTHERS' REPORT, 1985

AMERICA'S MOST PROFITABLE INVESTMENTS

Compounded Annual Rates of Return
(for the period ending June 1, 1985)

	15 Years	Rank	10 Years	Rank	5 Years	Rank	1 Year	Rank
Oil (a)	19.7%	1	8.0%	9	(5.4)%	12	(4.5)%	10
U.S. Coins	17.7	2	20.4	1	0.1	9	11.5	4
Gold Bullion	15.5	3	6.9	13	(11.0)	14	(20.3)	14
Chinese								
Ceramics (b)	14.3	4	17.1	2	1.0	8	5.9	6
Stamps	14.1	5	14.5	3	0.1	10	(9.6)	11
Diamonds	10.4	6	9.5	7	1.2	7	0.0	9
Old Masters (b)	9.1	7	10.7	4	1.5	6	13.6	3
Treasury Bills	9.1	8	10.0	6	12.0	3	9.5	5
Bonds	8.7	9	9.3	8	13.2	2	42.9	1
Silver Bullion	8.7	10	3.5	14	(15.9)	15	(34.3)	15
Stocks	8.5	11	10.4	5	15.2	1	28.7	2
U.S. Farmland	8.5	12	6.9	12	(1.7)	11	(10.0)	12
Housing	8.2	13	7.9	10	4.3	5	2.5	8
CPI	7.1	14	7.3	11	5.7	4	3.7	7
Foreign Exchange	2.0	15	(0.6)	15	(7.9)	13	(11.3)	13

Inflation Scorecard (Number of Assets That Outperformed Inflation)

Tangibles	10 out of 10	7 out of 10	0 out of 10	3 out of 10
^Collectibles	4 out of 4	4 out of 4	0 out of 4	3 out of 4
^Commodities	4 out of 4	2 out of 4	0 out of 4	0 out of 4
^Real Estate	2 out of 2	1 out of 2	0 out of 2	0 out of 2
Financials	3 out of 4	3 out of 4	3 out of 4	3 out of 4

(a) Reflects revision in oil index.
(b) Source: Sotheby's.
Chart Source: Salomon Brothers

The findings? Viewed across a ten-year period, U.S. coins ranked first among investments, at an annual gain of 20.4 percent; while gold was ranked 13th and stocks fifth. Across a 15-year span, coins ranked second only to oil, at 17.7 percent. Owing to a softening of the coin market since 1980— one which, at present, is seeing a dramatic reversal—coins did not post the same sort of impressive gains in 1985; yet they continued to finish high, and ranked fourth overall.

U.S. coins continue to outpace inflation and nearly all other tangible properties according to the survey. The 1985 survey prepared by the investment

CHART 2 SALOMON BROTHERS' REPORT, 1970–1985

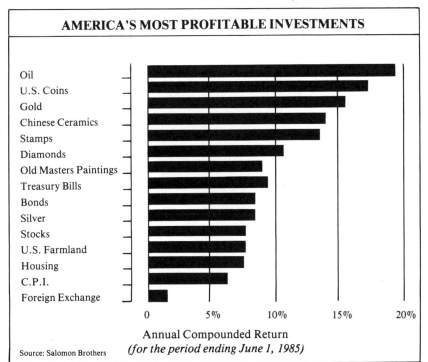

AMERICA'S MOST PROFITABLE INVESTMENTS

Oil
U.S. Coins
Gold
Chinese Ceramics
Stamps
Diamonds
Old Masters Paintings
Treasury Bills
Bonds
Silver
Stocks
U.S. Farmland
Housing
C.P.I.
Foreign Exchange

0   5%   10%   15%   20%

Annual Compounded Return
(for the period ending June 1, 1985)

Source: Salomon Brothers

banking house discloses that coins had an average return of 11.5 percent, substantially in excess of the 3.7 percent change in the consumer price index. The CPI is a common measure of the effects of inflation.

While coins have not always finished in first place, a close examination of the figures reveals that they have maintained a far greater consistency of return than the majority of other investments, whether tangible or financial, and did not demonstrate even remotely the instability that gripped other high performers.

Oil, the top gainer across a 15-year period, falls to ninth place in the ten-year overview. Bonds, number one for 1985, posted a dismal loss of −7.2 percent the previous year (not shown in the charts), placing them second to last. In 1983 (not shown), the study proclaimed silver the best investment; this year, it declined to last, reflecting the extraordinary instability of its market.

U.S. coins, however, have generally finished near the top, more than justifying their reputation for solid and consistent gains. While all other assets and investments were fluctuating, or even losing value, U.S. coins were keeping strong and gaining—always gaining.

CHART 3   SALOMON BROTHERS' REPORT, 1975–1985

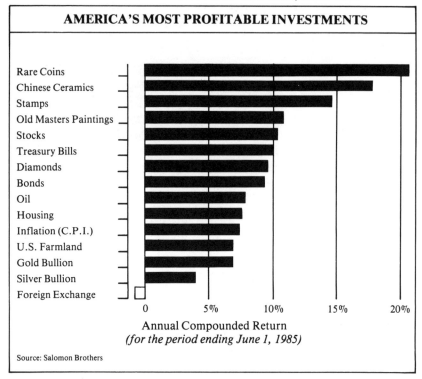

AMERICA'S MOST PROFITABLE INVESTMENTS

Rare Coins
Chinese Ceramics
Stamps
Old Masters Paintings
Stocks
Treasury Bills
Diamonds
Bonds
Oil
Housing
Inflation (C.P.I.)
U.S. Farmland
Gold Bullion
Silver Bullion
Foreign Exchange

0   5%   10%   15%   20%

Annual Compounded Return
(for the period ending June 1, 1985)

Source: Salomon Brothers

For the second year running, an inflation scorecard has been presented to show how financial as well as tangible assets fared in the war against depreciation of the dollar's purchasing power. Over the past 15 years, all collectibles, commodities and real estate surveyed outperformed inflation. Salomon's study makes one interesting conclusion about the nature of the collectibles' changes and the value of coins as an investment: Coin purchases (as well as other collectibles) are not as interest-sensitive as stocks and bonds are because of a conclusion that "purchases are rarely, if ever, financed with debt." While this ignores the pioneer efforts in lending money with numismatic collateral, it is generally true. This is not the case with the stock market, which is highly leveraged.

What is most exciting about the performance record of U.S. coins is not revealed by the chart: they could have done *even better* than the figures suggest. The Salomon study, to remain fair and unbiased in its measure of an asset's performance, must look at the overall picture presented by a given market. Stocks, bonds, precious metals and the like offer the examiner published figures upon which to base conclusions. This is not strictly possible in the case of U.S. coins, as many transactions remain anonymous, and there

CHART 4   SALOMON BROTHERS' REPORT, 1984–1985

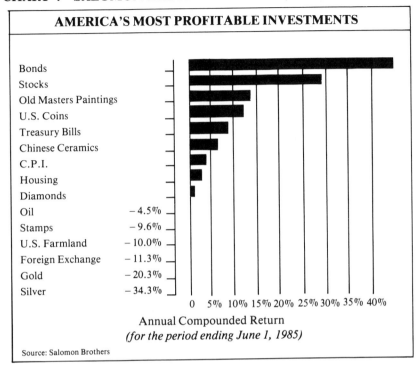

AMERICA'S MOST PROFITABLE INVESTMENTS

Bonds
Stocks
Old Masters Paintings
U.S. Coins
Treasury Bills
Chinese Ceramics
C.P.I.
Housing
Diamonds
Oil — 4.5%
Stamps — 9.6%
U.S. Farmland — 10.0%
Foreign Exchange — 11.3%
Gold — 20.3%
Silver — 34.3%

0   5% 10% 15% 20% 25% 30% 35% 40%

Annual Compounded Return
(for the period ending June 1, 1985)

Source: Salomon Brothers

is no widely accepted industry average. Thus, a specific portfolio cannot be assumed to represent the entire market. So, to cover all possible areas, Salomon Brothers uses a selection of 20 coins (compiled at Salomon Brothers' request by Stack's, a leading coin auction house), representing a number of different grades and levels of rarity.

COINS COMPRISING SALOMON BROTHERS' COIN INDEX

1795	Draped Bust Dollar—Brilliant Uncirculated
1881	Trade Dollar—Brilliant Uncirculated
1862	Liberty Seated Half Dime—Brilliant Uncirculated
1807	Draped Bust Dime—Brilliant Uncirculated
1866	Liberty Seated Dime—Brilliant Uncirculated
1876	Twenty Cents—Brilliant Uncirculated
1873	Arrows Quarter Dollar—Brilliant Uncirculated
1886	Liberty Seated Quarter Dollar—Brilliant Uncirculated
1847	Liberty Seated Dollar—Brilliant Uncirculated
1884-S	Morgan Dollar—Brilliant Uncirculated
1928	Hawaiian Half Dollar—Brilliant Uncirculated
1862	Three Cent Silver—Brilliant Uncirculated
1916	Liberty Standing Quarter—Brilliant Uncirculated
1815	Bust Half Dollar—Uncirculated

1834	Bust Half Dollar—Brilliant Uncirculated
1855-O	Liberty Seated Half Dollar—Brilliant Uncirculated
1921	Liberty Walking Half Dollar—Brilliant Uncirculated
1866	With Rays Shield Nickel—Brilliant Proof
1794	Liberty Capped Right Half Cent—Extremely Fine
1873	Two Cents—Brilliant Proof

No attempt has been made by Stack's to compile a portfolio of high-quality *type* coins, the sort a serious investor would unquestionably demand. Most numismatists, however, recommend only the best quality type coins when making *investment* purchases. Had Salomon Brothers based their research on investment-grade, common-date type coins, instead of mixing rare and common, circulated and uncirculated coins, the average gain for the preceding decade would have surpassed, not merely 20 percent, but fully *40 percent* per annum compounded. The advantages of quality *type* coins as opposed to rare date coins is explained in detail in the *"Quality"* section of Chapter Three.

The fact is that the U.S. coin market is uniquely able to withstand the ordinary problems that plague most investments. Silver, gold, diamonds, and other hard assets fall victim to high interest rates, and their markets are too often subject to manipulation; collectibles other than coins remain tied almost exclusively to inflation; and stocks, bonds and other financial investments, owing to unforeseeable political and economic forces, are endlessly unstable. Only U.S. coins—their increasingly finite supply in greater and greater demand—consistently show a reassuring steadiness.

This is not to say that we do not like other investments. We do. But we stress the importance of diversification to the success of all investment portfolios; and point out that, like every other investment, rare coins are not the ultimate investment. Nevertheless, a comparison of the real rates of return of rare coins versus other popular forms of investment indicates that coins have not just outperformed their competitors, but left them standing at the gate.

Let us consider gold and silver bullion. Both have done quite well by investors in the past, and will no doubt continue to do so. Apart from its traditional, and proven, value as a defense against war, revolution, economic collapse, and/or anarchy, gold is a good means of speculation, and can yield substantial profits if purchased at the proper moment during an inflationary cycle.

Silver, you may be surprised to learn, sees much of its price controlled or dictated by the industrial sector, which accounts almost entirely for its use. It does well during inflationary cycles, and poorly during recessions. We'll go more into detail about gold and silver shortly in another chapter.

One thousand (inflation adjusted) dollars, invested in choice quality U.S. type coins at the very beginning of 1970, would have yielded $25,933 in 1984. The same sum invested for the same time period in gold returned $3,911, while silver paid $1,689.

CHART 5

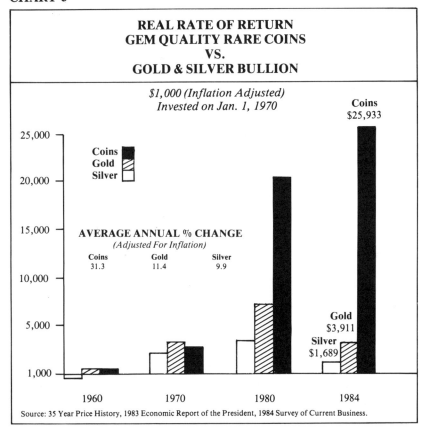

REAL RATE OF RETURN
GEM QUALITY RARE COINS
VS.
GOLD & SILVER BULLION

$1,000 (Inflation Adjusted)
Invested on Jan. 1, 1970

Coins
$25,933

Coins ■
Gold ▨
Silver □

AVERAGE ANNUAL % CHANGE
(Adjusted For Inflation)

Coins	Gold	Silver
31.3	11.4	9.9

Gold
$3,911

Silver
$1,689

25,000
20,000
15,000
10,000
5,000
1,000

1960   1970   1980   1984

Source: 35 Year Price History, 1983 Economic Report of the President, 1984 Survey of Current Business.

What about stocks and bonds? Also excellent investments. At present, the stock market seems firmly entrenched in a bullish trend, with records shattering, and new highs being reached regularly. Bonds offer not one but two means of return: guaranteed interest and, purchased at the top of an inflationary cycle, solid capital gains if sold when rates fall.

Sophisticated investors have made money with bonds, and gotten rich in the stock market. But, if they also diversified their portfolios with a five to 15 percent investment in rare coins, chances are they did a whole lot better.

Between 1950 and 1959, the average real rate of return on choice quality U.S. coins came to 10.9 percent, just behind stocks, at 11.9 percent, and well ahead of bonds, at 1.3 percent. Things changed dramatically in the following decade: between 1960 and 1969, coins went up at an average yearly rate of 12.7 percent, with stocks lagging badly at 1.5 percent, beaten even by bonds, at 2.7 percent.

In the decade that followed, between 1970 and 1979, U.S. coins skyrocketed, averaging 39.3 percent per year. Stocks, however, posted a loss of −6.8

CHART 6

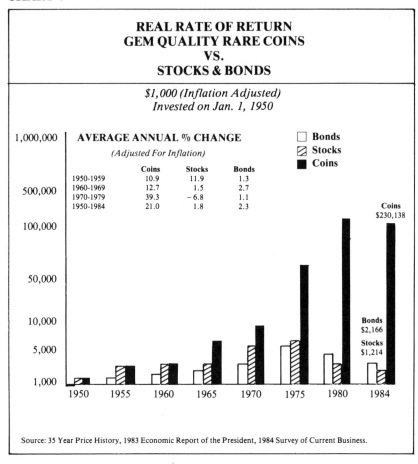

REAL RATE OF RETURN
GEM QUALITY RARE COINS
VS.
STOCKS & BONDS

$1,000 (Inflation Adjusted)
Invested on Jan. 1, 1950

AVERAGE ANNUAL % CHANGE

(Adjusted For Inflation)

	Coins	Stocks	Bonds
1950-1959	10.9	11.9	1.3
1960-1969	12.7	1.5	2.7
1970-1979	39.3	-6.8	1.1
1950-1984	21.0	1.8	2.3

☐ Bonds
▨ Stocks
■ Coins

Coins
$230,138

Bonds
$2,166

Stocks
$1,214

Source: 35 Year Price History, 1983 Economic Report of the President, 1984 Survey of Current Business.

percent, surpassed again by bonds' minuscule gain of 1.1 percent. Stocks and bonds? Nobody can say that there is not money to be made there. But, if you had invested only $1,000 in choice quality U.S. coins back in 1950, you could have sold them in 1984 for $230,138.

And how about Treasury-bills? They are popular these days. But the fact is, when the real rate of return is taken into account, three-month T-bills lost money, on the average every year in two out of the last three decades. Moreover, between 1950 and 1984, they posted a whopping average yearly gain (adjusted for inflation, of course) of 1.1 percent!

If you invested $1,000 in T-bills in 1950, you would have had a profit of $321 to celebrate New Year's with at the start of 1985.

If only you'd bought coins instead.

CHART 7

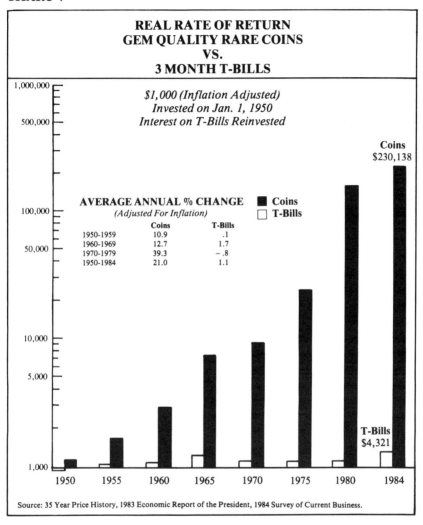

REAL RATE OF RETURN
GEM QUALITY RARE COINS
VS.
3 MONTH T-BILLS

$1,000 (Inflation Adjusted)
Invested on Jan. 1, 1950
Interest on T-Bills Reinvested

Coins
$230,138

AVERAGE ANNUAL % CHANGE ■ Coins
(Adjusted For Inflation) □ T-Bills

	Coins	T-Bills
1950-1959	10.9	.1
1960-1969	12.7	1.7
1970-1979	39.3	– .8
1950-1984	21.0	1.1

T-Bills
$4,321

Source: 35 Year Price History, 1983 Economic Report of the President, 1984 Survey of Current Business.

The Consumer Price Index (CPI) is a measure of the average change in prices over time in a fixed market basket of goods and services. The CPI is based on prices of food, clothing, shelter, and fuels, transportation fares, charges for doctors' and dentists' services, drugs, and the other goods and services that people buy for day-to-day living.

If you compare coins against the CPI, you will note that they outperformed the CPI index by 283 percent from 1950 to 1984. No other inflation-sensitive investment came even close. And in today's market, where there is no inflation, they continue to perform well. It is this outstanding performance in periods of both high and low inflation that adds to the appeal of coins as a diversification play in a well-rounded investment portfolio.

CHART 8

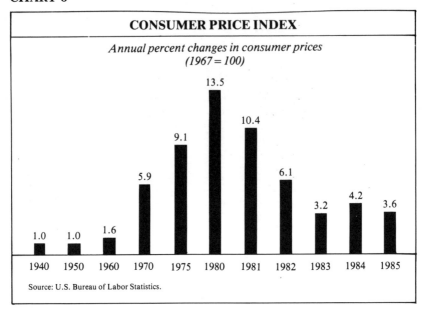

CONSUMER PRICE INDEX

Annual percent changes in consumer prices
(1967 = 100)

Source: U.S. Bureau of Labor Statistics.

CHART 9

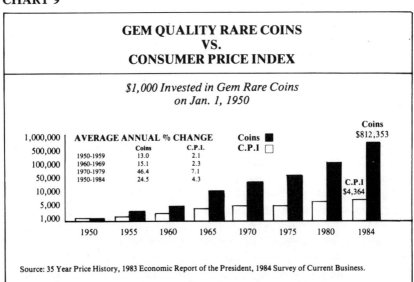

GEM QUALITY RARE COINS
VS.
CONSUMER PRICE INDEX

$1,000 Invested in Gem Rare Coins
on Jan. 1, 1950

AVERAGE ANNUAL % CHANGE		
	Coins	C.P.I.
1950-1959	13.0	2.1
1960-1969	15.1	2.3
1970-1979	46.4	7.1
1950-1984	24.5	4.3

Coins ■
C.P.I □

Coins
$812,353

C.P.I
$4,364

Source: 35 Year Price History, 1983 Economic Report of the President, 1984 Survey of Current Business.

The evidence is plain, and unmistakable. When it comes to performance—consistent, dependable, genuine capital gains—rare coins beat all other alternatives. They are the unquestioned best diversification for your portfolio. In the next chapter, you will find a complete price history of U.S. type coins—one that, in cold, hard, indisputable facts, reveals that no investment currently available has done as well, or earned as much money for those in the investment market.

Historic U.S. Coins

CONTINENTAL DOLLAR, 1776

With the advent of the American Revolution, the Continental Congress proposed coining a Continental Dollar. Coins were struck in pewter, brass and silver as patterns (coins meant only to test the proposed design and not meant for circulation). The obverse shows the rays of the sun striking a sundial, with a legend reading: "Continental Currency 1776; Fugio; Mind Your Business." On the reverse is the legend, "American Congress, We Are One," surrounded by an endless chain of 13 links, each inscribed with the name of one of the original colonies. The chain motif was used again later on the first U.S. Large Cent. Surviving specimens of the Continental Dollar are extremely rare.

FUGIO CENT, 1787

The Fugio Cent was the country's first federally sanctioned coin and the first coin to bear the name, United States. Similar in design to the Continental Dollar of 1776, it was also known as the Franklin Cent, as the motto: "Mind Your Business," as well as the chain design of 13 links, are believed to have been created by Benjamin Franklin. The word "Fugio" means "time flies." Most of the copper for the Fugio Cents came from the copper bands which held together the kegs of gunpowder sent to America by the French during the Revolutionary War.

Chapter Two
COMPLETE PRICE HISTORY
OF U.S. TYPE COINS

In this chapter, we will unveil the complete universe of choice quality United States type coins and their investment record over a period of 30 years, from 1955 to the present. *Every* type coin issued by the United States mint from 1793 to date is listed, illustrated, and annotated with dates issued, metal content, size, weight, designer's name, investment comments and price appreciation record in 30-, 20-, and 10-year intervals.

More than 250 coins are listed by type, and each represents the lowest priced, most common-date coin in its series. This is the first time ever that an historical investment record for all U.S. type coins has been presented in such a comprehensive, easy-to-follow format. For reasons that will shortly become apparent, type collecting, as opposed to date collecting, has proven the most popular method of investing in choice quality rare coins in the 1980s.

What is the difference between date and type collecting? Date collectors try to acquire every date and mintmark combination issued for every coin design within a given series. For example, to assemble a complete date set of Buffalo nickels would require a total of 68 coins. A collector putting together a type set, on the other hand, would require only two Buffalo nickels: one Type I (1913) and one Type II (any date between 1913 through 1938). A type collector is concerned with a multitude of designs which he wants to complete with a representative example of each. To build a complete "set" of type coins, he would go on to acquire one Barber dime, one Seated Liberty quarter, one Franklin half dollar, one Morgan dollar, etc., until he obtained one example of every type (or kind) of coin issued by the United States from the beginning to the present.

Note: All prices listed in this chapter are for coins in Choice Uncirculated condition, the highest quality coins, except where noted. Starting in 1975, they were graded by the numerical standard, Mint State-65; prior to that, they were not. Where Proof coins are priced, they are for choice Proof type coins likewise graded by the numerical standard Proof-65 starting in 1975. Grading is explained in detail in Chapter Five.

In date collecting, the emphasis is on rarity; in type collecting, the emphasis is on condition. Since only one representative coin of each design is needed, irrespective of date or mintmark, type collectors seek out the most common or semi-common dates in the series. Fortunately, these common coins also are the least expensive coins in the type. While in date collecting, the emphasis is, generally, on acquiring all the dates and mint mark combinations in the series, in type collecting the emphasis is on the *quality* of a single coin, since rarity is only an incidental consideration. However, there are date collectors who want only gem coins, and there are type collectors who want only circulated coins.

As quality (or condition) is everything, the specimens now on the rise in the current investment market are those available in the very best condition. Therefore, rare coins in poor condition are not as desirable. This accounts for the change in the kinds of coins on the performance lists. On the 30-year list of best performing type coins, *rarity* performed best; but on the 10-year list, *quality* was king.

How well have choice quality type coins performed? The charts that follow represent the highlights of the study and show the top ten performing type coins for the past 30-, 20-, and 10-year periods. They show how the tastes of collectors and investors have changed over the decades and they reveal insights into the new investment strategies that are fueling the new bull market.

The charts show the present value of $1,000 invested in each type coin over the past three decades.

30-YEAR PERFORMANCE RECORD

The best type coin performers over the 30-year period from 1955 to 1985, in order of their investment performance, are:

Rank	Type Coin	1985 VALUE (of $1,000 invested in 1955)
1	Capped Bust Dimes, Small Size, 1828–37	$1,580,000
2	Gold Dollars, Type II, 1854–56	1,300,000
3	Liberty Seated Quarters, No Motto, 1840–53, 1856–65	1,275,000
4	Capped Bust Half Dollars, Lettered Edge, 1807–36	1,272,727
5	Liberty Seated Half Dimes, Drapery, 1840–53, 1856–59	1,200,000
6	Capped Bust Half Dimes, 1829–37	1,188,888
7	Liberty Seated Half Dollars, Drapery, 1839–53, 1856–66	1,120,000
8	Liberty Seated Quarters, Arrows, 1854–55	1,080,000
9	Liberty Seated Dimes, Drapery, 1840–53, 1856–60	1,037,500
10	Liberty Seated Half Dollars, With Motto, 1866–73, 1875–91	1,020,000

20-YEAR PERFORMANCE RECORD

The best type coin performers over the 20-year
period from 1965 to 1985, in order of
their investment performance, are:

Rank	Type Coin	1985 VALUE (of $1,000 invested in 1965)
1	Liberty Seated Quarters, With Motto, 1866–73, 1875–91	$461,111
2	Capped Bust Half Dollars, Lettered Edge, 1807–36	388,888
3	Liberty Seated Quarters, Drapery, 1840–53, 1856–65	318,750
4	Liberty Seated Half Dollars, Drapery, 1839–53, 1856–66	280,000
5	Liberty Seated Dimes, Legend Obverse, 1860–73, 1875–91	278,947
6	Liberty Seated Half Dollars, With Motto, 1866–73, 1875–91	268,421
7	Liberty Seated Half Dimes, Drapery, 1840–53, 1856–59	257,142
8	Liberty Seated Dollars, With Motto, 1866–73	242,857
9	Trade Dollars, 1873–83	224,000
10	Liberty Seated Dimes, Drapery, 1840–53, 1856–60	207,500

10-YEAR PERFORMANCE RECORD

The best type coin performers over the 10-year
period from 1975 to 1985, in order of
their investment performances, are:

Rank	Type Coin	1985 VALUE (of $1,000 invested in 1975)
1	Peace Dollars, Low Relief, 1922–35	$75,925
2	Morgan Dollars, 1878–1921	69,565
3	Coronet (Liberty) Half Eagles, With Motto, 1866–1908	41,481
4	Peace Dollars, High Relief, 1921	31,924
5	Mercury Dimes, 1916–45	29,818
6	Liberty Nickels, With Cents, 1883–1913	27,727
7	Indian Quarter Eagles, 1908–29	25,666
8	Liberty Walking Half Dollars, 1916–47	24,166
9	Three Cent Silver, Type I, 1851–53	23,103
10	Barber Dimes, 1892–1916	22,666

The charts show that the value of choice uncirculated coins as an investment vehicle can be matched by few other assets.

The top ten performance leaders all showed gains ranging from 10,000% to 15,000% for the 30-year period. An original investment of $1,000 in 1955 grew to over one million dollars by 1985. That's an *average* appreciation of from 333% to 500% *a year.*

For the 20-year period, the top ten performance leaders showed gains ranging from 2,075% to 4,611%. An original investment of $1,000 grew to between $207,500 and $461,111 by 1985, an average *yearly* increase of 103% to 194%.

For the latest ten-year period, the top ten performance leaders showed gains of from 226% to 759%. An original investment of $1,000 grew to between $22,666 and $75,925, an average *yearly* increase of 22.6% to 75.9%.

The Prices

The prices listed in the *Price History of U.S. Type Coins* come from two sources: the venerable *Guide Book of United States Coins* by R. S. Yeoman (the *Redbook*) for 1955, 1965 and some 1975 prices, and the weekly *Coin Dealer Newsletter* (CDN) for 1975 and 1985 prices. The newer *CDN* was used for 1975 and beyond because it is a weekly publication, with valuations that are more up to date than those in the *Redbook,* and with prices based on MS-65 and PR-65 grades.

The 1975 and 1985 prices from the *Coin Dealer Newsletter* are from the issues of June 6, 1975; June 7, 1985, and the June 1985 Monthly Summary. The prices listed are retail prices, except for the price appreciation records showing the present value of $1,000 invested in 1955, 1965 and 1975. For that figure, we used the 1985 "bid" price, which represents the approximate amount which an investor would receive if he sold his coins to a dealer. For unusual or rare types for which there is no *Redbook* or *CDN* price, we have used auction records for the period in question. It should be noted that the *Redbook* and *CDN* prices are merely guides as to what the coins were valued at at the time, since, as with all trading markets, coin prices fluctuated above and below these figures on a daily basis.

The *Redbook* prices for 1955 and 1965 are for coins in uncirculated condition, the highest condition listed in the book at that time. The system of grading coins by Mint State numbers had not yet been universally accepted. What we know today as MS-65 or better coins were called BU, or Brilliant Uncirculated, in 1955 and 1965, and they sold at only a small premium over regular uncirculated pieces. At that time, most people collected coins by date, and while condition was important, it had not yet evolved into the science it is today. Coins as a major investment vehicle was an idea whose time had not yet come.

So, 1955's low price base led to the spectacular gains that came later on when investors took command of the hobby and opened their purse strings to obtain the finest specimens available.

By 1975, coin investment had become big business. Prices had risen significantly from 1955 levels, Mint State grading represented the industry standard and the quest for quality knew no limits. Consequently, the gains for the ten-year period, from 1975 to 1985, were not as spectacular as the 30- and 20-year increases. But in their own right, they are still very impressive when compared to any other form of investing. Few other investments, if any, can match the 10-year record of the top ten performing type coins, which produced average *annual* increases of up to 75%.

The charts also reflect the changing tastes of collectors and investors. From 1955 and 1965 to date, the largest increases were recorded by the classic rare coins that collectors have always favored—the Capped Bust dimes and quarters of the early 1800's and the Liberty Seated half dimes, dimes and quarters of the mid-1800's.

But from 1975 on, when it became legal to own gold bullion coins in the United States; when inflation reared its ugly head and investments in stocks, bonds, diamonds and real estate, as well as coins, zoomed in value, investors switched to more modern coin issues.

In the ten-year period from 1975 to 1985, when Mint State grading numbers became the standard of every coin collector and investor; when the silver value of the metal in dimes, quarters and halves surpassed their numismatic value, collectors switched their investment modes to that of obtaining the finest quality specimens available. Quality, i.e., condition, became all important; a coin's rarity was secondary.

Since most of the historic early coins were not readily available in any quantity or in the highest conditions demanded by investors, and since modern coins exist in greater abundance and are available in the highest Mint State conditions, it is not surprising that the investment leaders for the past ten years have been Peace dollars, Morgan dollars, Mercury dimes, Liberty nickels, Quarter Eagle gold pieces and Liberty Walking half dollars.

Not a single leader from the 30- and 20-year groups appears on the 10-year leadership list. This provides a dramatic picture of the complete change in investment direction and the importance in today's market of coin quality, i.e., the all-consuming desire of investors to obtain examples of coins as close to perfection as possible.

Surprisingly, gold coins and commemorative coins, both glamorous areas of the coin market, did relatively poorly as a group in relation to other coin series. Some rarities, like the proof Gobrecht dollars of 1838–1839, show very disappointing results. One thousand dollars invested in 1955 would be worth only $58,333 in 1985. Contrast this with $1,000 invested in common bronze Indian cents, which would be worth $304,000 today.

Another rarity that was disappointing is the Stella, or Four Dollar gold piece of 1879–1880. A $1,000 investment in 1955 would be worth only $69,230 today. And for the last ten years, a $1,000 investment in the coin grew to only $1,333; hardly a stella performance!

Is there a collector who would not want to own a magnificent Panama-Pacific Exposition 50 dollar gold piece? Probably not, and yet, this fabled coin, one of the most expensive U.S. coins, was one of the worst performers. A $1,000 investment in 1955 would be worth only $45,555 today.

And what collector back in 1975 would have guessed that a common type Peace dollar would outperform a 1921 Peace high-relief specimen? After all, the 1921 sold for $106.50 ten years ago, while the common type was only a mere $5.40. Yet, from 1975 to 1985, a $1,000 investment in a 1921 Peace high-relief dollar grew to $31,924, while the same investment in a 1922–1935 Peace common type dollar more than doubled that amount, swelling to an astounding $75,925!

Conclusions

The figures dramatically show the advantages of investing in coins for the long term. Thirty-year investments did far, far better than 20-year commitments, and 20-year investments did better than 10-year ones.

High priced coins are not always the best investment vehicles, as lower-priced coins often have more room to grow; if it is part of a neglected coin series, a lower-priced coin may have spectacular upside potential. Being more affordable, and also more available, there is a bigger market for lower-priced coins; and the increasing demand for a finite supply invariably drives prices up.

Expensive coins may have less liquidity. There tend to be fewer buyers for them. In troubled economic times, when money is tight, it may require more effort to find a buyer for a rare, expensive piece. Then, too, owners of rarities must often go the auction route to dispose of their coins. Auctions are held periodically, but a ready seller often must wait months to find a buyer. Contrast this with the market that exists for coins of average price, which are traded daily through a nationwide network of coin dealers. Although expensive rarities may require more effort to dispose of, they are always in demand and tend to retain their value.

When studying the *Price History of U.S. Type Coins* that follows, one should bear in mind that the prices shown are for the lowest-priced coins of each type in choice uncirculated condition. There are many other coins in each series, and all would command higher prices, according to date and rarity. But for common type coins, the bottom line, as you will see, remains the same: a staggering record of spectacular performances.

TYPE COINS INCLUDED IN THE PRICE HISTORY OF U.S. TYPE COINS

HALF CENTS

Flowing Hair, 1793
Liberty Cap, 1794
Liberty Cap, 1795–97
Draped Bust, 1800–08
Classic Head, 1809–35
Braided Hair, 1840–57

LARGE CENTS

Chain Reverse, 1793
Wreath Reverse, 1793
Liberty Cap, 1793
Liberty Cap, 1794–96
Draped Bust, 1796–1807
Classic Head, 1808–14
Coronet, 1816–39
Coronet, Braided Hair, 1840–57

SMALL CENTS

Flying Eagle, 1856–58
Indian, Copper-Nickel, 1859
Indian, Copper-Nickel, 1860–64
Indian, Bronze, 1864–1909
Lincoln, VDB on Reverse, 1909
Lincoln, VDB on Obverse, 1909–58
Lincoln, Steel, 1943
Lincoln, Memorial Reverse, 1959 to date

TWO-CENT PIECES

Two Cents, 1864–73

THREE-CENT PIECES

Three Cents, Silver, Type I, 1851–53
Three Cents, Silver, Type II, 1854–58
Three Cents, Silver, Type III, 1859–73
Three Cents, Nickel, 1865–89

FIVE-CENT PIECES

Shield, Rays, 1866–67
Shield, No Rays, 1867–83
Liberty, No "Cents," 1883
Liberty, With "Cents," 1883–1913
Buffalo, Type I, 1913
Buffalo, Type II, 1913–38
Jefferson, 1938–42, 1946 to date
Jefferson, Silver, 1942–45

HALF DIMES

Flowing Hair, 1794–95
Draped Bust, Small Eagle, 1796–97
Draped Bust, Large Eagle, 1800–05
Capped Bust, 1829–37
Liberty Seated, No Stars, 1837–38
Liberty Seated, No Drapery, 1838–40
Liberty Seated, Drapery, 1840–53, 1856–59
Liberty Seated, Arrows, 1853–55
Liberty Seated, Legend Obverse, 1860–73

DIMES

Draped Bust, Small Eagle, 1796–97
Draped Bust, Large Eagle, 1798–1807
Capped Bust, Large Size, 1809–28
Capped Bust, Small Size, 1828–37
Liberty Seated, No Stars, 1837–38
Liberty Seated, No Drapery, 1838–40
Liberty Seated, Drapery, 1840–53, 1856–60
Liberty Seated, Arrows, 1853–55
Liberty Seated, Legend Obverse, 1860–73, 1875–91
Liberty Seated, Arrows, 1873–74
Barber, 1892–1916
Mercury, 1916–45
Roosevelt, Silver, 1946–64
Roosevelt, Copper-Nickel, 1965 to date

TWENTY-CENT PIECES

Twenty Cents, 1875–78

QUARTER DOLLARS

Draped Bust, Small Eagle, 1796
Draped Bust, Large Eagle, 1804–07
Capped Bust, Large Size, 1815–28
Capped Bust, Reduced Size, 1831–38
Liberty Seated, No Drapery, 1838–40
Liberty Seated, Drapery, 1840–53, 1856–65
Liberty Seated, Arrows & Rays, 1853
Liberty Seated, Arrows, 1854–55
Liberty Seated, With Motto, 1866–73, 1875–91

Liberty Seated, Arrows, 1873–74
Barber, 1892–1916
Standing Liberty, Type I, 1916–17
Standing Liberty, Type II, 1917–30
Washington, Silver, 1932–64
Washington, Copper-Nickel Clad, 1965 to date
Washington, Silver Clad, 1976
Washington, Copper-Nickel, 1976

HALF DOLLARS

Flowing Hair, 1794–95
Draped Bust, Small Eagle, 1796–97
Draped Bust, Large Eagle, 1801–07
Capped Bust, Lettered Edge, 1807–36
Capped Bust, "50 Cents" on Reverse,
  1836–37
Capped Bust, "Half Dol." on Reverse,
  1838–39
Liberty Seated, No Drapery, 1839
Liberty Seated, Drapery, 1839–53, 1856–66
Liberty Seated, Arrows & Rays, 1853
Liberty Seated, Arrows, 1854–55
Liberty Seated, With Motto, 1866–73,
  1875–91
Liberty Seated, Arrows, 1873–74
Barber, 1892–1915
Liberty Walking, 1916–47
Franklin, 1948–63
Kennedy, Silver, 1964
Kennedy, Silver Clad, 1965–70
Kennedy, Copper-Nickel Clad, 1971 to date
Kennedy, Silver Clad, 1976
Kennedy, Copper-Nickel, 1976

SILVER DOLLARS

Flowing Hair, 1794–95
Draped Bust, Small Eagle, 1795–98
Draped Bust, Large Eagle, 1798–1804
Gobrecht, No Stars on Obverse, 1836
Gobrecht, Stars on Obverse, 1838–39
Liberty Seated, No Motto, 1840–65
Liberty Seated, With Motto, 1866–73
Morgan, 1878–1921
Peace, High Relief, 1921
Peace, Low Relief, 1922–35
Trade, 1873–83
Eisenhower, Silver Clad, 1971–78
Eisenhower, Copper Nickel, 1971–78
Eisenhower, Silver Clad, 1976
Eisenhower, Copper Nickel, 1976
Susan B. Anthony, 1979–81

GOLD DOLLARS

Liberty, Type I, 1849–54
Indian, Type II, 1854–56
Liberty, Type III, 1856–89

QUARTER EAGLES

Capped Bust, No Stars, 1796
Capped Bust, Stars, 1796–1807
Capped Bust Left, 1808
Capped Head, 1821–27
Capped Head, Reduced Size, 1829–34
Classic Head, 1834–39
Coronet, Large Arrows, 1840–59
Coronet, Small Arrows, 1860–1907
Indian, 1908–29

THREE DOLLAR GOLD PIECES

Three Dollars, 1854
Three Dollars, 1855–89

FOUR DOLLAR GOLD PIECES (STELLAS)

Flowing Hair, 1879–80
Coiled Hair, 1879–80

HALF EAGLES ($5 GOLD)

Capped Bust, Small Eagle, 1795–98
Capped Bust, Large Eagle, 1797–1807
Capped and Draped Bust, 1807–12
Capped Head, Large Diameter, 1813–29
Capped Head, Small Diameter, 1829–34
Classic Head, 1834–38
Coronet, No Motto, Small Letters, 1839
Coronet, No Motto, Large Letters, 1839–66
Coronet, With Motto, 1866–1908
Indian, 1908–29

EAGLES ($10 GOLD)

Capped Bust, Small Eagle, 1795–97
Capped Bust, Large Eagle, 1797–1804
Coronet, No Motto, Small Letters, 1838–39
Coronet, No Motto, Large Letters, 1839–66
Coronet, With Motto, 1866–1907
Indian, No Motto, 1907–08
Indian, With Motto, 1908–33

DOUBLE EAGLES ($20 GOLD)

Coronet, Type I, No Motto, 1849–66
Coronet, Type II, "Twenty D." on Reverse,
  1866–76

Coronet, Type III, "Twenty Dollars" on
Reverse, 1877–1907
St. Gaudens, High Relief, 1907
St. Gaudens, No Motto, 1907–08
St. Gaudens, With Motto, 1908–32

COMMEMORATIVE QUARTERS AND DOLLARS

Isabella Quarter Dollar, 1893
Lafayette Dollar, 1900
Los Angeles Olympics Dollar, 1983
Los Angeles Olympics Dollar, 1984
Statue of Liberty Dollar, 1986

COMMEMORATIVE HALF DOLLARS

Alabama, 1921
Albany, 1936
Antietam, 1937
Arkansas, 1935–39
Bay Bridge, 1936
Daniel Boone, 1934–38
Bridgeport, Connecticut, 1936
California Jubilee, 1925
Cincinnati, 1936
Cleveland, 1936
Columbia, South Carolina, 1936
Columbian Exposition, 1892–93
Connecticut, 1935
Delaware, 1936
Elgin, Illinois, 1936
Gettysburg, 1936
Grant Memorial, 1922
Hawaii, 1928
Hudson, New York, 1935
Huguenot-Walloon, 1924
Immigrant, 1986
Iowa, 1946
Lexington-Concord, 1925
Lincoln-Illinois, 1918
Long Island, 1936
Lynchburg, Virginia, 1936

Maine, 1920
Maryland, 1934
Missouri, 1921
Monroe Doctrine, 1923
New Rochelle, New York, 1938
Norfolk, Virginia, 1936
Oregon Trail, 1926–39
Panama-Pacific, 1915
Pilgrim, 1920–21
Rhode Island, 1936
Roanoke Island, North Carolina, 1937
Robinson-Arkansas, 1936
San Diego, 1935–36
Sesquicentennial of American Independence,
1926
Old Spanish Trail, 1935
Stone Mountain, 1925
Texas, 1934–38
Fort Vancouver, 1925
Vermont, 1927
Booker T. Washington, 1946–51
Washington-Carver, 1951–54
George Washington, 1982
Wisconsin, 1936
York County, Maine, 1936

COMMEMORATIVE GOLD COINS

Grant Memorial Gold Dollar, 1922
Lewis and Clark Gold Dollar, 1904–05
Louisiana Purchase Gold Dollar (Jefferson),
1903
Louisiana Purchase Gold Dollar (McKinley),
1903
McKinley Memorial Gold Dollar, 1916–17
Panama-Pacific Gold Dollar, 1915
Panama-Pacific Quarter Eagle, 1915
Philadelphia Sesquicentennial Quarter Eagle,
1926
Statue of Liberty Half Eagle, 1986
Los Angeles Olympics Ten Dollars Gold, 1984
Panama-Pacific 50 Dollars Gold, Round, 1915
Panama-Pacific 50 Dollars Gold, Octagonal,
1915

Note: In the section that follows, in the cases of some of the earlier dated coins and the few that are rare, such as the Type II Gold Dollars, we have used values that are theoretical to show the price appreciation of a $1,000 investment over a 30-year period. There just weren't enough of these coins extant in 1955 to accumulate $1,000 worth of them at one time. However, the projected value is based on the actual value of the coin at the time. For example, in the case of Type II Gold Dollars, even at the low $15 price of 1955, you would have had to acquire 67 coins to make a $1,000 investment and that would not have been likely even at that low price. That's why they are called "rare coins."

Coinage of the States

Before the establishment of the U.S. Mint, the Articles of Confederation granted the individual states the right to issue their own coins. During the period 1785–88, four states produced coins: Vermont, Connecticut and New Jersey issued copper cents; Massachusetts issued both cents and half-cents. As large quantities of the state issues were minted, they are readily available today and can be put together to form an interesting collection of early American coins. Two examples of the coinage are shown below.

1787 CONNECTICUT COPPER

The laureated bust on the obverse gives the Connecticut coppers a late-Roman Empire appearance. The figure of Liberty appears on the reverse. Most of the 1787 and 1788 coppers were crudely struck.

1787 NEW JERSEY COPPER

A horse's head, a plow and the legend, "Nova Caesarea" (New Jersey) appear on the obverse. The reverse features a shield and the legend, "E Pluribus Unum" (One out of many), the legend that appears on many later United States coins.

COMPLETE PRICE HISTORY
OF U.S. TYPE COINS

HALF CENTS—1793–1857

The Half Cent is one of the most difficult of the major type issues to find in choice uncirculated condition. All of the early types, which include the Liberty Capped Left, Liberty Capped Right and Draped Bust, are extremely rare in the top grades.

Because the early types are so infrequently found in uncirculated grades, the two major types of Half Cents available for investment purposes are the Classic Head (1809–1835) and the Braided Hair (1840–1857).

Coins with full original mint red luster are the most desirable and command the highest premium. This entire series has been undervalued in comparison to its rarity for over 20 years. Proofs are very scarce.

FLOWING HAIR, 1793

Head Facing Left.

Copper, 6.74 grams, 22 mm., lettered edge. Designer unknown.

Date	Fine Price		Date	Fine Price
1955	65.00		1975	700.00
1965	425.00		1985	2,300.00

Uncollectable in uncirculated condition.

$1,000 invested in 1955 would be worth $35,385 in 1985.
$1,000 invested in 1965 would be worth $5,412 in 1985.
$1,000 invested in 1975 would be worth $3,286 in 1985.

Note: Half Cents from 1793–1808 are so rare that they are virtually unavailable in choice uncirculated condition. Therefore, the prices quoted are for coins in Fine condition, the highest grade in which they are generally available.

LIBERTY CAP, 1794

Head Facing Right

Enlarged to 23.5 mm. Designed by Robert Scot. Other specifications same as previous issue.

Date	Fine Price		Date	Fine Price
1955	25.00		1975	175.00
1965	120.00		1985	750.00

Uncollectable in uncirculated condition.

$1,000 invested in 1955 would be worth $30,000 in 1985.
$1,000 invested in 1965 would be worth $6,250 in 1985.
$1,000 invested in 1975 would be worth $4,286 in 1985.

LIBERTY CAP, 1795–1797

Copper, 6.74 grams (1795), 5.44 grams (1795–1797), 23.5 mm., lettered edge (1795), plain edge (1795–1797). Designed by John Smith Gardner.

Date	Fine Price		Date	Fine Price
1955	22.50		1975	135.00
1965	100.00		1985	450.00

Uncollectable in uncirculated condition.

$1,000 invested in 1955 would be worth $20,000 in 1985.
$1,000 invested in 1965 would be worth $4,500 in 1985.
$1,000 invested in 1975 would be worth $3,333 in 1985.

DRAPED BUST, 1800–1808

Copper, 5.44 grams, 23.5 mm., plain edge. Designed by Robert Scot.

Date	Fine Price		Date	Fine Price
1955	6.00		1975	15.00
1965	15.00		1985	45.00

Uncollectable in uncirculated condition.

$1,000 invested in 1955 would be worth $7,500 in 1985.
$1,000 invested in 1965 would be worth $3,000 in 1985.
$1,000 invested in 1975 would be worth $1,800 in 1985.

CLASSIC HEAD, 1809–1835

Designed by John Reich. Other specifications same as previous issue.

Date	Unc. Price		Date	Unc. Price
1955	6.50		1975	420.00
1965	35.00		1985	3,600.00

$1,000 invested in 1955 would be worth $507,690 in 1985.
$1,000 invested in 1965 would be worth $94,285 in 1985.
$1,000 invested in 1975 would be worth $7,857 in 1985.

BRAIDED HAIR, 1840–1857

Diameter reduced to 23 mm. Designed by Christian Gobrecht. Other specifications same as previous issue.

Date	Unc. Price		Date	Unc. Price
1955	5.50		1975	410.00
1965	32.50		1985	3,900.00

$1,000 invested in 1955 would be worth $645,454 in 1985.
$1,000 invested in 1965 would be worth $109,230 in 1985.
$1,000 invested in 1975 would be worth $8,658 in 1985.

LARGE CENTS—1793–1857

Slightly larger than a quarter and twice as thick, Large Cents were minted for a period of 65 years. Along with the Half Cent, they were among the first coins struck by the newly formed United States government and were widely circulated.

Early date choice uncirculated Large Cents are extremely rare, although the later dates are only scarce. Coins with full original mint red luster are greatly desired and command a high premium. Numerous die varieties exist because the dies for the early coins were individually made. Large Cents were often poorly made because of low quality planchets. Proof Large Cents were first minted in 1817 and all dates are rare.

Note: Large Cents from 1793–1796 are virtually unavailable in choice uncirculated condition. Therefore, the prices quoted are for coins in Fine condition, the highest grade in which they are generally available.

CHAIN REVERSE, 1793

Copper, 13.48 grams, approximately 26–27 mm., lettered edge. Designed by Henry Voigt.

Date	Fine Price		Date	Fine Price
1955	135.00		1975	1,100.00
1965	525.00		1985	2,750.00

Uncollectable in uncirculated condition.

$1,000 invested in 1955 would be worth $20,370 in 1985.
$1,000 invested in 1965 would be worth $5,238 in 1985.
$1,000 invested in 1975 would be worth $2,500 in 1985.

WREATH REVERSE, 1793

Approximately 26–28 mm. Designed by Adam Eckfeldt. Other specifications same as previous issue.

Date	Fine Price		Date	Fine Price
1955	125.00		1975	725.00
1965	325.00		1985	1,450.00

Uncollectable in uncirculated condition.

$1,000 invested in 1955 would be worth $11,600 in 1985.
$1,000 invested in 1965 would be worth $4,461 in 1985.
$1,000 invested in 1975 would be worth $2,000 in 1985.

LIBERTY CAP, 1793

Lettered Edge

Copper, thick planchet, 13.48 grams, approximately 29 mm., lettered edge. Designed by Joseph Wright. Only one piece is known in mint state condition. It was in B. Max Mehl's Atwater sale, June 11, 1946, lot #14, and sold for $2,000.

Date	Fine Price		Date	Fine Price
1955	30.00		1975	110.00
1965	95.00		1985	300.00

Uncollectable in uncirculated condition.

> $1,000 invested in 1955 would be worth $10,000 in 1985.
> $1,000 invested in 1965 would be worth $3,158 in 1985.
> $1,000 invested in 1975 would be worth $2,727 in 1985.

LIBERTY CAP, 1794–1796

Copper, thin planchet, 10.89 grams, approximately 29 mm., plain edge. Designed by John Smith Gardner.

Date	Fine Price		Date	Fine Price
1955	15.00		1975	150.00
1965	60.00		1985	225.00

Uncollectable in uncirculated condition.

$1,000 invested in 1955 would be worth $15,000 in 1985.
$1,000 invested in 1965 would be worth $3,750 in 1985.
$1,000 invested in 1975 would be worth $1,500 in 1985.

DRAPED BUST, 1796–1807

Copper, 10.89 grams, 29 mm., plain edge. Designed by Robert Scot.

Date	Unc. Price		Date	Unc. Price
1955	—		1975	3,500.00
1965	—		1985	11,500.00

$1,000 invested in 1955 would be worth $— in 1985.
$1,000 invested in 1965 would be worth $— in 1985.
$1,000 invested in 1975 would be worth $3,285 in 1985.

CLASSIC HEAD, 1808–1814

Designed by John Reich. Other specifications same as previous issue.

Date	Unc. Price		Date	Unc. Price
1955	—		1975	3,100.00
1965	—		1985	16,000.00

$1,000 invested in 1955 would be worth $— in 1985.
$1,000 invested in 1965 would be worth $— in 1985.
$1,000 invested in 1975 would be worth $5,161 in 1985.

CORONET, 1816–1839

Copper, 10.89 grams, 28–29 mm., plain edge. Designed by Robert Scot.

Date	Unc. Price		Date	Unc. Price
1955	7.50		1975	375.00
1965	35.00		1985	3,300.00

$1,000 invested in 1955 would be worth $406,666 in 1985.
$1,000 invested in 1965 would be worth $87,142 in 1985.
$1,000 invested in 1975 would be worth $8,133 in 1985.

CORONET, 1840–1857

Braided Hair

Same specifications as previous issue.

Date	Unc. Price		Date	Unc. Price
1955	10.00		1975	380.00
1965	45.00		1985	3,150.00

$1,000 invested in 1955 would be worth $315,000 in 1985.
$1,000 invested in 1965 would be worth $70,000 in 1985.
$1,000 invested in 1975 would be worth $8,289 in 1985.

SMALL CENTS—1856 TO DATE

Flying Eagle Cents (1856–1858) share the distinction, along with Susan B. Anthony dollars, of being the shortest lived of all United States coins, having been issued in only three years. The 1856 cent was a pattern not intended for issue, and it is scarce in any grade. Many forgeries exist of this date, most of which are altered dates, and are clearly visible to an expert under a powerful magnifying glass.

Indian Cents (1860–1909) were produced for 50 years until the Lincoln Cent was issued in 1909 to commemorate the 100th anniversary of Abraham Lincoln's birth. While all Indian Cents are difficult to find in choice uncirculated condition, early copper-nickel cents (type of 1859, and type of 1860–64) are considerably scarcer than the later bronze issues. Spot-free coins with full original mint red color are particularly desirable.

Lincoln Cents (1909 to date) are one of the most popularly collected series, but the coins have not appreciated in value at the same rate as other coins of the 20th century. Original early dates may be difficult to find.

FLYING EAGLE, 1856–1858

88% copper, 12% nickel; 4.67 grams, 19 mm., plain edge. Designed by James B. Longacre.

Date	Price		Date	Price
1955	10.00		1975	450.00
1965	80.00		1985	2,750.00

$1,000 invested in 1955 would be worth $250,000 in 1985.
$1,000 invested in 1965 would be worth $31,250 in 1985.
$1,000 invested in 1975 would be worth $5,555 in 1985.

Note: It is the opinion of some dealers that a copper coin must have original full mint red color, and be spot-free, in addition to being MS-65, to be considered choice. Some disagree, and feel a copper coin can be red and brown so long as it is otherwise in choice uncirculated condition. With no other metal is color so important as with copper.

INDIAN, 1859–1909

INDIAN, 1859

Copper-Nickel, Wreath Reverse

Same specifications as previous issue.

Date	Price		Date	Price
1955	8.50		1975	300.00
1965	82.50		1985	1,800.00

$1,000 invested in 1955 would be worth $194,117 in 1985.
$1,000 invested in 1965 would be worth $20,000 in 1985.
$1,000 invested in 1975 would be worth $5,500 in 1985.

INDIAN, 1860–1864

Copper-nickel, Wreath and Shield Reverse

Same specifications as previous issue.

Date	Price		Date	Price
1955	2.00		1975	77.50
1965	22.50		1985	1,000.00

$1,000 invested in 1955 would be worth $450,000 in 1985.
$1,000 invested in 1965 would be worth $40,000 in 1985.
$1,000 invested in 1975 would be worth $11,612 in 1985.

INDIAN, 1864–1909

Bronze

Metal content changed to 95% copper and 5% tin and zinc. Weight reduced to 3.11 grams, 19 mm., plain edge.

Date	Price		Date	Price
1955	1.25		1975	29.00
1965	11.00		1985	415.00

$1,000 invested in 1955 would be worth $304,000 in 1985.
$1,000 invested in 1965 would be worth $34,545 in 1985.
$1,000 invested in 1975 would be worth $13,103 in 1985.

LINCOLN, 1909 TO DATE

LINCOLN, 1909

VDB on Reverse, Wheat Ears Reverse

95% copper, 5% tin and zinc; 3.11 grams, 19 mm., plain edge. Designed by Victor D. Brenner.

Date	Price		Date	Price
1955	.50		1975	9.50
1965	6.00		1985	50.00

$1,000 invested in 1955 would be worth $90,000 in 1985.
$1,000 invested in 1965 would be worth $7,500 in 1985.
$1,000 invested in 1975 would be worth $4,736 in 1985.

LINCOLN, 1909–1958

VDB on Obverse, Wheat Ears Reverse

Same specifications as previous issue. 1909 to 1917 have no VDB on obverse.

Date	Price		Date	Price
1955	.10		1975	.10
1965	.15		1985	.15

LINCOLN, 1943

Steel, Wheat Ears Reverse

Zinc-coated steel, 2.70 grams, 19 mm., plain edge. Same design as previous issue.

Date	Price		Date	Price
1955	.15		1975	.60
1965	1.00		1985	2.75

$1,000 invested in 1955 would be worth $16,666 in 1985.
$1,000 invested in 1965 would be worth $2,500 in 1985.
$1,000 invested in 1975 would be worth $4,166 in 1985.

LINCOLN, 1959 TO DATE

Memorial Reverse

1959–1962: 95% copper, 5% tin, and zinc.
1962–1982: 95% copper, 5% zinc.

1982 to date: Copper-plated zinc (97.6% zinc, 2.4% copper). 3.11 grams, 19 mm., plain edge. Both metal types issued in 1982. Victor D. Brenner designed the obverse, Frank Gasparro the reverse.

Date	Price		Date	Price
1955	—		1975	.10
1965	.05		1985	.10

TWO-CENT PIECES—1864–1873

Issued for only ten years, Two-Cent pieces were the first United States coins to bear the motto, "In God We Trust." These coins are very rare in full red choice uncirculated condition, especially the Proofs.

95% Copper, 5% tin and zinc; 6.22 grams, 23 mm., plain edge. Designed by James B. Longacre.

Date	Price		Date	Price
1955	2.50		1975	195.00
1965	15.00		1985	1,200.00

$1,000 invested in 1955 would be worth $440,000 in 1985.
$1,000 invested in 1965 would be worth $73,333 in 1985.
$1,000 invested in 1975 would be worth $5,641 in 1985.

THREE-CENT PIECES—1851–1889

One of the most popular type issues, Three-Cent pieces were made in both silver and copper-nickel. The coins are the smallest United States silver coins issued and choice uncirculated specimens are difficult to locate. Type II silver pieces (1854–1858) are much rarer than the other two varieties. Curiously, Three-Cent nickel pieces in choice uncirculated condition are rarer than the Proofs, but sell for less.

THREE CENTS, SILVER, 1851–1853

Type I: Plain Star

75% silver, 25% copper; .80 grams, 14 mm., plain edge. Designed by James B. Longacre.

Date	Price		Date	Price
1955	5.00		1975	145.00
1965	21.00		1985	3,650.00

$1,000 invested in 1955 would be worth $670,000 in 1985.
$1,000 invested in 1965 would be worth $159,523 in 1985.
$1,000 invested in 1975 would be worth $23,103 in 1985.

THREE CENTS, SILVER, 1854–1858

Type II: Star with Three Outlines

90% silver, 10% copper. Weight reduced to .75 grams.

Date	Price		Date	Price
1955	6.00		1975	485.00
1965	35.00		1985	4,600.00

$1,000 invested in 1955 would be worth $712,500 in 1985.
$1,000 invested in 1965 would be worth $122,142 in 1985.
$1,000 invested in 1975 would be worth $8,814 in 1985.

THREE CENTS, SILVER, 1859–1873

Type III: Star with Two Outlines

Same specifications as previous issue.

Date	Price		Date	Price
1955	5.00		1975	155.00
1965	26.50		1985	3,100.00

$1,000 invested in 1955 would be worth $560,000 in 1985.
$1,000 invested in 1965 would be worth $105,660 in 1985.
$1,000 invested in 1975 would be worth $18,064 in 1985.

THREE CENTS, NICKEL, 1865–1889

75% copper, 25% nickel; 1.94 grams, 17.9 mm., plain edge. Designed by James B. Longacre.

Date	Price		Date	Price
1955	2.00		1975	82.00
1965	10.00		1985	1,675.00

$1,000 invested in 1955 would be worth $762,500 in 1985.
$1,000 invested in 1965 would be worth $152,500 in 1985.
$1,000 invested in 1975 would be worth $18,597 in 1985.

FIVE-CENT PIECES (NICKELS), 1866 TO DATE

Shield Nickels (1866–1883) are the rarest type coin in the United States nickel series. Because the coins were poorly manufactured, few specimens have survived well struck, with full original mint luster, and no carbon spots. Choice uncirculated coins are harder to find than the Proofs, but the Proofs cost more. The "with Rays" type is extremely rare in Proof.

Liberty Nickels (1883–1913) first appeared with a large letter "V" on the reverse without the word CENTS. Unscrupulous individuals goldplated the coins and passed them as Five Dollar gold pieces, earning them the name "Racketeer Nickels." Later in the year, the word CENTS was added. A one-year type issue, NO CENTS nickels are popular in uncirculated condition. The 1913 Liberty Nickel is a classic rarity. Only five specimens are known, one of which was auctioned for $385,000 in January, 1985.

Buffalo Nickels (1913–1938) are popular with collectors and investors and although minted in large quantities, they nevertheless are rare in choice uncirculated condition. This is partially due to manufacturing problems caused by the hardness of the metal, which produced weakly struck coins, die-breaks and coins with poor luster. Few Proofs were made and they are scarce in choice condition. The 1937-D three-legged Buffalo Nickel shows the buffalo standing on only three legs, the result of a die defect obliterating the fourth leg. This series contains the rare overdate 1918-D with the 8 over 7.

Jefferson Nickels (1938 to date) have not proven to be a popular investment vehicle, except for the early Proof issues from 1938 to 1955. During the Second World War, this coin was struck in silver, to avoid using nickel, a strategic metal, which was needed for the war effort. This wartime series contains a number of interesting overstruck mint marks.

SHIELD NICKELS, 1866–1883

SHIELD, 1866–1867

Rays on Reverse

75% copper, 25% nickel; 5 grams, 20.5 mm., plain edge. Designed by James B. Longacre.

Date	Price		Date	Price
1955	13.50		1975	425.00
1965	85.00		1985	3,100.00

$1,000 invested in 1955 would be worth $207,407 in 1985.
$1,000 invested in 1965 would be worth $32,941 in 1985.
$1,000 invested in 1975 would be worth $6,588 in 1985.

SHIELD, 1867–1883

No Rays on Reverse

Same specifications as previous issue.

Date	Price		Date	Price
1955	4.50		1975	107.50
1965	17.50		1985	2,300.00

$1,000 invested in 1955 would be worth $466,666 in 1985.
$1,000 invested in 1965 would be worth $120,000 in 1985.
$1,000 invested in 1975 would be worth $19,534 in 1985.

LIBERTY NICKELS, 1883–1913

LIBERTY, 1883

No CENTS on Reverse

Diameter enlarged to 21.2 mm. Designed by Charles E. Barber. Other specifications same as previous issue.

Date	Price		Date	Price
1955	1.00		1975	36.00
1965	6.00		1985	835.00

$1,000 invested in 1955 would be worth $765,000 in 1985.
$1,000 invested in 1965 would be worth $127,500 in 1985.
$1,000 invested in 1975 would be worth $21,250 in 1985.

LIBERTY, 1883–1913

With CENTS on Reverse

Same specifications as previous issue.

Date	Price		Date	Price
1955	4.50		1975	55.00
1965	15.00		1985	1,650.00

$1,000 invested in 1955 would be worth $338,888 in 1985.
$1,000 invested in 1965 would be worth $101,666 in 1985.
$1,000 invested in 1975 would be worth $27,727 in 1985.

BUFFALO NICKELS, 1913–1938

BUFFALO, 1913

Type I: Bison on Raised Mound

75% copper, 25% nickel; 5 grams, 21.2 mm., plain edge. Designed by James Earle Fraser.

Date	Price		Date	Price
1955	1.25		1975	26.00
1965	7.00		1985	245.00

$1,000 invested in 1955 would be worth $180,000 in 1985.
$1,000 invested in 1965 would be worth $32,142 in 1985.
$1,000 invested in 1975 would be worth $8,653 in 1985.

BUFFALO, 1913–1938

Type II: Bison on Level Ground

Same specifications as previous issue.

Date	Price		Date	Price
1955	.25		1975	6.25
1965	3.00		1985	64.00

$1,000 invested in 1955 would be worth $236,000 in 1985.
$1,000 invested in 1965 would be worth $19,666 in 1985.
$1,000 invested in 1975 would be worth $9,440 in 1985.

JEFFERSON NICKELS, 1938 TO DATE

JEFFERSON, 1938–1942, 1946 TO DATE

75% copper, 25% nickel. Designed by Felix Schlag. Other specifications same as previous issue.

Date	Price		Date	Price
1955	.15		1975	.10
1965	.15		1985	.10

JEFFERSON, 1942–1945

Large P, D or S Mint Mark on Reverse

Metal content changed to 56% copper, 35% silver, 9% manganese. Net weight: .05626 oz. pure silver. Other specifications same as previous issue.

Date	Price		Date	Price
1955	.20		1975	1.75
1965	2.00		1985	5.00

$1,000 invested in 1955 would be worth $22,500 in 1985.
$1,000 invested in 1965 would be worth $2,250 in 1985.
$1,000 invested in 1975 would be worth $2,571 in 1985.

HALF DIMES—1794–1873

Early Half Dimes (1794–1805) The Flowing Hair and Draped Bust are scarce and expensive in all grades. Uncirculated coins are extremely rare.

The pre-1860 *Liberty Seated Half Dimes* were made in extremely limited quantities and are among the scarcest of all the major type coins in choice uncirculated condition. The dates 1837, 1838, and 1840 and 1853 each exist in two distinct types. Many of the coins carrying mint marks are extremely rare in uncirculated grades.

FLOWING HAIR, 1794–1795

89.24% silver, 10.76% copper; 1.35 grams, approximately 16.5 mm., reeded edge. Designed by Robert Scot.

Date	Price		Date	Price
1955	55.00		1975	5,250.00
1965	650.00		1985	25,000.00

$1,000 invested in 1955 would be worth $454,545 in 1985.
$1,000 invested in 1965 would be worth $38,461 in 1985.
$1,000 invested in 1975 would be worth $4,761 in 1985.

DRAPED BUST, 1796–1805

DRAPED BUST, 1796–1797

Small Eagle on Reverse

Same specifications as previous issue.

Date	Price		Date	Price
1955	110.00		1975	2,600.00
1965	800.00		1985	31,000.00

$1,000 invested in 1955 would be worth $281,818 in 1985.
$1,000 invested in 1965 would be worth $38,750 in 1985.
$1,000 invested in 1975 would be worth $11,923 in 1985.

DRAPED BUST, 1800–1805

Large (Heraldic) Eagle on Reverse

Same specifications as the previous issue.

Date	Price		Date	Price
1955	65.00		1975	3,850.00
1965	600.00		1985	26,000.00

$1,000 invested in 1955 would be worth $400,000 in 1985.
$1,000 invested in 1965 would be worth $43,333 in 1985.
$1,000 invested in 1975 would be worth $6,753 in 1985.

CAPPED BUST, 1829–1837

Diameter reduced to 15.5 mm. Designed by William Kneass. Other specifications same as previous issue.

Date	Price		Date	Price
1955	4.50		1975	345.00
1965	35.00		1985	5,800.00

$1,000 invested in 1955 would be worth $1,188,888 in 1985.
$1,000 invested in 1965 would be worth $152,857 in 1985.
$1,000 invested in 1975 would be worth $15,507 in 1985.

LIBERTY SEATED, 1837–1873

LIBERTY SEATED, 1837–1838

No Stars on Obverse

90% silver, 10% copper; 1.34 grams, 15.5 mm., reeded edge. Designed by Christian Gobrecht.

Date	Price		Date	Price
1955	15.00		1975	650.00
1965	175.00		1985	5,100.00

$1,000 invested in 1955 would be worth $313,333 in 1985.
$1,000 invested in 1965 would be worth $26,857 in 1985.
$1,000 invested in 1975 would be worth $7,230 in 1985.

LIBERTY SEATED, 1838–1840

Stars on Obverse, No Drapery from Elbow

Same specifications as previous issue.

Date	Price		Date	Price
1955	4.50		1975	260.00
1965	25.00		1985	4,300.00

$1,000 invested in 1955 would be worth $866,666 in 1985.
$1,000 invested in 1965 would be worth $156,000 in 1985.
$1,000 invested in 1975 would be worth $15,000 in 1985.

LIBERTY SEATED, 1840–1853, 1856–59

Stars on Obverse, Drapery from Elbow

Same specifications as previous issue.

Date	Price		Date	Price
1955	3.00		1975	200.00
1965	14.00		1985	3,900.00

$1,000 invested in 1955 would be worth $1,200,000 in 1985.
$1,000 invested in 1965 would be worth $257,142 in 1985.
$1,000 invested in 1975 would be worth $17,142 in 1985.

LIBERTY SEATED, 1853–1855

Stars on Obverse, Arrows at Date

Weight reduced to 1.24 grams. The arrows indicate a reduction in weight. Other specifications same as previous issue.

Date	Price		Date	Price
1955	4.00		1975	255.00
1965	20.00		1985 .	3,700.00

$1,000 invested in 1955 would be worth $850,000 in 1985.
$1,000 invested in 1965 would be worth $170,000 in 1985.
$1,000 invested in 1975 would be worth $13,333 in 1985.

LIBERTY SEATED, 1860–1873

"United States of America" Legend on Obverse

Same specifications as previous issue.

Date	Price		Date	Price
1955	3.00		1975	152.50
1965	15.00		1985	3,200.00

$1,000 invested in 1955 would be worth $983,333 in 1985.
$1,000 invested in 1965 would be worth $196,666 in 1985.
$1,000 invested in 1975 would be worth $19,344 in 1985.

DIMES—1796 TO DATE

From 1796 to 1891, the designs of the Dimes are similar to those of the Half Dimes.

Draped Bust Dimes (1796–1807) are very scarce and expensive in all grades. Uncirculated coins are extremely rare.

Capped Bust Dimes (1809–1837) are scarce in all grades and especially rare in uncirculated condition.

Liberty Seated Dimes (1837–1891) are one of the most popular U.S. type issues. The types "With Stars" and "No Stars" are scarce. Many of the mint-marked issues are extremely rare in uncirculated grades.

Barber Dimes (1892–1916) are among the few series that are sought after by both type and date collectors.

Mercury Dimes (1916–1945) have long been a favorite with collectors because of the beautiful winged head of Liberty design. The 1916-D is the lowest minted 20th century dime and is one of the best known of all United States rare coins. It is scarce in all grades. When the two horizontal bands that cross the center of the fasces (the vertical sticks) on the reverse of the Mercury Dime are sharply struck and have a distinct line separating them, they are called "Full bands." Gem quality Mercury Dimes with full bands command higher prices than those with non-full bands.

Roosevelt Dimes (1946 to date) are notable because a complete set of the silver pieces (1946–1964) comprises the least expensive U.S. silver coin set that can be assembled.

DRAPED BUST, 1796–1807

DRAPED BUST, 1796–1797

Small Eagle on Reverse

89.24% silver, 10.76% copper; 2.70 grams, approximately 19 mm., reeded edge. Designed by Robert Scot.

Date	Price		Date	Price
1955	150.00		1975	5,500.00
1965	1,350.00		1985	30,000.00

$1,000 invested in 1955 would be worth $200,000 in 1985.
$1,000 invested in 1965 would be worth $22,222 in 1985.
$1,000 invested in 1975 would be worth $5,454 in 1985.

DRAPED BUST, 1798–1807

Large (Heraldic) Eagle on Reverse

Same specifications as previous issue.

Date	Price		Date	Price
1955	45.00		1975	2,750.00
1965	325.00		1985	18,000.00

$1,000 invested in 1955 would be worth $400,000 in 1985.
$1,000 invested in 1965 would be worth $55,384 in 1985.
$1,000 invested in 1975 would be worth $6,545 in 1985.

CAPPED BUST, 1809–1837

CAPPED BUST, 1809–1828

Large Size

Diameter 18.8 mm. Designed by John Reich. Other specifications same as previous issue.

Date	Price		Date	Price
1955	12.50		1975	1,800.00
1965	75.00		1985	8,700.00

$1,000 invested in 1955 would be worth $696,000 in 1985.
$1,000 invested in 1965 would be worth $116,000 in 1985.
$1,000 invested in 1975 would be worth $4,833 in 1985.

CAPPED BUST, 1828–1837

Small Size

Same specifications as previous issue.

Date	Price		Date	Price
1955	5.00		1975	1,000.00
1965	40.00		1985	8,600.00

$1,000 invested in 1955 would be worth $1,580,000 in 1985.
$1,000 invested in 1965 would be worth $197,500 in 1985.
$1,000 invested in 1975 would be worth $7,900 in 1985.

LIBERTY SEATED, 1837–1891

LIBERTY SEATED, 1837–1838

No Stars on Obverse

90% silver, 10% copper; 2.67 grams, 17.9 mm., reeded edge. Designed by Christian Gobrecht.

Date	Price		Date	Price
1955	25.00		1975	1,500.00
1965	200.00		1985	5,600.00

$1,000 invested in 1955 would be worth $204,000 in 1985.
$1,000 invested in 1965 would be worth $25,500 in 1985.
$1,000 invested in 1975 would be worth $3,400 in 1985.

LIBERTY SEATED, 1838–1840

Stars on Obverse, No drapery from Elbow

Same specifications as previous issue.

Date	Price		Date	Price
1955	6.00		1975	385.00
1965	30.00		1985	4,500.00

$1,000 invested in 1955 would be worth $683,333 in 1985.
$1,000 invested in 1965 would be worth $136,666 in 1985.
$1,000 invested in 1975 would be worth $10,649 in 1985.

LIBERTY SEATED, 1840–1853, 1856–60

Stars on Obverse, Drapery from Elbow

Same specifications as previous issue.

Date	Price		Date	Price
1955	4.00		1975	280.00
1965	20.00		1985	4,500.00

$1,000 invested in 1955 would be worth $1,037,500 in 1985.
$1,000 invested in 1965 would be worth $207,500 in 1985.
$1,000 invested in 1975 would be worth $14,821 in 1985.

LIBERTY SEATED, 1853–1855

Stars on Obverse, Arrows at Date

Weight reduced to 2.49 grams. The arrows indicate a reduction in weight. Other specifications same as previous issue.

Date	Price		Date	Price
1955	4.50		1975	365.00
1965	22.50		1985	3,600.00

$1,000 invested in 1955 would be worth $733,333 in 1985.
$1,000 invested in 1965 would be worth $146,666 in 1985.
$1,000 invested in 1975 would be worth $9,041 in 1985.

LIBERTY SEATED, 1860–1873, 1875–91

"United States of America" Legend on Obverse

Same specifications as previous issue.

Date	Price		Date	Price
1955	2.75		1975	135.00
1965	9.50		1985	2,900.00

$1,000 invested in 1955 would be worth $963,636 in 1985.
$1,000 invested in 1965 would be worth $278,947 in 1985.
$1,000 invested in 1975 would be worth $19,629 in 1985.

LIBERTY SEATED, 1873–1874

Legend on Obverse, Arrows at Date

Weight increased to 2.50 grams. The arrows indicate an increase in weight. Other specifications same as previous issue.

Date	Price		Date	Price
1955	10.00		1975	465.00
1965	75.00		1985	5,000.00

$1,000 invested in 1955 would be worth $450,000 in 1985.
$1,000 invested in 1965 would be worth $60,000 in 1985.
$1,000 invested in 1975 would be worth $9,677 in 1985.

BARBER, 1892–1916

90% silver, 10% copper; 2.50 grams, 17.9 mm., reeded edge. Designed by Charles E. Barber. Net weight: .07234 oz. pure silver.

Date	Price		Date	Price
1955	3.00		1975	75.00
1965	9.00		1985	1,850.00

$1,000 invested in 1955 would be worth $566,666 in 1985.
$1,000 invested in 1965 would be worth $188,888 in 1985.
$1,000 invested in 1975 would be worth $22,666 in 1985.

MERCURY, 1916–1945

Designed by Adolph A. Weinman. Other specifications same as previous issue. Net weight: .07234 oz. pure silver. Prices are for coins with full bands.

Date	Price		Date	Price
1955	.25		1975	2.75
1965	.75		1985	87.00

$1,000 invested in 1955 would be worth $328,000 in 1985.
$1,000 invested in 1965 would be worth $109,333 in 1985.
$1,000 invested in 1975 would be worth $29,818 in 1985.

ROOSEVELT, 1946 TO DATE

ROOSEVELT, 1946–1964

Silver

Designed by John R. Sinnock. Other specifications same as previous issue. Net weight: .07234 oz. pure silver.

Date	Price		Date	Price
1955	.15		1975	.75
1965	.20		1985	2.00

$1,000 invested in 1955 would be worth $11,666 in 1985.
$1,000 invested in 1965 would be worth $8,750 in 1985.
$1,000 invested in 1975 would be worth $2,333 in 1985.

ROOSEVELT, 1965 TO DATE

Copper-Nickel Clad

75% copper, 25% nickel outer layer bonded to inner core of pure copper. 2.27 grams, 17.9 mm., reeded edge.

Date	Price		Date	Price
1955	—		1975	.20
1965	—		1985	.20

TWENTY-CENT PIECES, 1875–1878

Because of its similarity in design and size to the Liberty Seated Quarter Dollar, the Twenty-Cent piece was not popular with the public. After only four years of production, it was discontinued. Now, more than 100 years later, the once-shunned coin has become one of the most wanted type issues. It is also one of the rarest type coins in all grades, and the date 1876-CC is a classic rarity.

TWENTY-CENT PIECES, 1875–1878

90% silver, 10% copper; 5 grams, 22 mm., plain edge. Designed by William Barber.

Date	Price		Date	Price
1955	15.00		1975	800.00
1965	70.00		1985	6,800.00

$1,000 invested in 1955 would be worth $413,333 in 1985.
$1,000 invested in 1965 would be worth $88,571 in 1985.
$1,000 invested in 1975 would be worth $7,750 in 1985.

QUARTER DOLLARS—1796 TO DATE

Draped Bust Quarters (1796–1807) are scarce in all grades and extremely difficult to obtain in uncirculated condition. Investors should be aware that early quarters are difficult for a layman to grade.

Capped Bust Quarters (1815–1838) are also extremely rare. In fact, they are the rarest of all the four silver Capped Bust issues (Half Dimes, Dimes, Quarters and Halves).

Liberty Seated Quarters (1838–1891). The six types are popular and expensive in choice uncirculated condition. The "no motto" quarters are much scarcer than the "with motto" variety, which start in 1866.

Barber Quarters (1892–1916) are among the few series that are sought after by both type and date collectors. Truly choice uncirculated Barber Quarters, with full mint luster, are difficult to locate.

Standing Liberty Quarters (1916–1930) are the rarest silver coins issued in the 20th century. The first variety achieved notoriety in 1916 when the bare breast of Liberty caused such a public outcry that the design was changed and Liberty's breast was covered after two years. Quarters with a fully struck head of Liberty are known as "full heads" and they command higher prices than quarters without full heads. This popular series contains the classic rarity, the 1918-S, 8 over 7, which is virtually unknown in Gem uncirculated or with a full head.

Washington Quarters (1932 to date) are popular because their recent vintage makes it possible for them to be assembled into a silver set that can still be completed. Quarters in gem uncirculated and gem Proof condition from 1932 to 1945 are much scarcer than the later issues.

DRAPED BUST, 1796–1807

DRAPED BUST, 1796

Small Eagle on Reverse

89.24% silver, 10.76% copper; 6.74 grams, 27.5 mm., reeded edge. Designed by Robert Scot.

Date	Price		Date	Price
1955	275.00		1975	10,000.00
1965	3,750.00		1985	40,000.00

$1,000 invested in 1955 would be worth $145,454 in 1985.
$1,000 invested in 1965 would be worth $10,666 in 1985.
$1,000 invested in 1975 would be worth $4,000 in 1985.

DRAPED BUST, 1804–1807

Large (Heraldic) Eagle on Reverse

Same specifications as previous issue.

Date	Price		Date	Price
1955	60.00		1975	4,750.00
1965	550.00		1985	27,500.00

$1,000 invested in 1955 would be worth $458,333 in 1985.
$1,000 invested in 1965 would be worth $50,000 in 1985.
$1,000 invested in 1975 would be worth $5,789 in 1985.

CAPPED BUST, 1815–1838

CAPPED BUST, 1815–1828

Large Size, Motto Above Eagle

Diameter 27 mm. Designed by John Reich. Other specifications same as previous issue.

Date	Price		Date	Price
1955	22.50		1975	2,850.00
1965	175.00		1985	12,250.00

$1,000 invested in 1955 would be worth $544,444 in 1985.
$1,000 invested in 1965 would be worth $70,000 in 1985.
$1,000 invested in 1975 would be worth $4,298 in 1985.

CAPPED BUST, 1831–1838

Small Size, No Motto Above Eagle

Diameter reduced to 24.3 mm. Designed by William Kneass. Other specifications same as previous issue.

Date	Price		Date	Price
1955	11.00		1975	1,500.00
1965	75.00		1985	11,250.00

$1,000 invested in 1955 would be worth $954,545 in 1985.
$1,000 invested in 1965 would be worth $140,000 in 1985.
$1,000 invested in 1975 would be worth $7,000 in 1985.

LIBERTY SEATED, 1838–1891

LIBERTY SEATED, 1838–1840

No Motto Above Eagle, No Drapery from Elbow

90% silver, 10% copper; 6.68 grams, 24.3 mm., reeded edge. Designed by Christian Gobrecht.

Date	Price		Date	Price
1955	12.50		1975	1,450.00
1965	65.00		1985	12,000.00

$1,000 invested in 1955 would be worth $960,000 in 1985.
$1,000 invested in 1965 would be worth $184,615 in 1985.
$1,000 invested in 1975 would be worth $8,275 in 1985.

LIBERTY SEATED, 1840–1853, 1856–65

No Motto Above Eagle, Drapery from Elbow

Same specifications as previous issue.

Date	Price		Date	Price
1955	4.00		1975	335.00
1965	16.00		1985	5,500.00

$1,000 invested in 1955 would be worth $1,275,000 in 1985.
$1,000 invested in 1965 would be worth $318,750 in 1985.
$1,000 invested in 1975 would be worth $15,223 in 1985.

LIBERTY SEATED, 1853

No Motto Above Eagle; With Arrows at Date, Rays Around Eagle

Weight reduced to 6.22 grams. The arrows indicate a reduction in weight. Other specifications same as previous issue.

Date	Price		Date	Price
1955	9.00		1975	1,050.00
1965	55.00		1985	8,800.00

$1,000 invested in 1955 would be worth $888,888 in 1985.
$1,000 invested in 1965 would be worth $145,454 in 1985.
$1,000 invested in 1975 would be worth $7,619 in 1985.

LIBERTY SEATED, 1854–1855

No Motto Above Eagle; With Arrows at Date

Same specifications as previous issue.

Date	Price		Date	Price
1955	5.00		1975	640.00
1965	40.00		1985	5,900.00

$1,000 invested in 1955 would be worth $1,080,000 in 1985.
$1,000 invested in 1965 would be worth $135,000 in 1985.
$1,000 invested in 1975 would be worth $8,437 in 1985.

LIBERTY SEATED, 1866–1873, 1875–91

Motto "In God We Trust" Above Eagle

Same specifications as previous issue.

Date	Price		Date	Price
1955	4.00		1975	280.00
1965	9.00		1985	4,500.00

$1,000 invested in 1955 would be worth $1,037,500 in 1985.
$1,000 invested in 1965 would be worth $461,111 in 1985.
$1,000 invested in 1975 would be worth $14,821 in 1985.

LIBERTY SEATED, 1873–1874

Motto Above Eagle, Arrows at Date

Weight increased to 6.25 grams. The arrows indicate an increase in weight. Other specifications same as previous issue.

Date	Price		Date	Price
1955	15.00		1975	525.00
1965	120.00		1985	5,000.00

$1,000 invested in 1955 would be worth $306,666 in 1985.
$1,000 invested in 1965 would be worth $38,333 in 1985.
$1,000 invested in 1975 would be worth $8,761 in 1985.

BARBER, 1892–1916

90% silver, 10% copper; 6.25 grams, 24.3 mm., reeded edge. Designed by Charles E. Barber. Net weight: .18084 oz. pure silver.

Date	Price		Date	Price
1955	5.00		1975	180.00
1965	17.00		1985	3,150.00

$1,000 invested in 1955 would be worth $580,000 in 1985.
$1,000 invested in 1965 would be worth $170,588 in 1985.
$1,000 invested in 1975 would be worth $16,111 in 1985.

STANDING LIBERTY, 1916–1930

STANDING LIBERTY, 1916–1917

Type I: Bare Breast

Designed by Herman A. MacNeil. Other specifications same as previous issue. Net weight: .18084 oz. pure silver. Prices are for coins with a full head.

Date	Price		Date	Price
1955	5.00		1975	195.00
1965	30.00		1985	2,325.00

$1,000 invested in 1955 would be worth $420,000 in 1985.
$1,000 invested in 1965 would be worth $70,000 in 1985.
$1,000 invested in 1975 would be worth $10,769 in 1985.

STANDING LIBERTY, 1917–1930

Type II: Covered Breast, Stars below Eagle

Same specifications as previous issue. Prices are for coins with a full head.

Date	Price		Date	Price
1955	3.00		1975	110.00
1965	15.00		1985	2,325.00

$1,000 invested in 1955 would be worth $700,000 in 1985.
$1,000 invested in 1965 would be worth $140,000 in 1985.
$1,000 invested in 1975 would be worth $19,090 in 1985.

WASHINGTON, 1932 TO DATE

WASHINGTON, 1932–1964

Designed by John Flanagan. Other specifications same as previous issue. Net weight: .18084 oz. pure silver.

Date	Price		Date	Price
1955	.50		1975	1.75
1965	.50		1985	4.00

$1,000 invested in 1955 would be worth $7,000 in 1985.
$1,000 invested in 1965 would be worth $7,000 in 1985.
$1,000 invested in 1975 would be worth $2,000 in 1985.

WASHINGTON, 1965 TO DATE

Copper-Nickel Clad

75% copper, 25% nickel outer layers bonded to inner core of pure copper. Weight reduced to 5.67 grams. 24.3 mm., reeded edge.

Date	Price		Date	Price
1955	—		1975	.50
1965	.50		1985	.50

WASHINGTON, Dated 1776–1976

Silver-Clad Bicentennial Quarter

80% silver, 20% copper outer layers bonded to inner core of 20.9% silver, 79.1% copper. 5.75 grams, 24.3 mm., reeded edge. Designed by John Flanagan (obverse) and Jack L. Ahr (reverse). Net weight: .0739 oz. pure silver.

Date	Price		Date	Price
1976	2.00		1985	2.50

WASHINGTON, Dated 1776–1976

Copper-Nickel Clad Bicentennial Quarter

Designed by John Flanagan (obverse) and Jack L. Ahr (reverse). Other specifications same as previous Washington copper-nickel clad issue.

Date	Price		Date	Price
1976	.50		1985	.50

HALF DOLLARS—1794 TO DATE

Flowing Hair and Draped Bust Half Dollars (1794–1807), as with early Dimes and Quarters, are historic coins and rare in all grades.

Bust Half Dollars (1807–1839) are monumentally difficult to locate in uncirculated condition and MS-65 coins are almost non-existent. The coins in this period are rich in varieties. There are overdates, small and large dates, small and large letters, etc.

Liberty Seated Half Dollars (1839–1891) are scarce in uncirculated condition. The series was issued for 52 years and features many important varieties (motto, no motto, arrows, arrows and rays, no arrows, etc.).

Barber Halves (1892–1915) are very popular in uncirculated and proof with both collectors and investors.

Liberty Walking Halves (1916–1947) are one of our most beautiful and popular coins. Although struck in relatively large quantities, they are harder to find in uncirculated condition than the mintage figures would indicate. Consequently, all MS-65 Liberty Walking halves are relatively expensive and the early issues (1916–1929) are all very scarce. San Francisco-minted coins usually come weakly struck. The 1933-S Half Dollar was the only silver coin issued by the United States in that year.

Franklin Half Dollars (1948–1963) are difficult to find in Gem uncirculated condition. Because of the coin's design, it attracts bag marks readily. Coins with fully struck lines in the Liberty Bell (known as "full bell lines") are more desirable and command higher prices than non-full bell line coins.

Kennedy Half Dollars (1964 to date) have not attracted much investor interest, except for the 1964 Proof issue, and the 1970-D.

Note: Half Dollars from 1794–1797 are so rare, they are virtually unavailable in choice uncirculated condition. Therefore, the prices quoted are for coins in Fine condition, the highest grade in which they are generally available.

FLOWING HAIR, 1794–1795

89.24% silver, 10.76% copper; 13.48 grams, 32.5 mm., lettered edge. Designed by Robert Scot.

Date	Fine Price		Date	Fine Price
1955	27.50		1975	3,750.00
1965	185.00		1985	45,000.00

Uncollectable in uncirculated condition.

$1,000 invested in 1955 would be worth $1,636,363 in 1985.
$1,000 invested in 1965 would be worth $243,243 in 1985.
$1,000 invested in 1975 would be worth $12,000 in 1985.

DRAPED BUST 1796–1807

DRAPED BUST, 1796–1797

Small Eagle on Reverse

Same specifications as previous issue.

Date	Fine Price		Date	Fine Price
1955	275.00		1975	4,100.00
1965	2,100.00		1985	15,000.00

Uncollectable in uncirculated condition.

$1,000 invested in 1955 would be worth $54,545 in 1985.
$1,000 invested in 1965 would be worth $7,143 in 1985.
$1,000 invested in 1975 would be worth $3,658 in 1985.

DRAPED BUST, 1801–1807

Large (Heraldic) Eagle on Reverse

Same specifications as previous issue.

Date	Price		Date	Price
1955	25.00		1975	4,500.00
1965	160.00		1985	20,000.00

$1,000 invested in 1955 would be worth $800,000 in 1985.
$1,000 invested in 1965 would be worth $125,000 in 1985.
$1,000 invested in 1975 would be worth $4,444 in 1985.

CAPPED BUST, 1807–1839

CAPPED BUST, 1807–1836

Lettered Edge

89.24% silver, 10.76% copper; 13.48 grams, 32.5 mm., lettered edge. Designed by John Reich.

Date	Price		Date	Price
1955	5.50		1975	410.00
1965	18.00		1985	7,650.00

$1,000 invested in 1955 would be worth $1,272,727 in 1985.
$1,000 invested in 1965 would be worth $388,888 in 1985.
$1,000 invested in 1975 would be worth $17,073 in 1985.

CAPPED BUST, 1836–1837

Reeded Edge, "50 Cents" on Reverse

90% silver, 10% copper; 13.36 grams, 30 mm., reeded edge. Designed by Christian Gobrecht.

Date	Price		Date	Price
1955	11.50		1975	925.00
1965	80.00		1985	8,000.00

$1,000 invested in 1955 would be worth $695,652 in 1985.
$1,000 invested in 1965 would be worth $100,000 in 1985.
$1,000 invested in 1975 would be worth $8,648 in 1985.

CAPPED BUST, 1838–1839

Reeded Edge, "HALF DOL." on Reverse

Same specifications as previous issue.

Date	Price		Date	Price
1955	12.50		1975	925.00
1965	75.00		1985	8,000.00

$1,000 invested in 1955 would be worth $640,000 in 1985.
$1,000 invested in 1965 would be worth $106,666 in 1985.
$1,000 invested in 1975 would be worth $8,648 in 1985.

LIBERTY SEATED, 1839–1891

LIBERTY SEATED, 1839

No Motto Above Eagle, No Drapery from Elbow

90% silver, 10% copper; 13.36 grams, 30.6 mm., reeded edge. Designed by Christian Gobrecht.

Date	Price		Date	Price
1955	30.00		1975	5,000.00
1965	200.00		1985	20,000.00

$1,000 invested in 1955 would be worth $666,666 in 1985.
$1,000 invested in 1965 would be worth $100,000 in 1985.
$1,000 invested in 1975 would be worth $4,000 in 1985.

LIBERTY SEATED, 1839–1853, 1856–1866

No Motto Above Eagle, Drapery from Elbow

Same specifications as previous issue.

Date	Price		Date	Price
1955	5.00		1975	360.00
1965	20.00		1985	6,100.00

$1,000 invested in 1955 would be worth $1,120,000 in 1985.
$1,000 invested in 1965 would be worth $280,000 in 1985.
$1,000 invested in 1975 would be worth $15,555 in 1985.

LIBERTY SEATED, 1853

No Motto Above Eagle, Arrows at Date, Rays Around Eagle

Weight reduced to 12.44 grams. The arrows indicate the reduction in weight. Other specifications same as previous issue.

Date	Price		Date	Price
1955	15.00		1975	1,850.00
1965	80.00		1985	14,500.00

$1,000 invested in 1955 would be worth $866,666 in 1985.
$1,000 invested in 1965 would be worth $162,500 in 1985.
$1,000 invested in 1975 would be worth $7,027 in 1985.

LIBERTY SEATED, 1854–1855

No Motto Above Eagle, Arrows at Date

Same specifications as previous issue.

Date	Price		Date	Price
1955	8.00		1975	550.00
1965	40.00		1985	7,400.00

$1,000 invested in 1955 would be worth $850,000 in 1985.
$1,000 invested in 1965 would be worth $170,000 in 1985.
$1,000 invested in 1975 would be worth $12,363 in 1985.

LIBERTY SEATED, 1866–1873, 1875–1891

Motto "In God We Trust" Above Eagle

Same specifications as previous issue.

Date	Price		Date	Price
1955	5.00		1975	315.00
1965	19.00		1985	5,600.00

$1,000 invested in 1955 would be worth $1,020,000 in 1985.
$1,000 invested in 1965 would be worth $268,421 in 1985.
$1,000 invested in 1975 would be worth $16,190 in 1985.

LIBERTY SEATED, 1873–1874

Motto Above Eagle, Arrows at Date

Weight increased to 12.50 grams. The arrows indicate an increase in weight. Other specifications same as previous issue.

Date	Price		Date	Price
1955	15.00	|	1975	620.00
1965	135.00	|	1985	6,600.00

$1,000 invested in 1955 would be worth $406,666 in 1985.
$1,000 invested in 1965 would be worth $45,185 in 1985.
$1,000 invested in 1975 would be worth $9,838 in 1985.

BARBER, 1892–1915

90% silver, 10% copper; 12.50 grams, 30.6 mm., reeded edge. Designed by Charles E. Barber.

Date	Price		Date	Price
1955	7.50	|	1975	395.00
1965	25.00	|	1985	5,000.00

$1,000 invested in 1955 would be worth $620,000 in 1985.
$1,000 invested in 1965 would be worth $186,000 in 1985.
$1,000 invested in 1975 would be worth $11,772 in 1985.

LIBERTY WALKING, 1916–1947

Designed by Adolph A. Weinman. Other specifications same as previous issue. Net weight: .36169 oz. pure silver.

Date	Price		Date	Price
1955	1.25	|	1975	12.00
1965	2.25	|	1985	310.00

$1,000 invested in 1955 would be worth $232,000 in 1985.
$1,000 invested in 1965 would be worth $128,888 in 1985.
$1,000 invested in 1975 would be worth $24,166 in 1985.

FRANKLIN, 1948–1963

Designed by John R. Sinnock. Other specifications same as previous issue. Net weight: .36169 oz. pure silver. Prices are for coins with full bell lines.

Date	Price		Date	Price
1955	1.00		1975	3.75
1965	1.15		1985	36.00

$1,000 invested in 1955 would be worth $33,000 in 1985.
$1,000 invested in 1965 would be worth $28,695 in 1985.
$1,000 invested in 1975 would be worth $8,800 in 1985.

KENNEDY, 1964 TO DATE

KENNEDY, 1964

Silver

Designed by Gilroy Roberts (obverse) and Frank Gasparro (reverse). Other specifications same as previous issue. Net weight: .36169 oz. pure silver.

SILVER AMERICAN EAGLE ONE DOLLAR
COIN SPECIFICATIONS

CONDITION: Proof
DATE: 1987
MINT: San Francisco Assay Office
MINT MARK: "S"
DIAMETER: 1.598 inches (40.60 mm)
THICKNESS (EST.): .120 inches (3.04 mm)
COMPOSITION: 99.9% Silver
WEIGHT: 1.000 troy oz. (31.103 g)
CONTENT: Silver .999 troy oz. (31.072 g) balance Copper

OBV: Adolph A. Weinman's full length figure of Liberty in full stride, enveloped in folds of the flag, with her right hand extended and branches of laurel and oak in her left.
REV: Heraldic eagle with shield, an olive branch in the right talon and arrows in the left.

COIN ARTISTS: OBV: Adolph A. Weinman (1870-1952). REV: John Mercanti, Sculptor Engraver, United States Mint.

FURTHER INFORMATION: United States Mint. Washington, DC 20220

Date	Price		Date	Price
	1.00		1985	7.00
	3.00			

...ted in 1964 would be worth $6,500 in 1985.
... in 1975 would be worth $2,166 in 1985.

KENNEDY, 1965–1970

Silver Clad

...silver, 20% copper outer layers bonded to inner core of 20.9% silver, 79.1% copper. 11.50 grams, 30.6 mm., reeded edge. Net weight: .1479 oz. pure silver.

Date	Price		Date	Price
1965	1.00		1985	3.00
1975	1.25			

$1,000 invested in 1965 would be worth $3,000 in 1985.
$1,000 invested in 1975 would be worth $2,400 in 1985.

KENNEDY, 1971 TO DATE

Copper-Nickel Clad

75% copper, 25% nickel outer layers bonded to inner core of pure copper. 11.34 grams, 30.6 mm., reeded edge.

Date	Price		Date	Price
1971	1.00		1985	1.00
1975	1.00			

KENNEDY, Dated 1776–1976

Silver Clad Bicentennial Half Dollar

Designed by Gilroy Roberts (obverse) and Seth G. Huntington (reverse). Other specifications same as previous Kennedy silver-clad issue. Net weight: .14792 oz. pure silver.

Date	Price		Date	Price
1976	4.00		1985	5.50

KENNEDY, Dated 1776–1976

Copper-Nickel Clad Bicentennial Half Dollar

Designed by Gilroy Roberts (obverse) and Seth G. Huntington (reverse). Other specifications same as previous Kennedy copper-nickel clad issue.

Date	Price		Date	Price
1976	1.00		1985	1.50

SILVER DOLLARS—1794 TO DATE

With all of the interest in silver dollars, it comes as a surprise to many of today's investors to learn that silver dollars were not popular and did not circulate to any great extent in the United States after 1803. The North and East in particular disliked the coins and they were virtually unused there. But later on, as a political favor to Western mining interests, the government produced more silver dollars than were needed and a huge quantity of the coins were stored unused in Treasury vaults for more than half a century. In the 1960's, the government finally released the coins and, because of their great availability, they have become very popular with collectors and investors. From an investment standpoint, choice uncirculated silver dollars have been one of the best performing United States coins. One of the reasons for this is that, at a starting price of under $1,000, they are still very affordable, while other rarer coin series have gone sky-high.

Early Dollars (1794–1804). Flowing Hair and Draped Bust dollars are almost impossible to find in high grades and are priced accordingly. This series includes a classic rarity, the 1804 dollar, of which 15 are known. The Idler specimen sold for $308,000 in 1985.

Gobrecht Dollars (1836, 1838 and 1839) are patterns, with a design similar to the Liberty Seated Dollars. They were struck in Proof only and come in two major types and several varieties, all of which are rare.

Liberty Seated Dollars (1840–1873) in MS-65 condition are one of the scarcest U.S. coin issues. There are less than a handful of known uncirculated specimens for many dates in the series, and for many other dates, choice specimens are unknown. Choice Proof Liberty Seated dollars are also scarce; mintages were only in the 460 to 1,300 range for even the more common dates.

Trade Dollars (1873–1885) were issued for circulation in the Orient to compete with the dollar-size coins of other countries, particularly Mexico. They are slightly heavier than a regular silver dollar and are a popular type issue. Trade Dollars are more available than Liberty Seated dollars. Proof Trade Dollars are scarce, with mintages between 500 and 1,900 for the common dates.

Morgan Dollars (1878–1921) are the most available and most popularly collected coins of the silver dollar series. Most uncirculated Morgan dollars have marks as a result of having banged against one another when stored in mint bags. Also, improper handling and storage of the coins resulted in a large number of hairlined, cleaned or otherwise less than choice coins. As a result, MS-65 specimens are highly prized for their pristine beauty and almost blemish-free surfaces. Sharply struck, "Proof-like" coins have a highly reflective surface and are even more desirable, although they are much harder to locate. Morgan dollars in choice Proof condition are not as plentiful as mintage figures would indicate.

Peace Dollars (1921–1935) were issued to commemorate the peace that followed the first World War. Even though they are of more recent vintage, they are much scarcer than Morgan Dollars in MS-65 condition.

Eisenhower Dollars (1971–1978) honor both Dwight D. Eisenhower and the first moon landing. But here on earth, the coin has not had a good investment record.

Susan B. Anthony Dollars (1979–1981) were so disliked by the public that their production was stopped after only three years. As far as their investment performance is concerned, perhaps they should be renamed the Anthony adverse dollars.

FLOWING HAIR, 1794–1795

89.24% silver, 10.76% copper; 26.96 grams, approximately 39–40 mm., lettered edge. Designed by Robert Scot.

Date	Price		Date	Price
1955	150.00		1975	6,500.00
1965	950.00		1985	25,000.00

$1,000 invested in 1955 would be worth $150,000 in 1985.
$1,000 invested in 1965 would be worth $23,684 in 1985.
$1,000 invested in 1975 would be worth $3,461 in 1985.

DRAPED BUST, 1795–1804

DRAPED BUST, 1795–1798

Small Eagle on Reverse

Same specifications as previous issue.

Date	Price		Date	Price
1955	135.00		1975	7,650.00
1965	600.00		1985	45,000.00

$1,000 invested in 1955 would be worth $333,333 in 1985.
$1,000 invested in 1965 would be worth $75,000 in 1985.
$1,000 invested in 1975 would be worth $5,882 in 1985.

DRAPED BUST, 1798–1804

Large (Heraldic) Eagle on Reverse

Same specifications as previous issue.

Date	Price		Date	Price
1955	85.00		1975	6,500.00
1965	230.00		1985	32,500.00

$1,000 invested in 1955 would be worth $382,352 in 1985.
$1,000 invested in 1965 would be worth $141,304 in 1985.
$1,000 invested in 1975 would be worth $5,000 in 1985.

GOBRECHT DOLLARS, 1836–1839

All coins were struck in Proof only.

GOBRECHT DOLLARS, 1836

No Stars on Obverse, Stars on Reverse

26.96 grams, plain edge. Engraved by Christian Gobrecht from designs by Thomas Sully and Titian Peale. Other specifications same as previous issue.

Date	Price		Date	Price
1955	185.00		1975	2,700.00
1965	1,350.00		1985	17,500.00

$1,000 invested in 1955 would be worth $94,594 in 1985.
$1,000 invested in 1965 would be worth $12,962 in 1985.
$1,000 invested in 1975 would be worth $6,481 in 1985.

GOBRECHT DOLLARS, 1838–1839

Stars on Obverse, No Stars on Reverse

Weight reduced to 26.73 grams, reeded edge. Other specifications same as previous issue.

Date	Price		Date	Price
1955	300.00		1975	4,500.00
1965	2,750.00		1985	17,500.00

$1,000 invested in 1955 would be worth $58,333 in 1985.
$1,000 invested in 1965 would be worth $6,363 in 1985.
$1,000 invested in 1975 would be worth $3,888 in 1985.

LIBERTY SEATED, 1840–1873

LIBERTY SEATED, 1840–1865

No Motto on Reverse

90% silver, 10% copper; 26.73 grams, 38.1 mm., reeded edge. Designed by Christian Gobrecht. Net weight: .77344 oz. pure silver.

Date	Price		Date	Price
1955	21.00		1975	575.00
1965	52.50		1985	9,000.00

$1,000 invested in 1955 would be worth $395,238 in 1985.
$1,000 invested in 1965 would be worth $158,095 in 1985.
$1,000 invested in 1975 would be worth $14,434 in 1985.

LIBERTY SEATED, 1866–1873

With Motto "In God We Trust" on Reverse

Same specifications as previous issue.

Date	Price		Date	Price
1955	17.50		1975	600.00
1965	35.00		1985	9,200.00

$1,000 invested in 1955 would be worth $485,714 in 1985.
$1,000 invested in 1965 would be worth $242,857 in 1985.
$1,000 invested in 1975 would be worth $14,166 in 1985.

MORGAN, 1878–1921

Liberty Head

90% silver, 10% copper; 26.73 grams, 38.1 mm., reeded edge. Designed by George T. Morgan. Net weight: .77344 oz. pure silver.

Date	Price		Date	Price
1955	2.50		1975	5.75
1965	2.00		1985	435.00

$1,000 invested in 1955 would be worth $160,000 in 1985.
$1,000 invested in 1965 would be worth $200,000 in 1985.
$1,000 invested in 1975 would be worth $69,565 in 1985.

PEACE, 1921–1935

PEACE, 1921

High Relief

Designed by Anthony De Francisci. Other specifications same as previous issue. Net weight: .77344 oz. pure silver.

Date	Price		Date	Price
1955	6.00		1975	106.50
1965	30.00		1985	3,750.00

$1,000 invested in 1955 would be worth $566,666 in 1985.
$1,000 invested in 1965 would be worth $113,333 in 1985.
$1,000 invested in 1975 would be worth $31,924 in 1985.

PEACE, 1922–1935

Low Relief

Same specifications as previous issue.

Date	Price		Date	Price
1955	2.00		1975	5.40
1965	2.00		1985	460.00

$1,000 invested in 1955 would be worth $205,000 in 1985.
$1,000 invested in 1965 would be worth $205,000 in 1985.
$1,000 invested in 1975 would be worth $75,925 in 1985.

TRADE, 1873–1883

90% silver, 10% copper; 27.22 grams, 38.1 mm., reeded edge. Designed by William Barber.

Date	Price		Date	Price
1955	10.00		1975	395.00
1965	25.00		1985	6,100.00

$1,000 invested in 1955 would be worth $560,000 in 1985.
$1,000 invested in 1965 would be worth $224,000 in 1985.
$1,000 invested in 1975 would be worth $14,177 in 1985.

EISENHOWER, 1971–1978

EISENHOWER, 1971–1978

Silver Clad

80% silver, 20% copper outer layers bonded to inner core of 20.9% silver, 79.1% copper. 24.59 grams, 38.1 mm., reeded edge. Designed by Frank Gasparro. Net weight: .3161 oz. pure silver.

Date	Price		Date	Price
1975	4.75		1985	7.00

$1,000 invested in 1975 would be worth $1,368 in 1985.

EISENHOWER, 1971–1978

Copper-Nickel Clad

75% copper, 25% nickel outer layers bonded to inner core of pure copper. 22.68 grams, 38.1 mm., reeded edge.

Date	Price		Date	Price
1975	1.50		1985	2.25

$1.000 invested in 1975 would be worth $1,333 in 1985.

EISENHOWER, Dated 1776–1976

Silver-Clad Bicentennial Dollar

Reverse design by Dennis R. Williams. Other specifications same as previous Eisenhower silver-clad issue.

Date	Price		Date	Price
1976	6.00		1985	8.00

EISENHOWER, Dated 1776–1976

Copper-Nickel Clad Bicentennial Dollar

Reverse design by Dennis R. Williams. Same specifications as previous Eisenhower copper-nickel clad issue.

Date	Price		Date	Price
1976	1.60		1985	2.25

SUSAN B. ANTHONY, 1979–1981

75% copper, 25% nickel outer layers bonded to inner core of pure copper. 8.1 grams, 26.5 mm., reeded edge. Designed by Frank Gasparro.

Date	Price		Date	Price
1979	1.00		1985	1.50

GOLD COINS

As a group, gold coins are the rarest United States coins to obtain in choice uncirculated condition. They were struck in smaller quantities than other coins and the number surviving is much less than the mintages would indicate.

Many issues were stored at the Treasury and used as backing for paper currency and later melted. The rarity of the early gold pieces is due to the fact that the gold content was reduced in 1834, making the previous issues' gold value greater than face value, causing both official and unofficial melting.

Small denomination gold coins weren't saved or hoarded to the extent that larger denominations were and fewer have survived in choice condition. As a result of the 1933 order prohibiting United States citizens from holding monetary gold, a vast quantity of coins were surrendered to the government, and these, in addition to all of the gold coins held by the Treasury at the time, were melted in 1933. Finally, because of the softness of the metal, gold coins become scratched and nicked more readily than other coins. Ideally, the coins should be sharply struck, free of marks and abrasions and possess original mint luster.

GOLD DOLLARS—1849–1889

Type One Dollars (1849–1854) are the smallest in size and the second rarest of the three types. While the luster and strike are good on Type Ones, blemish-free, and mint-marked specimens are hard to locate.

Type Two Dollars (1854–1856) are among the rarest of all U.S. gold coins. Very few have survived in choice uncirculated condition and they are priced out of the range of all but the wealthiest investors. Gems are desirable and very expensive.

Type Three Dollars (1856–1889) are generally considered the most beautiful of the three types, and are one of the easiest U.S. gold coins to acquire in choice or gem uncirculated condition. The obverse on a Type III Gold Dollar is the same design that appears on the Three Dollar Gold Piece. Because of the popularity of their design, they are more in demand and more expensive than Type One Dollars, which are actually rarer. The late dates, especially, have survived in excellent condition and in goodly quantities.

LIBERTY, 1849–1854

Type I, Small Planchet

90% gold, 10% copper; 1.672 grams, 13 mm., reeded edge. Designed by James B. Longacre. Net weight .04837 oz. pure gold.

Date	Price		Date	Price
1955	10.00		1975	410.00
1965	45.00		1985	6,100.00

$1,000 invested in 1955 would be worth $560,000 in 1985.
$1,000 invested in 1965 would be worth $124,444 in 1985.
$1,000 invested in 1975 would be worth $13,658 in 1985.

INDIAN, 1854–1856

Type II, Small Head

The diameter was increased to 15 mm. Other specifications same as previous issue.

Date	Price		Date	Price
1955	15.00		1975	2,800.00
1965	200.00		1985	19,500.00

$1,000 invested in 1955 would be worth $1,300,000 in 1985.
$1,000 invested in 1965 would be worth $97,500 in 1985.
$1,000 invested in 1975 would be worth $6,964 in 1985.

LIBERTY, 1856–1889

Type III, Large Head

Same specifications as previous issue.

Date	Price		Date	Price
1955	11.00		1975	410.00
1965	50.00		1985	5,100.00

$1,000 invested in 1955 would be worth $422,727 in 1985.
$1,000 invested in 1965 would be worth $93,000 in 1985.
$1,000 invested in 1975 would be worth $11,341 in 1985.

QUARTER EAGLES (TWO AND A HALF DOLLAR GOLD PIECES)—1796–1929

Early Quarter Eagles (1796–1839) are rare in all grades and expensive. These coins are best suited to the portfolios of only the wealthiest investors.

Coronet (Liberty) Quarter Eagles (1840–1907) are relatively common, although many of the pre-Civil War issues are rare or uncollectable in uncirculated condition. The 1859 and 1861 come with both large and small arrows. The 20th century issues are easier to acquire. Proof specimens, on the other hand, are rare coins, with mintages in the 20 to 200 coin range. This series contains two of my personal favorite coins, the 1864 and 1865 Coronet Quarter Eagles.

Indian Quarter Eagles (1908–1929), although of more recent vintage, are actually as scarce in top condition as the late date Liberties and true gem uncirculated specimens are hard to come by. Along with the Indian Half Eagle, it is unique in U.S. coinage in that it has an incuse design. Because of this design, the coin is difficult for the novice to grade accurately.

CAPPED BUST, 1796–1807

CAPPED BUST, 1796

No Stars on Obverse

91.67% gold, 8.33% copper; 4.37 grams, 20 mm., reeded edge. Designed by Robert Scot.

Date	Price		Date	Price
1955	375.00		1975	11,000.00
1965	6,750.00		1985	55,000.00

$1,000 invested in 1955 would be worth $146,666 in 1985.
$1,000 invested in 1965 would be worth $8,148 in 1985.
$1,000 invested in 1975 would be worth $5,000 in 1985.

CAPPED BUST, 1796–1807

Stars on Obverse

Same specifications as previous issue.

Date	Price		Date	Price
1955	100.00		1975	1,900.00
1965	1,250.00		1985	27,500.00

$1,000 invested in 1955 would be worth $275,000 in 1985.
$1,000 invested in 1965 would be worth $22,000 in 1985.
$1,000 invested in 1975 would be worth $14,473 in 1985.

CAPPED BUST LEFT, 1808

Head Facing Left, Large Size

Designed by John Reich. Other specifications same as previous issue.

Date	Price		Date	Price
1955	300.00		1975	10,000.00
1965	6,000.00		1985	55,000.00

$1,000 invested in 1955 would be worth $183,333 in 1985.
$1,000 invested in 1965 would be worth $9,166 in 1985.
$1,000 invested in 1975 would be worth $5,500 in 1985.

CAPPED HEAD, 1821–1834

CAPPED HEAD, 1821–1827

Head Facing Left, Reduced Size, Large Planchet

Diameter reduced to 18.5 mm. Other specifications same as previous issue.

Date	Price		Date	Price
1955	125.00		1975	4,500.00
1965	1,250.00		1985	26,000.00

$1,000 invested in 1955 would be worth $208,000 in 1985.
$1,000 invested in 1965 would be worth $20,800 in 1985.
$1,000 invested in 1975 would be worth $5,777 in 1985.

CAPPED HEAD, 1829–1834

Head Facing Left, Reduced Size, Small Planchet

Same specifications as previous issue.

Date	Price		Date	Price
1955	75.00		1975	2,600.00
1965	800.00		1985	22,000.00

$1,000 invested in 1955 would be worth $293,333 in 1985.
$1,000 invested in 1965 would be worth $27,500 in 1985.
$1,000 invested in 1975 would be worth $8,461 in 1985.

CLASSIC HEAD, 1834–1839

89.92% gold, 10.08% copper; 4.18 grams, 18.2 mm., reeded edge. Designed by William Kneass. 1835 through 1839 have a slightly different head.

Date	Price		Date	Price
1955	17.50		1975	2,950.00
1965	100.00		1985	10,000.00

$1,000 invested in 1955 would be worth $571,428 in 1985.
$1,000 invested in 1965 would be worth $100,000 in 1985.
$1,000 invested in 1975 would be worth $3,389 in 1985.

CORONET (LIBERTY), 1840–1907

CORONET (LIBERTY), 1840–1859

Large Arrows on Reverse

90% gold, 10% copper; 4.18 grams, 18 mm., reeded edge. Designed by Christian Gobrecht. Net weight: .12094 oz. pure gold.

Date	Price		Date	Price
1955	15.00		1975	180.00
1965	55.00		1985	4,100.00

$1,000 invested in 1955 would be worth $256,666 in 1985.
$1,000 invested in 1965 would be worth $70,000 in 1985.
$1,000 invested in 1975 would be worth $21,388 in 1985.

CORONET (LIBERTY), 1860–1907

Small Arrows on Reverse

Same specifications as previous issue.

Date	Price		Date	Price
1955	15.00		1975	180.00
1965	50.00		1985	4,100.00

$1,000 invested in 1955 would be worth $256,666 in 1985.
$1,000 invested in 1965 would be worth $77,000 in 1985.
$1,000 invested in 1975 would be worth $21,388 in 1985.

INDIAN, 1908–1929

Designed by Bela Lyon Pratt. Other specifications same as previous issue. Net weight: .12094 oz. pure gold.

Date	Price		Date	Price
1955	10.00		1975	150.00
1965	32.00		1985	4,100.00

$1,000 invested in 1955 would be worth $385,000 in 1985.
$1,000 invested in 1965 would be worth $120,312 in 1985.
$1,000 invested in 1975 would be worth $25,666 in 1985.

THREE DOLLAR GOLD—1854–1889

Three Dollar gold pieces were never popular with the public and only a relatively small number were saved. As a result, they are the second rarest U.S. gold type coin of the 12 modern gold coins. Both choice Uncirculated and choice Proof specimens of this Liberty-headed coin are rare and expensive. Gem coins of all dates are extremely rare. It is said that this coin was created to make it easy for the public to buy sheets of three cent stamps. This series contains the classic rarities of 1875 and 1876, and the unique 1870-S which brought $687,500 in the 1982 Eliasberg auction.

THREE DOLLARS, 1854

Small "Dollars" on Reverse

90% gold, 10% copper; 5.015 grams, 20.5 mm., reeded edge. Designed by James B. Longacre. Net weight: .14512 oz. pure gold.

Date	Price		Date	Price
1955	35.00		1975	2,100.00
1965	245.00		1985	11,000.00

$1,000 invested in 1955 would be worth $314,285 in 1985.
$1,000 invested in 1965 would be worth $44,897 in 1985.
$1,000 invested in 1975 would be worth $5,238 in 1985.

THREE DOLLARS, 1855–1889

Large "Dollars" on Reverse

Same specifications as previous issue.

Date	Price		Date	Price
1955	35.00		1975	2,100.00
1965	240.00		1985	11,000.00

$1,000 invested in 1955 would be worth $314,285 in 1985.
$1,000 invested in 1965 would be worth $45,833 in 1985.
$1,000 invested in 1975 would be worth $5,238 in 1985.

FOUR DOLLAR GOLD PIECES ("STELLAS")—1879–1880

Four Dollar gold pieces are technically "pattern" coins, designed to serve as an international coinage based on the metric system. They are the rarest type of the U.S. gold series, and although they were never officially issued, advanced collectors and wealthy investors often include them in their holdings. Struck in Proof only. The Coiled Hair type is extremely rare.

FOUR DOLLARS, 1879–1880

Flowing Hair

90% gold, 10% copper, 108 grains, 22 mm., reeded edge, (Restrikes of 1879 Flowing Hair: 103.2–109.0 grains). Designed by Charles E. Barber.

Date	Price		Date	Price
1955	800.00		1975	15,000.00
1965	6,000.00		1985	48,000.00

$1,000 invested in 1955 would be worth $60,000 in 1985.
$1,000 invested in 1965 would be worth $8,000 in 1985.
$1,000 invested in 1975 would be worth $3,200 in 1985.

FOUR DOLLARS, 1879–1880

Coiled Hair

Designed by George T. Morgan. Other specifications same as previous issue.

Date	Price		Date	Price
1955	1,300.00		1975	* 67,500.00
1965	14,500.00		1985	100,000.00

$1,000 invested in 1955 would be worth $69,230 in 1985.
$1,000 invested in 1965 would be worth $6,206 in 1985.
$1,000 invested in 1975 would be worth $1,333 in 1985.

* Paramount 1980 Davis Sale.

HALF EAGLES (FIVE DOLLAR GOLD)—1795–1929

Early Half Eagles (1795–1838) are extremely rare in uncirculated condition and have more rare and uncollectable dates than any other U.S. coin series. The dates 1795, 1797, 1798, 1807 and 1834 each exist in two distinct types. The 1822 Five Dollar gold piece is considered the most valuable regular issue coin of the entire U.S. series. This coin brought $687,500 at the Eliasberg Sale in 1982. This type also includes the classic rarity, the 1815 Half Eagle.

Coronet (Liberty) Half Eagles, particularly the "No motto" type of 1839, and "No motto" type of 1839–1866) are extremely expensive in uncirculated condition, particularly the early issues, most of which are unknown in MS-65 condition, and many are unknown uncirculated. The later "With motto" dates are occasionally available, although very popular and expensive. Proofs, with mintages in the 20 to 230 coin range, are even rarer than the Liberty Quarter Eagles.

Indian Half Eagles (1908–1929) are among the most desirable of this century's gold type coins in uncirculated condition. Like the Indian Quarter Eagles, the Indian Half Eagles have Bela Lyon Pratt's incuse designs and lettering, making them difficult for the novice to grade accurately. These coins are also scarce in choice Proof.

CAPPED BUST, 1795–1807

CAPPED BUST, 1795–1798

Small Eagle on Reverse

91.67% gold, 8.33% copper; 8.75 grams, 25 mm., reeded edge. Designed by Robert Scot.

Date	Price		Date	Price
1955	225.00		1975	4,250.00
1965	1,600.00		1985	42,500.00

$1,000 invested in 1955 would be worth $188,888 in 1985.
$1,000 invested in 1965 would be worth $26,562 in 1985.
$1,000 invested in 1975 would be worth $10,000 in 1985.

CAPPED BUST, 1795–1807

Large (Heraldic) Eagle on Reverse

Same specifications as previous issue.

Date	Price		Date	Price
1955	65.00		1975	1,250.00
1965	475.00		1985	22,000.00

$1,000 invested in 1955 would be worth $338,461 in 1985.
$1,000 invested in 1965 would be worth $46,315 in 1985.
$1,000 invested in 1975 would be worth $17,600 in 1985.

CAPPED AND DRAPED BUST, 1807–1812

Head Facing Left

Designed by John Reich. Other specifications same as previous issue.

Date	Price		Date	Price
1955	65.00		1975	1,100.00
1965	450.00		1985	20,000.00

$1,000 invested in 1955 would be worth $307,692 in 1985.
$1,000 invested in 1965 would be worth $44,444 in 1985.
$1,000 invested in 1975 would be worth $18,181 in 1985.

CAPPED HEAD, 1813–1834

CAPPED HEAD, 1813–1829

Large Diameter

Same specifications as previous issue.

Date	Price		Date	Price
1955	90.00		1975	1,300.00
1965	650.00		1985	25,000.00

$1,000 invested in 1955 would be worth $277,777 in 1985.
$1,000 invested in 1965 would be worth $38,461 in 1985.
$1,000 invested in 1975 would be worth $19,230 in 1985.

CAPPED HEAD, 1829–1834

Small Diameter

In addition to a reduced diameter, these coins also have smaller letters, dates and stars. Other specifications same as previous issue.

Date	Price		Date	Price
1955	325.00		1975	3,800.00
1965	1,350.00		1985	35,000.00

$1,000 invested in 1955 would be worth $107,692 in 1985.
$1,000 invested in 1965 would be worth $25,925 in 1985.
$1,000 invested in 1975 would be worth $9,210 in 1985.

CLASSIC HEAD, 1834–1838

89.92% gold, 10.08% copper; 8.36 grams, 22.5 mm., reeded edge. Designed by William Kneass. 1835 through 1838 have a slightly different head.

Date	Price		Date	Price
1955	25.00		1975	2,800.00
1965	100.00		1985	12,000.00

$1,000 invested in 1955 would be worth $480,000 in 1985.
$1,000 invested in 1965 would be worth $120,000 in 1985.
$1,000 invested in 1975 would be worth $4,285 in 1985.

CORONET (LIBERTY), 1839–1866

CORONET (LIBERTY), 1839

No Motto Above Eagle, Small Letters

90% gold, 10% copper; 8.359 grams, 22.5 mm., reeded edge. Designed by Christian Gobrecht. Net weight: .24187 oz. pure gold.

Date	MS-60 Price		Date	MS-60 Price
1955	25.00		1975	750.00
1965	50.00		1985	1,900.00

This type is rarely available in uncirculated grades.

> $1,000 invested in 1955 would be worth $76,000 in 1985.
> $1,000 invested in 1965 would be worth $38,000 in 1985.
> $1,000 invested in 1975 would be worth $2,533 in 1985.

CORONET (LIBERTY), 1839–1866

No Motto Above Eagle, Large Letters

Diameter, 1839–40: 22.5 mm.; 1840–1929: 21.6 mm. Other specifications same as previous issue. Some coins of 1840 have the larger diameter.

Date	Price		Date	Price
1955	25.00		1975	750.00
1965	50.00		1985	9,000.00

This type is scarce in uncirculated grades.

> $1,000 invested in 1955 would be worth $360,000 in 1985.
> $1,000 invested in 1965 would be worth $180,000 in 1985.
> $1,000 invested in 1975 would be worth $12,000 in 1985.

CORONET (LIBERTY) 1866–1908

Motto "In God We Trust" Above Eagle

Same specifications as previous issue.

Date	Price		Date	Price
1955	16.00		1975	135.00
1965	32.50		1985	5,600.00

$1,000 invested in 1955 would be worth $350,000 in 1985.
$1,000 invested in 1965 would be worth $172,307 in 1985.
$1,000 invested in 1975 would be worth $41,481 in 1985.

INDIAN, 1908–1929

Designed by Bela Lyon Pratt. Other specifications same as previous issue.

Date	Price		Date	Price
1955	15.00		1975	265.00
1965	35.00		1985	6,100.00

$1,000 invested in 1955 would be worth $373,333 in 1985.
$1,000 invested in 1965 would be worth $160,000 in 1985.
$1,000 invested in 1975 would be worth $21,132 in 1985.

EAGLES (TEN DOLLAR GOLD)—1795–1933

Early Eagles (1795–1804) are among the rarest of all of the early issues of U.S. gold coins and all are very expensive. The rarest regular issue date is 1798. Many of these early coins have adjustment marks from the Mint's practice of adjusting planchet weight. The date 1797 exists in two distinct types. No Ten Dollar gold pieces were struck from 1805 to 1837.

Coronet (Liberty) Eagles, particularly the "No motto" types of 1838–39, and 1839–1866 are extremely difficult to find in uncirculated condition. Before the turn of the century, many of the early dates are unknown in even MS-60 condition. This is one of the toughest types to find nice, and this series is uncollectable by date. Proofs are also extremely rare; only 20 to 120 pieces were minted in the years they were produced. The "With motto" types (1866–1907) are much in demand, and very expensive.

Indian Eagles (1907–1933) were designed by Augustus Saint-Gaudens, considered by many to be the greatest of modern American sculptors. The Ten Dollar Indian was only minted in 15 of the 26 years the series existed. Although it is of more recent vintage, it is even rarer than the late date Ten Dollar Liberties in choice uncirculated condition. The dates 1907 and 1908 exist in two distinct types. The 1933 Ten Dollar Indian is the rarest coin in the series and was the only U.S. gold coin of any kind officially issued in 1933.

CAPPED BUST, 1795–1804

CAPPED BUST, 1795–1797

Small Eagle on Reverse

91.67% gold, 8.33% copper; 17.50 grams, 33 mm., reeded edge. Designed by Robert Scot.

Date	Price		Date	Price
1955	275.00		1975	7,000.00
1965	1,800.00		1985	50,000.00

$1,000 invested in 1955 would be worth $181,818 in 1985.
$1,000 invested in 1965 would be worth $27,777 in 1985.
$1,000 invested in 1975 would be worth $7,142 in 1985.

CAPPED BUST, 1797–1804

Large (Heraldic) Eagle on Reverse

Same specifications as previous issue.

Date	Price		Date	Price
1955	130.00		1975	2,500.00
1965	725.00		1985	30,000.00

$1,000 invested in 1955 would be worth $230,769 in 1985.
$1,000 invested in 1965 would be worth $41,379 in 1985.
$1,000 invested in 1975 would be worth $12,000 in 1985.

CORONET (LIBERTY), 1838–1907

CORONET (LIBERTY), 1838–1839

No Motto Above Eagle, Large Letters

90% gold, 10% copper; 16.718 grams, 27 mm., reeded edge. Designed by Christian Gobrecht. Net weight: .48375 oz. pure gold.

Date	Price		Date	Price
1955	90.00		1975	2,800.00
1965	550.00		1985	14,500.00

This type is rarely available in uncirculated grades.

$1,000 invested in 1955 would be worth $161,111 in 1985.
$1,000 invested in 1965 would be worth $26,363 in 1985.
$1,000 invested in 1975 would be worth $5,178 in 1985.

CORONET (LIBERTY), 1839–1866

No Motto Above Eagle, Small Letters

Same specifications as previous issue.

Date	MS-63 Price		Date	MS-63 Price
1955	37.50		1975	2,800.00
1965	70.00		1985	17,500.00

This type is rarely available in uncirculated grades.

$1,000 invested in 1955 would be worth $466,666 in 1985.
$1,000 invested in 1965 would be worth $250,000 in 1985.
$1,000 invested in 1975 would be worth $6,250 in 1985.

CORONET (LIBERTY), 1866–1907

Motto "In God We Trust" Above Eagle

Same specifications as previous issue.

Date	Price		Date	Price
1955	35.00		1975	220.00
1965	45.00		1985	5,200.00

$1,000 invested in 1955 would be worth $131,428 in 1985.
$1,000 invested in 1965 would be worth $102,222 in 1985.
$1,000 invested in 1975 would be worth $20,909 in 1985.

INDIAN, 1907–1933

INDIAN, 1907–1908

No Motto on Reverse

90% pure gold, 10% copper; 16.718 grams, 27 mm. Edge: 46 raised stars. Designed by Augustus Saint-Gaudens. Net weight: .48375 oz. pure gold.

Date	Price		Date	Price
1955	35.00		1975	350.00
1965	70.00		1985	5,700.00

$1,000 invested in 1955 would be worth $151,428 in 1985.
$1,000 invested in 1965 would be worth $75,714 in 1985.
$1,000 invested in 1975 would be worth $15,142 in 1985.

INDIAN, 1908–1933

Motto "In God We Trust" on Reverse

Edge: 46 raised stars (1908–1911), 48 raised stars (1912–1933). Other specifications same as previous issue.

Date	Price		Date	Price
1955	32.50		1975	295.00
1965	50.00		1985	5,700.00

$1,000 invested in 1955 would be worth $163,076 in 1985.
$1,000 invested in 1965 would be worth $106,000 in 1985.
$1,000 invested in 1975 would be worth $17,966 in 1985.

DOUBLE EAGLES (TWENTY DOLLAR GOLD)— 1849–1933

Coronet (Liberty) Double Eagles, Type I, 1849–1866, and Type II, 1866–1876, are extremely difficult to find in choice uncirculated condition, although they are common in lesser grades. The more common Type III, 1877–1907 is much in demand. The most frequently encountered date is 1904.

St. Gaudens Double Eagles (1907–1933) are considered by many to be our most beautiful coins and are the most popular gold coins with investors. Although they are easier to locate than the Liberty type in uncirculated condition, pre-World War I issues in top grade condition are still difficult to find. The date 1907 exists in three distinct types and 1908 exists in two distinct types. Proof St. Gaudens were minted only between 1908 and 1915 in very low quantities and are extremely rare and expensive.

CORONET (LIBERTY), 1849–1907

CORONET (LIBERTY), 1849–1866

Type I: No Motto Above Eagle

90% gold, 10% copper; 33.436 grams, 34 mm., reeded edge. Designed by James B. Longacre. Net weight: .96750 oz. pure gold.

Date	Price		Date	Price
1955	80.00		1975	2,800.00
1965	120.00		1985	10,000.00

$1,000 invested in 1955 would be worth $125,000 in 1985.
$1,000 invested in 1965 would be worth $83,333 in 1985.
$1,000 invested in 1975 would be worth $3,571 in 1985.

CORONET (LIBERTY), 1866–1876

Type II: Motto Above Eagle, "Twenty D." on Reverse

Same specifications as previous issue.

Date	Price		Date	Price
1955	70.00		1975	600.00
1965	95.00		1985	7,200.00

$1,000 invested in 1955 would be worth $92,857 in 1985.
$1,000 invested in 1965 would be worth $68,421 in 1985.
$1,000 invested in 1975 would be worth $10,833 in 1985.

CORONET (LIBERTY), 1877–1907

Type III: Motto Above Eagle, "Twenty Dollars" on Reverse

Same specifications as previous issue.

Date	Price		Date	Price
1955	70.00		1975	285.00
1965	80.00		1985	4,400.00

$1,000 invested in 1955 would be worth $57,857 in 1985.
$1,000 invested in 1965 would be worth $50,625 in 1985.
$1,000 invested in 1975 would be worth $14,210 in 1985.

ST. GAUDENS, 1907–1932

ST. GAUDENS, 1907

High Relief, Date in Roman Numerals

90% gold, 10% copper; 33.436 grams, 34 mm., plain and lettered edge varieties. Designed by Augustus Saint-Gaudens. Net weight: .96750 oz. pure gold.

Date	Price		Date	Price
1955	145.00		1975	3,000.00
1965	850.00		1985	20,000.00

$1,000 invested in 1955 would be worth $124,137 in 1985.
$1,000 invested in 1965 would be worth $21,176 in 1985.
$1,000 invested in 1975 would be worth $6,000 in 1985.

ST. GAUDENS, 1907–1908

Low Relief, No Motto Below Eagle, Date in Arabic Numerals

Same specifications as previous issue.

Date	Price		Date	Price
1955	75.00		1975	375.00
1965	87.50		1985	3,100.00

$1,000 invested in 1955 would be worth $36,666 in 1985.
$1,000 invested in 1965 would be worth $31,428 in 1985.
$1,000 invested in 1975 would be worth $7,333 in 1985.

ST. GAUDENS, 1908–1932

Low Relief, Motto Below Eagle

Same specifications as previous issue.

Date	Price		Date	Price
1955	50.00		1975	270.00
1965	80.00		1985	3,100.00

$1,000 invested in 1955 would be worth $55,000 in 1985.
$1,000 invested in 1965 would be worth $34,375 in 1985.
$1,000 invested in 1975 would be worth $10,185 in 1985.

COMMEMORATIVE SILVER COINS—1892–1986

Commemorative coins are like numismatic history books; they are authorized by Congress from time to time to honor events and to fund monuments and festivities that commemorate historical persons, places and things. Commemoratives represent a fascinating, artistic record of this nation's development.

First authorized by the Coinage Act of August 5, 1892, the United States issued only 50 different types of silver commemorative coins between 1892 and 1954, and then issued one in 1982, one in 1983, two in 1984, and three in 1986, for a total of 57 types of coins. Because of the relatively small number of issues, it is still possible to assemble a complete type set of these coins. Most of the commemorative issues have relatively low mintage and the supply of choice uncirculated pieces is shrinking due to investor demand.

As a rule, commemoratives issued from 1892 to 1928 were not saved in large quantities and they are difficult to find in choice uncirculated condition. The later commemoratives were saved and are abundant in the top grades.

COMMEMORATIVE QUARTER DOLLARS

ISABELLA QUARTER DOLLAR, 1893

Issued for the World's Columbian Exposition in Chicago, it is our only commemorative quarter. Head of Queen Isabella of Spain. Reverse: Kneeling female spinner. Designed by Charles E. Barber. Mintage: 24,200. 90% silver, 10% copper; 6.25 grams, 24.3 mm., reeded edge. Net weight .18084 oz. pure silver. Very rare in uncirculated condition.

Date	Price		Date	Price
1955	17.50		1975	175.00
1965	90.00		1985	3,700.00

$1,000 invested in 1955 would be worth $191,428 in 1985.
$1,000 invested in 1965 would be worth $37,222 in 1985.
$1,000 invested in 1975 would be worth $19,142 in 1985.

COMMEMORATIVE DOLLARS

LAFAYETTE DOLLAR, 1900

Conjoined heads of Washington and Lafayette. Reverse: The statue of Lafayette that was erected in Paris as a gift from the youth of the United States. The dies were prepared by Charles E. Barber. In uncirculated condition, this coin is among the rarest in the commemorative series. Mintage: 36,026. 90% silver, 10% copper; 26.73 grams, 38.1 mm., reeded edge. Net weight .77344 oz. pure silver. Extremely rare in uncirculated condition.

Date	Price		Date	Price
1955	32.50		1975	525.00
1965	140.00		1985	8,200.00

$1,000 invested in 1955 would be worth $227,692 in 1985.
$1,000 invested in 1965 would be worth $52,857 in 1985.
$1,000 invested in 1975 would be worth $14,095 in 1985.

LOS ANGELES OLYMPICS DOLLAR, 1983

Discuss thrower. Reverse: American eagle. Designed by Elizabeth Jones. Same specifications as previous issue. Mintage: Unc.—642,571. Proof—1,557,025.

Date	Price		Date	Price
1983	28.00		1985	28.00

LOS ANGELES OLYMPICS DOLLAR, 1984

Sculpture at entrance to Coliseum. Reverse: American eagle. Designed by Robert Graham. Same specifications as previous issue. Mintage: Unc.—451,304. Proof—1,801,210.

Date	Price		Date	Price
1984	28.00		1985	28.00

STATUE OF LIBERTY DOLLAR, 1986

Statue of Liberty, with Ellis Island in background. Reverse: Hand holding torch. Same specifications as previous issue. Mintage: 10,000,000 total Proof and Uncirculated authorized by Congress for 1986. Struck to order.

Date	Proof Price
1986	24.50

COMMEMORATIVE HALF DOLLARS

All Commemorative Half Dollars are of the following standards, except where otherwise noted: Metal content: 90% silver, 10% copper. Weight: 12.50 grams. Diameter: 30.6 mm. Reeded edge. Net weight: .36169 oz. pure silver.

ALABAMA CENTENNIAL, 1921

Conjoined heads of Governor Bibb (1821) and Governor Kilby (1921). Reverse: Eagle. Designed by Laura Gardin Fraser. Extremely rare in gem uncirculated condition. Mintage: 50,000.

Date	Price		Date	Price
1955	30.00		1975	170.00
1965	60.00		1985	2,800.00

$1,000 invested in 1955 would be worth $85,000 in 1985.
$1,000 invested in 1965 would be worth $42,500 in 1985.
$1,000 invested in 1975 would be worth $15,000 in 1985.

ALBANY—250TH ANNIVERSARY, 1936

Beaver. Reverse: Governor Dongan, Peter Schuyler and Robert Livingston. Designed by Gertrude K. Lathrop. Mintage: 17,000.

Date	Price		Date	Price
1955	15.00		1975	131.50
1965	65.00		1985	875.00

$1,000 invested in 1955 would be worth $54,000 in 1985.
$1,000 invested in 1965 would be worth $12,461 in 1985.
$1,000 invested in 1975 would be worth $6,159 in 1985.

BATTLE OF ANTIETAM, 1937

Seventy-fifth anniversary of the Civil War battle. Generals McClellan and Lee. Reverse: Burnside Bridge. Designed by William Marks. Mintage: 18,028.

Date	Price		Date	Price
1955	25.00		1975	160.00
1965	115.00		1985	900.00

$1,000 invested in 1955 would be worth $32,800 in 1985.
$1,000 invested in 1965 would be worth $7,130 in 1985.
$1,000 invested in 1975 would be worth $5,125 in 1985.

ARKANSAS CENTENNIAL, 1935–1939

Conjoined Liberty and Indian heads. Reverse: Eagle. Designed by Edward Everett Burr. This coin is usually poorly struck; choice uncirculated coins are rarer than the mintage would indicate. Mintage: 85,300.

Date	Price		Date	Price
1955	4.00		1975	36.00
1965	12.00		1985	540.00

$1,000 invested in 1955 would be worth $123,750 in 1985.
$1,000 invested in 1965 would be worth $41,250 in 1985.
$1,000 invested in 1975 would be worth $13,750 in 1985.

BAY BRIDGE: SAN FRANCISCO-OAKLAND, 1936

Grizzly bear. Reverse: Bridge. Designed by Jacques Schnier. Mintage: 71,424.

Date	Price		Date	Price
1955	8.00		1975	50.00
1965	40.00		1985	510.00

$1,000 invested in 1955 would be worth $58,750 in 1985.
$1,000 invested in 1965 would be worth $11,750 in 1985.
$1,000 invested in 1975 would be worth $9,400 in 1985.

DANIEL BOONE BICENTENNIAL, 1934–1938

Head of Boone. Reverse: Boone with Chief Black Fish. Designed by Augustus Lukeman. One of the more common commemorative issues. Mintage: 87,185.

Date	Price		Date	Price
1955	4.50		1975	40.00
1965	13.50		1985	360.00

$1,000 invested in 1955 would be worth $74,444 in 1985.
$1,000 invested in 1965 would be worth $24,814 in 1985.
$1,000 invested in 1975 would be worth $8,375 in 1985.

BRIDGEPORT, CONNECTICUT CENTENNIAL, 1936

Head of P. T. Barnum. Reverse: Stylized eagle. Designed by Henry Kreiss. Mintage: 25,015.

Date	Price		Date	Price
1955	7.50		1975	66.50
1965	40.00		1985	615.00

$1,000 invested in 1955 would be worth $75,333 in 1985.
$1,000 invested in 1965 would be worth $14,125 in 1985.
$1,000 invested in 1975 would be worth $8,496 in 1985.

CALIFORNIA DIAMOND JUBILEE, 1925

A forty-niner panning gold. Reverse: Grizzly bear. Designed by Jo Mora. Mintage: 86,500. Coins in gem uncirculated condition are much rarer than the mintage would indicate.

Date	Price		Date	Price
1955	9.50		1975	44.00
1965	30.00		1985	800.00

$1,000 invested in 1955 would be worth $76,842 in 1985.
$1,000 invested in 1965 would be worth $24,333 in 1985.
$1,000 invested in 1975 would be worth $16,590 in 1985.

CINCINNATI MUSIC CENTER, 1936

Head of Stephen Foster. Reverse: Harpist. Designed by Constance Ortmayer. Mintage: 15,016. Scarce in gem uncirculated condition.

Date	Price		Date	Price
1955	18.50		1975	180.00
1965	150.00		1985	1,350.00

$1,000 invested in 1955 would be worth $66,216 in 1985.
$1,000 invested in 1965 would be worth $8,166 in 1985.
$1,000 invested in 1975 would be worth $6,805 in 1985.

CLEVELAND-GREAT LAKES EXPOSITION, 1936

Head of Moses Cleaveland. Reverse: Map of the Great Lakes. Designed by Brenda Putnam. Mintage: 50,030.

Date	Price		Date	Price
1955	4.00		1975	35.00
1965	25.00		1985	360.00

$1,000 invested in 1955 would be worth $83,750 in 1985.
$1,000 invested in 1965 would be worth $13,400 in 1985.
$1,000 invested in 1975 would be worth $9,571 in 1985.

COLUMBIA, SOUTH CAROLINA SESQUICENTENNIAL, 1936

Justice standing. Reverse: Palmetto tree. Designed by A. Wolfe Davidson. Mintage: 25,023.

Date	Price		Date	Price
1955	9.50		1975	84.00
1965	37.50		1985	590.00

$1,000 invested in 1955 would be worth $56,842 in 1985.
$1,000 invested in 1965 would be worth $14,400 in 1985.
$1,000 invested in 1975 would be worth $6,428 in 1985.

COLUMBIAN EXPOSITION, 1892–1893

Head of Columbus. Reverse: His flagship, the Santa Maria. Designed by Charles E. Barber (obverse) and George T. Morgan (reverse). This was the first American commemorative coin authorized by Congress. Mintage: 2,500,405.

Date	Price		Date	Price
1955	1.75		1975	19.00
1965	4.00		1985	390.00

$1,000 invested in 1955 would be worth $205,714 in 1985.
$1,000 invested in 1965 would be worth $90,000 in 1985.
$1,000 invested in 1975 would be worth $18,947 in 1985.

CONNECTICUT TERCENTENARY, 1935

The famous Charter Oak tree. Reverse: Eagle. Designed by Henry Kreiss. Mintage: 25,018. Scarce in choice uncirculated condition.

Date	Price		Date	Price
1955	20.00		1975	121.50
1965	57.50		1985	1,060.00

$1,000 invested in 1955 would be worth $48,250 in 1985.
$1,000 invested in 1965 would be worth $16,782 in 1985.
$1,000 invested in 1975 would be worth $7,942 in 1985.

DELAWARE TERCENTENARY, 1936

Old Swedes Church in Wilmington. Reverse: The Swedish ship, Kalmar Nyckel. Designed by Carl L. Schmitz. Mintage: 20,993. (A Two Kronor coin was issued in Sweden to commemorate the same event.) Scarce in choice uncirculated condition.

Date	Price		Date	Price
1955	10.00		1975	95.00
1965	55.00		1985	900.00

$1,000 invested in 1955 would be worth $82,500 in 1985.
$1,000 invested in 1965 would be worth $15,000 in 1985.
$1,000 invested in 1975 would be worth $8,684 in 1985.

ELGIN, ILLINOIS CENTENNIAL, 1936

Pioneer's head. Reverse: Pioneer memorial statue. Designed by Trygve Rovelstad. Mintage: 20,015. Rare in gem uncirculated condition.

Date	Price		Date	Price
1955	10.00		1975	86.00
1965	55.00		1985	900.00

$1,000 invested in 1955 would be worth $81,000 in 1985.
$1,000 invested in 1965 would be worth $14,727 in 1985.
$1,000 invested in 1975 would be worth $9,418 in 1985.

BATTLE OF GETTSBURY 75TH ANNIVERSARY, 1936

Conjoined heads of a Union and Confederate soldier. Reverse: Union and Confederate shields. Designed by Frank Vittor. Mintage: 26,928.

Date	Price		Date	Price
1955	10.00		1975	71.00
1965	57.50		1985	710.00

$1,000 invested in 1955 would be worth $65,000 in 1985.
$1,000 invested in 1965 would be worth $11,304 in 1985.
$1,000 invested in 1975 would be worth $9,154 in 1985.

GRANT MEMORIAL, 1922

General Ulysses S. Grant. Reverse: Log cabin. Designed by Laura Gardin Fraser, who also designed the Grant Commemorative Gold Dollar. Mintage: 4,256 with star, 67,405 without star. The Grant Memorial with star is rare.

Date	Price		Date	Price
1955	8.50		1975	53.50
1965	27.50		1985	800.00

$1,000 invested in 1955 would be worth $86,470 in 1985.
$1,000 invested in 1965 would be worth $26,727 in 1985.
$1,000 invested in 1975 would be worth $13,738 in 1985.

HAWAIIAN SESQUICENTENNIAL, 1928

Captain James Cook. Reverse: Native chief. Designed by Juliette May Fraser. Mintage: 9,958 uncirculated coins and 50 proofs. This is the lowest minted silver commemorative coin and is rare in uncirculated condition. Some sandblast proofs are known.

Date	Price		Date	Price
1955	80.00		1975	875.00
1965	600.00		1985	4,100.00

$1,000 invested in 1955 would be worth $46,250 in 1985.
$1,000 invested in 1965 would be worth $6,166 in 1985.
$1,000 invested in 1975 would be worth $4,228 in 1985.

HUDSON, NEW YORK SESQUICENTENNIAL, 1935

Hendrik Hudson's flagship, the Half Moon. Reverse: City seal. Designed by Chester Beach. Mintage: 10,008. Second lowest minted silver commemorative coin. Scarce in choice uncirculated condition.

Date	Price		Date	Price
1955	50.00		1975	385.00
1965	325.00		1985	1,900.00

$1,000 invested in 1955 would be worth $34,500 in 1985.
$1,000 invested in 1965 would be worth $5,307 in 1985.
$1,000 invested in 1975 would be worth $4,480 in 1985.

HUGUENOT-WALLOON TERCENTENARY, 1924

Conjoined heads of Admiral Coligny and William the Silent. Reverse: The ship
New Netherlands. Designed by George T. Morgan. Mintage: 142,080. Rarer in choice
uncirculated condition than the mintage would indicate.

Date	Price		Date	Price
1955	8.50		1975	42.00
1965	27.50		1985	700.00

$1,000 invested in 1955 would be worth $74,705 in 1985.
$1,000 invested in 1965 would be worth $23,090 in 1985.
$1,000 invested in 1975 would be worth $15,119 in 1985.

IMMIGRANT, 1986

Statue of Liberty at sunrise. Reverse: Immigrant family. Obverse designed by
Edgar Z. Steever, IV. Reverse designed by Sherl Joseph Winter. 75% copper, 25%
nickel outer layers bonded to inner core of pure copper. 11.34 grams, 30.6 mm.,
reeded edge. Mintage: 25,000,000 total Proof and Uncirculated authorized by Congress
for 1986. Struck to order.

IOWA CENTENNIAL, 1946

Iowa state seal. Reverse: Old Capitol building in Iowa City. Designed by Adam Pietz. Mintage: 100,057. A common commemorative in choice uncirculated condition.

Date	Price		Date	Price
1955	7.50		1975	35.50
1965	25.00		1985	290.00

$1,000 invested in 1955 would be worth $35,333 in 1985.
$1,000 invested in 1965 would be worth $10,600 in 1985.
$1,000 invested in 1975 would be worth $7,464 in 1985.

LEXINGTON-CONCORD SESQUICENTENNIAL, 1925

Minute Man statue at Concord. Reverse: The Old Belfry at Lexington. Designed by Chester Beach. Mintage: 162,013.

Date	Price		Date	Price
1955	5.00		1975	45.00
1965	16.00		1985	525.00

$1,000 invested in 1955 would be worth $95,000 in 1985.
$1,000 invested in 1965 would be worth $29,687 in 1985.
$1,000 invested in 1975 would be worth $10,555 in 1985.

LINCOLN-ILLINOIS CENTENNIAL, 1918

Head of Lincoln. Reverse: Illinois state seal. Designed by George T. Morgan (obverse) and J. R. Sinnock (reverse). Mintage: 100,058. Rare in choice uncirculated condition.

Date	Price		Date	Price
1955	8.50		1975	44.50
1965	25.00		1985	765.00

$1,000 invested in 1955 would be worth $83,529 in 1985.
$1,000 invested in 1965 would be worth $28,400 in 1985.
$1,000 invested in 1975 would be worth $15,955 in 1985.

LONG ISLAND TERCENTENARY, 1936

Conjoined heads of a Dutch settler and an Indian. Reverse: Sailing ship. Designed by Howard K. Weinman. Mintage: 81,800.

Date	Price		Date	Price
1955	4.50		1975	32.50
1965	22.50		1985	440.00

$1,000 invested in 1955 would be worth $91,111 in 1985.
$1,000 invested in 1965 would be worth $18,222 in 1985.
$1,000 invested in 1975 would be worth $12,615 in 1985.

LYNCHBURG, VIRGINIA SESQUICENTENNIAL, 1936

Head of Senator Carter Glass. Reverse: Liberty standing at The Old Courthouse. Designed by Charles Keck. Mintage: 20,013. Scarce in choice uncirculated condition.

Date	Price		Date	Price
1955	10.00		1975	69.00
1965	55.00		1985	950.00

$1,000 invested in 1955 would be worth $87,500 in 1985.
$1,000 invested in 1965 would be worth $15,909 in 1985.
$1,000 invested in 1975 would be worth $12,681 in 1985.

MAINE CENTENNIAL, 1920

Coat-of-arms of Maine. Reverse: Wreath of pines and cones. Designed by Anthony De Francisci. Mintage: 50,028. Scarce only in gem uncirculated condition.

Date	Price		Date	Price
1955	9.00		1975	59.50
1965	32.50		1985	1,000.00

$1,000 invested in 1955 would be worth $102,777 in 1985.
$1,000 invested in 1965 would be worth $28,461 in 1985.
$1,000 invested in 1975 would be worth $15,546 in 1985.

MARYLAND TERCENTENARY, 1934

Head of Lord Baltimore, who issued coins himself 300 years earlier in Maryland. Reverse: Coat-of-arms of Maryland. Designed by Hans Schuler. Mintage: 25,015. Scarce in choice uncirculated condition.

Date	Price		Date	Price
1955	10.00		1975	54.50
1965	50.00		1985	1,000.00

$1,000 invested in 1955 would be worth $90,000 in 1985.
$1,000 invested in 1965 would be worth $18,000 in 1985.
$1,000 invested in 1975 would be worth $16,513 in 1985.

MISSOURI CENTENNIAL, 1921

Bust of frontiersman. Reverse: Pioneer and Indian standing. Designed by Robert Aitken. Mintage: 20,428. Scarce in choice uncirculated condition.

Date	Price		Date	Price
1955	50.00		1975	465.00
1965	145.00		1985	3,650.00

$1,000 invested in 1955 would be worth $67,000 in 1985.
$1,000 invested in 1965 would be worth $23,103 in 1985.
$1,000 invested in 1975 would be worth $7,204 in 1985.

MONROE DOCTRINE CENTENNIAL, 1923

Conjoined heads of James Monroe and John Quincy Adams. Reverse: Two female figures in the shape of North and South America. Designed by Chester Beach. Mintage: 274,077. Despite the high mintage, the coin is scarce in choice uncirculated condition.

Date	Price		Date	Price
1955	6.50		1975	46.00
1965	17.50		1985	710.00

$1,000 invested in 1955 would be worth $100,000 in 1985.
$1,000 invested in 1965 would be worth $37,142 in 1985.
$1,000 invested in 1975 would be worth $14,130 in 1985.

NEW ROCHELLE 250TH ANNIVERSARY, 1938

John Pell with fattened calf. Reverse: Fleur-de-lis. Designed by Gertrude K. Lathrop. Mintage: 15,266. Scarce in choice uncirculated condition.

Date	Price		Date	Price
1955	18.00		1975	152.50
1965	85.00		1985	910.00

$1,000 invested in 1955 would be worth $46,388 in 1985.
$1,000 invested in 1965 would be worth $9,823 in 1985.
$1,000 invested in 1975 would be worth $5,475 in 1985.

NORFOLK, VIRGINIA BICENTENNIAL, 1936

Seal of the city. Reverse: The Royal Mace of Norfolk. Designed by William Marks Simpson and his wife, Marjorie. Mintage: 16,936.

Date	Price		Date	Price
1955	15.00		1975	142.50
1965	85.00		1985	765.00

$1,000 invested in 1955 would be worth $46,666 in 1985.
$1,000 invested in 1965 would be worth $8,235 in 1985.
$1,000 invested in 1975 would be worth $4,912 in 1985.

OREGON TRAIL MEMORIAL, 1926–1939

Covered wagon. Reverse: Indian superimposed over a map of the U.S. Designed by James Earle Fraser and his wife, Laura Gardin Fraser. Mintage: 203,100. One of our most beautiful commemorative coins.

Date	Price		Date	Price
1955	4.00		1975	35.00
1965	15.00		1985	445.00

$1,000 invested in 1955 would be worth $102,500 in 1985.
$1,000 invested in 1965 would be worth $27,333 in 1985.
$1,000 invested in 1975 would be worth $11,714 in 1985.

PANAMA-PACIFIC EXPOSITION, 1915

Columbia and child standing at the Golden Gate in San Francisco. Reverse: Eagle and shield. Designed by Charles E. Barber. Mintage: 27,134. Rare in gem uncirculated condition.

Date	Price		Date	Price
1955	35.00		1975	270.00
1965	110.00		1985	4,150.00

$1,000 invested in 1955 would be worth $107,142 in 1985.
$1,000 invested in 1965 would be worth $34,090 in 1985.
$1,000 invested in 1975 would be worth $13,888 in 1985.

PILGRIM TERCENTENARY, 1920–1921

Governor Bradford. Reverse: The ship, Mayflower. Designed by Cyrus E. Dallin. Mintage: 172,165.

Date	Price		Date	Price
1955	3.75		1975	34.50
1965	12.50		1985	460.00

$1,000 invested in 1955 would be worth $113,333 in 1985.
$1,000 invested in 1965 would be worth $34,000 in 1985.
$1,000 invested in 1975 would be worth $12,318 in 1985.

RHODE ISLAND TERCENTENARY, 1936

Roger Williams in a canoe being welcomed by an Indian. Reverse: An anchor. Designed by Arthur G. Carey and John H. Benson. Mintage: 50,034.

Date	Price		Date	Price
1955	5.85		1975	42.00
1965	20.00		1985	675.00

$1,000 invested in 1955 would be worth $106,837 in 1985.
$1,000 invested in 1965 would be worth $31,250 in 1985.
$1,000 invested in 1975 would be worth $14,880 in 1985.

ROANOKE ISLAND, NORTH CAROLINA, 1937

350th anniversary. Head of Sir Walter Raleigh. Reverse: Mother holding Virginia Dare, the first white child born in America. Designed by William Marks Simpson. Mintage: 29,030.

Date	Price		Date	Price
1955	10.00		1975	51.50
1965	37.50		1985	650.00

$1,000 invested in 1955 would be worth $59,500 in 1985.
$1,000 invested in 1965 would be worth $15,866 in 1985.
$1,000 invested in 1975 would be worth $11,553 in 1985.

ROBINSON-ARKANSAS CENTENNIAL, 1936

Head of Senator Joseph T. Robinson. Reverse: Eagle. Designed by Henry Kreiss (obverse) and Everett Burr (reverse). Mintage: 25,265. Same reverse as Arkansas Centennial issues of 1935–1939, but with different obverse; the only instance of the same event being commemorated by two different types of Half Dollars.

Date	Price		Date	Price
1955	8.00		1975	58.50
1965	35.00		1985	480.00

$1,000 invested in 1955 would be worth $55,000 in 1985.
$1,000 invested in 1965 would be worth $12,571 in 1985.
$1,000 invested in 1975 would be worth $7,521 in 1985.

SAN DIEGO: CALIFORNIA-PACIFIC INTERNATIONAL EXPOSITION, 1935–1936

Seated female and bear. Reverse: Exposition buildings. Designed by Robert Aitken. Mintage: 100,224.

Date	Price		Date	Price
1955	5.00		1975	35.50
1965	21.00		1985	390.00

$1,000 invested in 1955 would be worth $71,000 in 1985.
$1,000 invested in 1965 would be worth $16,904 in 1985.
$1,000 invested in 1975 would be worth $10,000 in 1985.

SESQUICENTENNIAL OF AMERICAN INDEPENDENCE, 1926

Conjoined heads of Presidents Washington and Coolidge. Reverse: The Liberty Bell. Commemorates the 150th anniversary of the signing of the Declaration of Independence. Designed by John R. Sinnock. Mintage: 141,120. Because of low-relief dies, there is much loss of detail in the coin.

Date	Price		Date	Price
1955	7.50		1975	35.00
1965	22.50		1985	685.00

$1,000 invested in 1955 would be worth $83,333 in 1985.
$1,000 invested in 1965 would be worth $27,777 in 1985.
$1,000 invested in 1975 would be worth $17,857 in 1985.

OLD SPANISH TRAIL, 1935

Head of a cow. Reverse: Yucca tree and map of the Trail. Commemorates the 400th anniversary of the deVaca Expedition through the Gulf states. Designed by L. W. Hoffecker. Mintage: 10,008. Scarce.

Date	Price		Date	Price
1955	30.00		1975	435.00
1965	290.00		1985	1,650.00

$1,000 invested in 1955 would be worth $50,000 in 1985.
$1,000 invested in 1965 would be worth $5,172 in 1985.
$1,000 invested in 1975 would be worth $3,448 in 1985.

STONE MOUNTAIN MEMORIAL, 1925

Generals "Stonewall" Jackson and Robert E. Lee on horseback. Reverse: Eagle on mountain top, with the inscription, "Memorial to the Valor of the Soldier of the South." Designed by Gutzon Borglum. Mintage: 1,314,709. Of the early issues, this is the easiest to locate in gem uncirculated condition.

Date	Price		Date	Price
1955	3.00		1975	19.00
1965	8.00		1985	235.00

$1,000 invested in 1955 would be worth $71,666 in 1985.
$1,000 invested in 1965 would be worth $26,875 in 1985.
$1,000 invested in 1975 would be worth $11,315 in 1985.

TEXAS CENTENNIAL, 1934–1938

Eagle on a "Lone Star." Reverse: Winged Victory between the heads of Sam Houston and Stephen Austin. Designed by Pompeo Coppini. Mintage: 149,500.

Date	Price		Date	Price
1955	3.00		1975	36.00
1965	17.00		1985	400.00

$1,000 invested in 1955 would be worth $123,333 in 1985.
$1,000 invested in 1965 would be worth $21,764 in 1985.
$1,000 invested in 1975 would be worth $10,277 in 1985.

FORT VANCOUVER CENTENNIAL, 1925

Head of Dr. John McLoughlin, who built the fort. Reverse: Pioneer standing before the fort. Designed by Laura Gardin Fraser. Mintage: 14,994. Rare in gem uncirculated condition.

Date	Price		Date	Price
1955	37.50		1975	205.00
1965	125.00		1985	1,335.00

$1,000 invested in 1955 would be worth $32,666 in 1985.
$1,000 invested in 1965 would be worth $9,800 in 1985.
$1,000 invested in 1975 would be worth $5,975 in 1985.

VERMONT SESQUICENTENNIAL, 1927

Head of Ira Allen, founder of Vermont. Reverse: Mountain lion. Designed by Charles Keck. Mintage: 28,142. Scarce in choice uncirculated condition.

Date	Price		Date	Price
1955	12.50		1975	84.00
1965	60.00		1985	1,000.00

$1,000 invested in 1955 would be worth $72,000 in 1985.
$1,000 invested in 1965 would be worth $15,000 in 1985.
$1,000 invested in 1975 would be worth $10,714 in 1985.

BOOKER T. WASHINGTON MEMORIAL, 1946–1951

Head of Booker T. Washington. Reverse: View of the log cabin of his birth and of the Hall of Fame for Great Americans where he is enshrined. Designed by Isaac Scott Hathaway. Mintage: 3,000,000. The most common commemorative.

Date	Price		Date	Price
1955	1.25		1975	6.00
1965	3.00		1985	49.00

$1,000 invested in 1955 would be worth $36,000 in 1985.
$1,000 invested in 1965 would be worth $15,000 in 1985.
$1,000 invested in 1975 would be worth $7,500 in 1985.

WASHINGTON-CARVER, 1951–1954

Conjoined heads of George Washington Carver and Booker T. Washington. Reverse: Map of the U.S. Designed by Isaac Scott Hathaway. Mintage: 2,422,392.

Date	Price		Date	Price
1955	3.35		1975	6.00
1965	3.00		1985	49.00

$1,000 invested in 1955 would be worth $13,432 in 1985.
$1,000 invested in 1965 would be worth $15,000 in 1985.
$1,000 invested in 1975 would be worth $7,500 in 1985.

GEORGE WASHINGTON, 1982

Commemorates the 250th anniversary of Washington's birth. Washington on horse-back. Reverse: Mount Vernon. Designed by Elizabeth Jones. The first silver half dollar struck since 1964. Mintage: Uncirculated—2,210,364. Proof—4,893,799. The uncirculated version was struck at Denver and the Proof at San Francisco.

Date	MS-65	PR-65
1982	8.50	10.50
1985	10.00	12.00

WISCONSIN TERRITORIAL CENTENNIAL, 1936

A badger on a log. Reverse: A forearm holding a pickaxe over lead ore. Designed by David Parsons. Mintage: 25,015.

Date	Price		Date	Price
1955	10.00		1975	76.00
1965	40.00		1985	625.00

$1,000 invested in 1955 would be worth $57,500 in 1985.
$1,000 invested in 1965 would be worth $14,375 in 1985.
$1,000 invested in 1975 would be worth $7,565 in 1985.

YORK COUNTY, MAINE TERCENTENARY, 1936

Brown's Garrison on the Saco River. Reverse: The York County seal. Designed by Walter H. Rich. Mintage: 25,015.

Date	Price		Date	Price
1955	7.50		1975	73.00
1965	32.50		1985	600.00

$1,000 invested in 1955 would be worth $73,333 in 1985.
$1,000 invested in 1965 would be worth $16,923 in 1985.
$1,000 invested in 1975 would be worth $7,534 in 1985.

COMMEMORATIVE GOLD COINS—1903–1986

Until the Los Angeles Olympic Ten Dollar gold piece was issued in 1984, and the Statue of Liberty Half Eagle in 1986, the United States had produced only 11 gold commemorative coins. They were all issued between 1903 and 1926 in very low mintages, ranging from a low of 5,000 to a high of 46,019.

In common with most other gold coin issues, the survival rates are low for the commemoratives. Many of them weren't handled properly, and others were mounted in jewelry. As a result, the original 11 gold commemoratives are scarce in all grades and very rare in choice uncirculated condition.

Although not inexpensive, the 11-piece gold commemorative set can still be assembled, and it is a collection that is of interest to both the collector and the investor.

GRANT MEMORIAL GOLD DOLLAR, 1922

The designs by Laura Gardin Fraser are the same as for the Grant Commemorative Half Dollar. Head of General Grant. Reverse: Log cabin. Mintage: 10,016. Scarce.

90% gold, 10% copper; 1.672 grams, 15 mm., reeded edge. Net weight: .04837 oz. pure gold.

Date	Price		Date	Price
1955	50.00		1975	770.00
1965	325.00		1985	5,000.00

$1,000 invested in 1955 would be worth $92,000 in 1985.
$1,000 invested in 1965 would be worth $14,153 in 1985.
$1,000 invested in 1975 would be worth $5,974 in 1985.

LEWIS AND CLARK EXPOSITION GOLD DOLLAR, 1904–1905

Head of Lewis. Reverse: Head of Clark. Designed by Charles E. Barber. Mintage: 20,066. The coins of this issue were frequently used as jewelry and should be examined for signs of such use. Scarce. Other specifications same as previous issue.

Date	Price		Date	Price
1955	90.00		1975	950.00
1965	395.00		1985	6,850.00

$1,000 invested in 1955 would be worth $68,888 in 1985.
$1,000 invested in 1965 would be worth $15,696 in 1985.
$1,000 invested in 1975 would be worth $6,526 in 1985.

LOUISIANA PURCHASE EXPOSITION GOLD DOLLAR, 1903

Head of President Jefferson. Reverse: Value and date. Designed by Charles E. Barber. Mintage: 17,500. Among the easiest gold commemoratives to find in choice uncirculated condition. Other specifications same as previous issue.

Date	Price		Date	Price
1955	22.50		1975	385.00
1965	120.00		1985	3,500.00

$1,000 invested in 1955 would be worth $142,222 in 1985.
$1,000 invested in 1965 would be worth $26,666 in 1985.
$1,000 invested in 1975 would be worth $8,311 in 1985.

LOUISIANA PURCHASE EXPOSITION GOLD DOLLAR, 1903

Head of President McKinley. Reverse: Value and date. Designed by Charles
E. Barber. Mintage: 17,500. Other specifications same as previous issue.

Date	Price		Date	Price
1955	25.00		1975	385.00
1965	120.00		1985	3,625.00

$1,000 invested in 1955 would be worth $133,000 in 1985.
$1,000 invested in 1965 would be worth $27,708 in 1985.
$1,000 invested in 1975 would be worth $8,636 in 1985.

MCKINLEY MEMORIAL GOLD DOLLAR, 1916–1917

Head of President McKinley. Reverse: The McKinley memorial building in Niles,
Ohio. Designed by Charles E. Barber (obverse) and George T. Morgan (reverse).
Mintage: 19,977. The 1917 dollar is slightly rarer than the 1916. Other specifications
same as previous issue.

Date	Price		Date	Price
1955	19.00		1975	230.00
1965	125.00		1985	4,400.00

$1,000 invested in 1955 would be worth $213,157 in 1985.
$1,000 invested in 1965 would be worth $32,400 in 1985.
$1,000 invested in 1975 would be worth $17,608 in 1985.

PANAMA-PACIFIC EXPOSITION GOLD DOLLAR, 1915

Commemorates the opening of the Panama Canal. Head of a canal worker. Reverse: The value encircled by two dolphins. Designed by Charles Keck. Mintage: 15,000. Other specifications same as previous issue.

Date	Price		Date	Price
1955	15.00		1975	220.00
1965	90.00		1985	3,500.00

$1,000 invested in 1955 would be worth $213,333 in 1985.
$1,000 invested in 1965 would be worth $35,555 in 1985.
$1,000 invested in 1975 would be worth $14,545 in 1985.

PANAMA-PACIFIC EXPOSITION QUARTER EAGLE, 1915

A $2.50 gold piece featuring Columbia with a caduceus on a hippocampus. Reverse: American eagle. Designed by Charles E. Barber and George T. Morgan. Mintage: 6,749. 90% gold, 10% copper, 4.18 grams, 18 mm., reeded edge. Net weight: .12094 oz. pure gold. Rare in uncirculated condition.

Date	Price		Date	Price
1955	75.00		1975	1,250.00
1965	390.00		1985	7,300.00

$1,000 invested in 1955 would be worth $89,333 in 1985.
$1,000 invested in 1965 would be worth $17,179 in 1985.
$1,000 invested in 1975 would be worth $5,360 in 1985.

PHILADELPHIA SESQUICENTENNIAL QUARTER EAGLE, 1926

This $2.50 gold piece commemorates the 150th anniversary of the signing of the Declaration of Independence. Liberty standing. Reverse: Independence Hall. Designed by John R. Sinnock. Mintage: 46,019. Other specifications same as previous issue.

Date	Price		Date	Price
1955	16.50		1975	220.00
1965	80.00		1985	3,850.00

$1,000 invested in 1955 would be worth $218,181 in 1985.
$1,000 invested in 1965 would be worth $45,000 in 1985.
$1,000 invested in 1975 would be worth $16,363 in 1985.

STATUE OF LIBERTY HALF EAGLE, 1986

Face of Statue of Liberty. Reverse: Attacking Eagle. 90% gold, 10% copper, 8.36 grams, 21.6 mm., reeded edge. Net weight: .24187 oz. pure gold. Mintage: Uncirculated—95,875. Proof—404,916. Mint: West Point. Designed by Elizabeth Jones. The uncirculated piece is rarer than the proof.

Date	Unc. Price	Proof Price
1986	160.00	170.00

LOS ANGELES OLYMPIC TEN DOLLAR GOLD, 1984

Two runners holding the Olympic torch. Reverse: American eagle. Designed by John Mercanti. Mintage: Unc.—100,000. Proof—800,000. This is the first coin ever to bear the West Point "W" mint mark. 90% gold, 10% copper, 16.718 grams, 27 mm., reeded edge. Net weight: .48375 oz. pure gold.

Date	MS-65	PR-65
1984	339.00	352.00

PANAMA-PACIFIC EXPOSITION FIFTY DOLLAR GOLD, ROUND, 1915

Helmeted head of Minerva. Reverse: Owl. Designed by Robert Aitken. Mintage: 483. Along with the Octagonal piece, it is rare in any grade. One of the most expensive U.S. coins. 90% gold, 10% copper, 83.59 grams, 41 mm., reeded edge. Net weight: 2.41875 oz. pure gold.

Date	Price		Date	Price
1955	900.00		1975	14,000.00
1965	5,500.00		1985	41,000.00

$1,000 invested in 1955 would be worth $45,555 in 1985.
$1,000 invested in 1965 would be worth $7,454 in 1985.
$1,000 invested in 1975 would be worth $2,928 in 1985.

PANAMA-PACIFIC EXPOSITION 50 DOLLARS GOLD, OCTAGONAL, 1915

Same design as the 50 Dollar round piece. Mintage: 645. Rare. Same specifications as previous issue.

Date	Price		Date	Price
1955	750.00		1975	11,500.00
1965	4,250.00		1985	34,000.00

$1,000 invested in 1955 would be worth $45,333 in 1985.
$1,000 invested in 1965 would be worth $8,000 in 1985.
$1,000 invested in 1975 would be worth $2,956 in 1985.

CHART 10—PRICE PERFORMANCE OF MS-65 U.S. TYPE COINS

1955 to 1985
(By Percentages)

	30 Years 1955–1985			20 Years 1965–1985			10 Years 1975–1985		
	Rank	Total Gain	Yearly Increase	Rank	Total Gain	Yearly Increase	Rank	Total Gain	Yearly Increase
All MS-65 TYPE COINS	64	+15,895%	+529%	73	+2,020%	+101%	70	+534%	+53%
I. SMALL CENTS (ALL TYPES)	46	26,746	891	63	2,961	148	52	694	69
A. Flying Eagle	43	27,500	916	58	3,437	171	63	611	61
B. Indian	44	27,361	912	67	2,771	138	48	790	79
C. Lincoln	75	7,066	235	84	736	36	72	514	51
II. TWO-CENT PIECES	25	48,000	1,600	38	8,000	400	62	615	61
III. THREE-CENT PIECES (ALL TYPES)	12	72,361	2,412	12	14,081	704	20	1,502	150
A. Three-cent silver (All Types)	13	70,937	2,364	14	13,757	687	22	1,445	144
1. Type I	11	73,000	2,433	8	17,380	869	7	2,517	251
2. Type II	10	76,666	2,555	18	13,142	657	38	948	94
3. Type III	18	62,000	2,066	25	11,698	584	12	2,000	200
B. Three-cent nickel	6	83,750	2,791	9	16,750	837	11	2,042	204
IV. NICKELS (ALL TYPES)	40	32,343	1,078	43	6,044	302	26	1,246	124
A. Shield	42	30,000	1,000	46	5,268	263	33	1,014	101
B. Liberty	30	45,181	1,506	24	11,833	591	5	2,730	273
C. Buffalo	52	20,600	686	61	3,090	154	37	958	95
D. Jefferson	84	1,457	48	86	237	11	84	275	27
V. HALF DIMES (ALL TYPES)	32	40,909	1,363	48	4,627	231	47	795	79
A. Flowing Hair	28	45,454	1,515	54	3,846	192	74	476	47
B. Draped Bust	38	32,571	1,085	51	4,071	203	39	883	88
C. Capped Bust	2	128,888	4,296	10	16,571	828	15	1,681	168
D. Liberty Seated	15	68,474	2,282	37	8,112	405	23	1,322	132
VI. DIMES (ALL TYPES)	36	34,808	1,160	50	4,327	216	55	654	65
A. Draped Bust	49	24,615	820	65	2,865	143	66	581	58
B. Capped Bust	3	98,857	3,295	11	15,043	752	61	617	61
C. Liberty Seated	24	49,952	1,665	42	7,310	365	44	833	83
D. Barber	19	61,666	2,055	5	20,555	1,027	8	2,466	246
E. Mercury	37	34,800	1,160	26	11,600	580	3	3,163	316
F. Roosevelt	83	1,466	48	80	1,100	55	85	231	23

CHART 10 Continued

	30 Years 1955–1985			20 Years 1965–1985			10 Years 1975–1985		
	Rank	Total Gain	Yearly Increase	Rank	Total Gain	Yearly Increase	Rank	Total Gain	Yearly Increase
VII. TWENTY-CENT PIECES	29	45,333	1,511	32	9,714	485	41	850	85
VIII. QUARTERS (ALL TYPES)	39	32,564	1,085	66	2,857	142	64	588	58
A. Draped Bust	55	20,149	671	76	1,569	78	76	457	45
B. Capped Bust	14	70,149	2,338	34	9,400	470	69	540	54
C. Liberty Seated	5	84,242	2,808	15	13,672	683	35	974	97
D. Barber	17	63,000	2,100	6	18,529	926	14	1,750	175
E. Standing Liberty	21	58,125	1,937	28	10,333	516	19	1,524	152
F. Washington	82	2,900	96	64	2,900	145	57	644	64
IX. HALF DOLLARS (ALL TYPES)	34	35,382	1,179	47	4,785	239	51	696	69
A. Flowing Hair	60	17,404	580	72	2,122	106	50	712	71
B. Draped Bust	8	80,000	2,666	20	12,500	625	77	444	44
C. Capped Bust	7	80,169	2,672	2	22,631	1,131	32	1,046	104
D. Liberty Seated	9	77,179	2,572	22	12,186	609	53	692	69
E. Barber	16	66,666	2,222	7	20,000	1,000	25	1,265	126
F. Liberty Walking	48	24,800	826	13	13,777	688	6	2,583	258
G. Franklin	81	3,600	120	82	960	48	36	960	96
H. Kennedy	—	—	—	77	1,500	75	83	285	28
X. SILVER DOLLARS (ALL TYPES)	59	18,212	607	68	2,762	138	67	563	56
A. Flowing Hair	63	16,683	556	69	2,631	131	79	384	38
B. Draped Bust	35	35,227	1,174	35	9,337	466	68	547	54
C. Gobrecht	74	7,216	240	83	853	42	73	486	48
D. Liberty Seated	26	47,272	1,575	4	20,800	1,040	10	1,548	154
E. Morgan	61	17,400	580	3	21,750	1,087	1	7,565	756
F. Peace	23	52,625	1,754	17	13,156	657	2	3,762	376
G. Trade	20	61,000	2,033	1	24,400	1,220	17	1,544	154
H. Eisenhower	—	—	—	—	—	—	83	285	28

XI. GOLD DOLLARS (ALL TYPES)	4	85,277	2,842	27	10,406	520	42	848	84
A. Type I	20	61,000	2,033	16	13,555	677	21	1,487	148
B. Type II	1	130,000	4,333	31	9,750	487	51	696	69
C. Type III	27	46,363	1,545	29	10,200	510	27	1,243	124
XII. $2.50 GOLD (ALL TYPES)	56	20,125	670	78	1,275	63	59	621	62
A. Capped Bust and Head	58	19,025	634	79	1,155	57	60	618	61
B. Classic Head	22	57,142	1,904	30	10,000	500	82	338	33
C. Coronet (Liberty)	45	27,333	911	39	7,809	390	10	2,277	227
D. Indian	31	41,000	1,366	19	12,812	640	4	2,733	273
XIII. $3.00 GOLD	41	31,428	1,047	49	4,536	226	71	523	52
XIV. $4.00 GOLD	76	7,047	234	85	721	36	85	179	17
XV. $5.00 GOLD (ALL TYPES)	53	20,445	681	55	3,737	186	31	1,092	109
A. Capped Bust	50	23,802	793	59	3,346	167	24	1,280	128
B. Capped Head	66	14,457	481	62	3,000	150	29	1,176	117
C. Classic Head	25	48,000	1,600	23	12,000	600	78	428	32
D. Coronet (Liberty)	47	25,000	833	21	12,452	622	34	1,009	100
E. Indian	33	40,666	1,355	7	17,428	871	9	2,301	230
XVI. $10.00 GOLD (ALL TYPES)	54	20,251	675	52	3,885	194	46	805	80
A. Capped Bust	57	19,753	658	60	3,168	158	43	842	84
B. Coronet (Liberty)	51	22,892	763	44	5,593	279	58	639	63
C. Indian	62	16,888	562	33	9,500	475	13	1,767	176
XVII. $20.00 GOLD (ALL TYPES)	71	9,755	325	56	3,641	182	56	652	65
A. Coronet (Liberty) (All Types)	70	9,818	327	41	7,322	366	65	586	58
1. Type I—No Motto	68	12,500	416	36	8,333	416	81	357	35
2. Type II	69	10,285	342	40	7,578	378	28	1,200	120
3. Type III	77	6,285	209	45	5,500	275	18	1,543	154
B. Saint Gaudens (All Types)	72	9,703	323	70	2,574	128	49	718	71
1. High Relief	67	13,793	459	71	2,352	117	54	666	66
2. No Motto	80	4,133	137	57	3,542	177	45	826	82
3. With Motto	78	6,200	206	53	3,875	193	30	1,148	114
XVIII. GOLD (ALL TYPES—$1–$20)	65	14,581	486	75	1,626	81	75	467	46
XIX. COMMEMORATIVE SILVER	73	8,100	270	74	1,685	84	40	853	85
XX. COMMEMORATIVE GOLD	79	5,774	192	81	994	49	80	378	37

Note: Half Cents and Large Cents have been excluded from this table because the early date coins are seldom encountered in uncirculated grades.

CHART 11—PRICE PERFORMANCE OF MS-65 U.S. TYPE COINS

1955 to 1985
(By Dollar Amounts)

	1955	1965	1975	1985
ALL MS-65 TYPE COINS	$10,258.70	$80,688.70	$305,178.25	$1,630,640.10
I. SMALL CENTS				
(ALL TYPES)	22.50	203.20	866.80	6,018.00
A. Flying Eagle	10.00	80.00	450.00	2,750.00
B. Indian	11.75	116.00	406.50	3,215.00
C. Lincoln	.75	7.20	10.30	53.00
II. TWO-CENT PIECES	2.50	15.00	195.00	1,200.00
III. THREE-CENT PIECES				
(ALL TYPES)	18.00	92.50	867.00	13,025.00
A. Three-cent silver				
(All Types)	16.00	82.50	785.00	11,350.00
1. Type I	5.00	21.00	145.00	3,650.00
2. Type II	6.00	35.00	485.00	4,600.00
3. Type III	5.00	26.50	155.00	3,100.00
B. Three-Cent				
pieces, nickel	2.00	10.00	82.00	1,675.00
IV. NICKELS				
(ALL TYPES)	25.35	135.65	657.60	8,199.10
A. Shield	18.00	102.50	532.50	5,400.00
B. Liberty	5.50	21.00	91.00	2,485.00
C. Buffalo	1.50	10.00	32.25	309.00
D. Jefferson	.35	2.15	1.85	5.10
V. HALF DIMES				
(ALL TYPES)	264.00	2,334.00	13,572.50	108,000.00
A. Flowing Hair	55.00	650.00	5,250.00	25,000.00
B. Draped Bust	175.00	1,400.00	6,450.00	57,000.00
C. Capped Bust	4.50	35.00	345.00	5,800.00
D. Liberty Seated	29.50	249.00	1,527.50	20,200.00
VI. DIMES				
(ALL TYPES)	268.15	2,156.95	14.258.70	93,339.20
A. Draped Bust	195.00	1,675.00	8,250.00	48,000.00
B. Capped Bust	17.50	115.00	2,800.00	17,300.00
C. Liberty Seated	52.25	357.00	3,130.00	26,100.00
D. Barber	3.00	9.00	75.00	1,850.00
E. Mercury	.25	.75	2.75	87.00
F. Roosevelt	.15	.20	.95	2.20
VII. TWENTY-CENT				
PIECES	15.00	70.00	800.00	6,800.00
VIII. QUARTERS				
(ALL TYPES)	431.50	4,917.50	23,867.25	140,514.50
A. Draped Bust	335.00	4,300.00	14,750.00	67,500.00
B. Capped Bust	33.50	250.00	4,350.00	23,500.00
C. Liberty Seated	49.50	305.00	4,280.00	41,700.00
D. Barber	5.00	17.00	180.00	3,150.00
E. Standing Liberty	8.00	45.00	305.00	4,650.00
F. Washington	.50	.50	2.25	14.50

CHART 11 *Continued*

	1955	1965	1975	1985
IX. HALF DOLLARS				
(ALL TYPES)	469.75	3,472.90	23,871.00	166,211.00
A. Flowing Hair	327.50	2,685.00	8,000.00	57,000.00
B. Draped Bust	25.00	160.00	4,500.00	20,000.00
C. Capped Bust	29.50	104.50	2,260.00	23,650.00
D. Liberty Seated	78.00	494.00	8,695.00	60,200.00
E. Barber	7.50	25.00	395.00	5,000.00
F. Liberty Walking	1.25	2.25	12.00	310.00
G. Franklin	1.00	1.15	3.75	36.00
H. Kennedy	—	1.00	5.25	15.00
X. SILVER DOLLARS				
(ALL TYPES)	914.00	6,026.50	29,543.90	166,464.35
A. Flowing Hair	150.00	950.00	6,500.00	25,000.00
B. Draped Bust	220.00	830.00	14,150.00	77,500.00
C. Gobrecht	485.00	4,100.00	7,200.00	35,000.00
D. Liberty Seated	38.50	87.50	1,175.00	18,200.00
E. Morgan	2.50	2.00	5.75	435.00
F. Peace	8.00	32.00	111.90	4,210.00
G. Trade	10.00	25.00	395.00	6,100.00
H. Eisenhower	—	—	6.25	17.85
I. Anthony	—	—	—	1.50
XI. GOLD DOLLARS				
(ALL TYPES)	36.00	295.00	3,620.00	30,700.00
A. Type I	10.00	45.00	410.00	6,100.00
B. Type II	15.00	200.00	2,800.00	19,500.00
C. Type III	11.00	50.00	410.00	5,100.00
XII. $2.50 GOLD				
(ALL TYPES)	1,032.50	16,287.00	33,460.00	207,800.00
A. Capped Bust and				
Head	975.00	16,050.00	30,000.00	185,000.00
B. Classic Head	17.50	100.00	2,950.00	10,000.00
C. Coronet (Liberty)	30.00	105.00	360.00	8,200.00
D. Indian	10.00	32.00	150.00	4,100.00
XIII. $3.00 GOLD	70.00	485.00	4,200.00	22,000.00
XIV. $4.00 GOLD	2,100.00	20,500.00	82,500.00	148,000.00
XV. $5.00 GOLD				
(ALL TYPES)	876.00	4,792.50	16,400.00	179,100.00
A. Capped Bust	355.00	2,525.00	6,600.00	84,500.00
B. Capped Head	415.00	2,000.00	5,100.00	60,000.00
C. Classic Head	25.00	100.00	2,800.00	12,000.00
D. Coronet (Liberty)	66.00	132.50	1,635.00	16,500.00
E. Indian	15.00	35.00	265.00	6,100.00
XVI. $10.00 GOLD				
(ALL TYPES)	635.00	3,310.00	15,965.00	128,600.00
A. Capped Bust	405.00	2,525.00	9,500.00	80,000.00
B. Coronet (Liberty)	162.50	665.00	5,820.00	37,200.00
C. Indian	67.50	120.00	645.00	11,400.00

CHART 11 *Continued*

	1955	1965	1975	1985
XVII. $20.00 GOLD				
(ALL TYPES)	490.00	1,312.50	7,330.00	47,800.00
A. Coronet (Liberty)				
(All Types)	220.00	295.00	3,685.00	21,600.00
1. Type I—No				
Motto	80.00	120.00	2,800.00	10,000.00
2. Type II	70.00	95.00	600.00	7,200.00
3. Type III	70.00	80.00	285.00	4,400.00
B. Saint Gaudens				
(All Types)	270.00	1,017.50	3,645.00	26,200.00
1. High Relief	145.00	850.00	3,000.00	20,000.00
2. No Motto	75.00	87.50	375.00	3,100.00
3. With Motto	50.00	80.00	270.00	3,100.00
XVIII. GOLD				
(ALL TYPES—$1–$20)	5,239.50	46,982.00	163,475.00	764,000.00
XIX. COMMEMORATIVE				
SILVER	715.45	3,437.50	6,793.50	57,953.00
XX. COMMEMORATIVE				
GOLD	1,963.00	11,395.00	29,910.00	113,350.00

Note: Half Cents and Large Cents have been excluded from this table because the early date coins are seldom encountered in uncirculated grades.

Chapter Three
ADVANTAGES OF RARE COIN INVESTMENT

What makes rare coins such a solid and profitable investment? Actually, there is no one answer. In fact, a number of positive factors combine uniquely in coins, foremost among them rarity, quality and demand. The more perfect the combination of these elements, the better the investment.

Of the tens of thousands of gold coins minted between 1795 and 1933, fewer than four percent have survived in "mint state," or investment grade, condition. On a lesser scale, much the same is true of silver coins; the last of the regular issue silver coins were minted in 1964. Because there are relatively few, and because these are held in strong and diversified hands, top-quality merchandise becomes harder to find with each passing year, and therefore, their value continues to rise.

Rare coins also offer historical value, representing different periods, movements and events in the life of America and the world. As many were designed by some of the nation's finest artisans, they have additional, and valid worth as collectibles; and their metal content, whether .900 fine gold or silver, gives them bullion value, too. Rare coins, moreover, offer certain practical advantages not found in other investments. They are portable, highly liquid, easily bought and sold, and cheaply stored or insured. Tucked away in a safe deposit box, they require little management to make you money.

As investments, rare coins offer two features that might conceivably be seen as drawbacks: they must be held, ordinarily, for at least five years; and they yield no interest. On the other hand, they are not as susceptible to the boom-and-bust syndrome as many other options.

Even following the worst depression in the nation's history, coins recovered at a more rapid rate than stocks. In 1929, after the Crash, all assets dropped in value, including coins. But while it took the stock market 23 years to recover to its previous highs, by that same recovery year, 1952, the coin market had not only recovered, but was up more than 300 percent over 1929. (See Chart 12 on page 146.)

The fact is that because most numismatic investors can afford to hold onto their merchandise, it is unusual to find a high-grade coin offered for less than its current market value by a knowledgeable investor, even in the hardest of times and the softest of markets. While prices, *in theory,* may be off, seldom does one sell a rare MS-65 specimen cheaply, any more than he would throw away a Rembrandt, unless he is under duress. In bad times, the bulk of the coin market simply puts itself on hold, and resumes when things pick up, usually during growth and inflationary periods. This is a feat that remains unmatched—and perhaps unmatchable—by most other investment options.

CHART 12

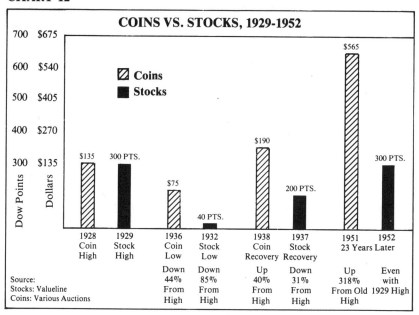

| | COINS VS. STOCKS, 1929-1952 | | | | | | |

Five Major Advantages of Rare Coin Investment

Apart from their inherent value, rare coins also offer the investor a variety of other advantages not found in other assets:

1. Rare Coins Are a Hedge Against Inflation. With the federal deficit exploding, the money supply increasing with alarming rapidity, and economic growth beginning to level out, the U.S. may well be into the incubation period for a major inflation. The current economic situation, in fact, resembles nothing so much as that of 1978–79, when a comparable combination of uncertain politics and finance ignited the coin and bullion markets. While rare coins have been performing well of late, we are at, or near, the bottom of the inflationary cycle; and, as we head for the top (and beyond), they will continue to do better.

Inflation, moreover, has a devastating effect on the vast majority of other investment options. Between 1950 and 1981, for example, inflation remained relatively under control, averaging only four percent per annum. Yet, even

CHART 13

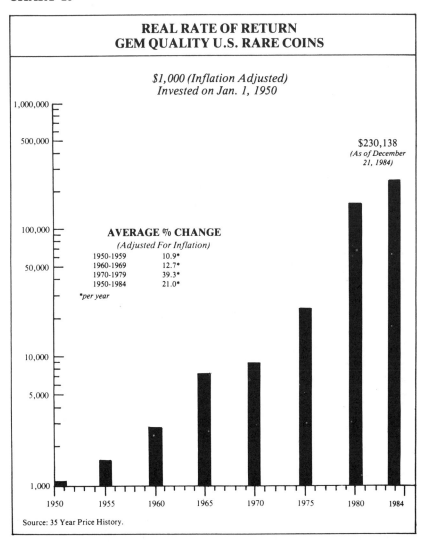

**REAL RATE OF RETURN
GEM QUALITY U.S. RARE COINS**

*$1,000 (Inflation Adjusted)
Invested on Jan. 1, 1950*

$230,138
*(As of December
21, 1984)*

AVERAGE % CHANGE
(Adjusted For Inflation)

1950-1959	10.9*
1960-1969	12.7*
1970-1979	39.3*
1950-1984	21.0*

per year

Source: 35 Year Price History.

at this moderate level, inflation during this same period served to flatten out much of the gain realized on investments in stocks and bonds. With economists such as Milton Friedman predicting a minimum inflation rate of between six and eight percent over the next few years, and estimates ranging as high as 13 percent or better, you will require an extraordinary hedge to keep your head above water. That is the virtue of rare coins: not only do they gain in value during periods of inflation, they remain consistent profit-makers. In the double-digit phase several years ago, many choice quality specimens increased an average of 141 percent!

2. *Rare Coins Are Less Risky than Bullion.* All dependable indicators suggest that gold and silver prices, for many of the reasons previously noted, are on the way up. Because of their metal content, rare coins inevitably ride the wave of bullion increases. The difference is that coins reap the benefits without falling prey to the pitfalls. The laws governing the purchase and sale of precious metals do not affect numismatic coins, which are judged collectibles. Moreover, gold and silver remain subject to volatile price swings, booming and busting with abandon; and, while coins tend to boom along, their collectible status and numismatic value again save them when prices tumble. Rare coins, apart from their other benefits, enable you to own gold and silver without having to endure most of the downside risk. They may suffer somewhat when bullion prices drop off; but coin values never fall victim to the widespread fluctuations to which precious metals are subject.

3. *Privacy.* Unlike the great majority of major investments, rare coins are not subject to federal disclosure rules. The purchase of any coin that does not carry a premium of at least 15 percent over its metal content must be reported on a 1099B tax form. As only bullion coins fall into this category, a rare coin portfolio may be constructed in relative privacy—a substantial advantage to the investor.

4. *Tax-deferred.* The tax situation for rare coin investors remains extremely advantageous. In the course of the minimum five years it is recommended that you hold your coins, their value should increase substantially. This increase can be tabulated on a per annum basis, giving you a good idea of your paper profits. Uncle Sam, however, does not require his payment until the moment of sale, which means that rare coins accrue their value, essentially tax-free until sold. Moreover, coins held for more than six months are currently taxable at the lower capital gains rate—another substantial savings.

5. *Supply and Demand.* There is really only one thing to say on the subject: demand has never been higher than it is today, and supplies have never been lower and more dispersed.

In truth, this represents no more than the culmination of a situation that has been developing for decades. A number of major coin hoards have appeared in the last quarter-century. Between 1959 and 1964, the U.S. Treasury dispersed somewhere in excess of ten million uncirculated silver dollars. For five years, beginning in 1974, the government sold nearly two million uncirculated Carson City silver dollars. Between 1976 and 1980, the estate of LaVere Redfield sold almost half a million Morgan and Peace Dollars. Recently, several millions of dollars came out of the Continental Bank failure. Other hoards have appeared from Europe, particularly of Double Eagles. Yet, staggering though it may seem, these coins, particularly those of investment grade quality, have been absorbed into the market.

Ten years ago, or even less, a collector or investor seeking top-quality gold coins might simply drop in at a numismatist's office, peruse his extensive inventory, and make purchases, usually at an eminently affordable price.

Today, only the St. Gaudens Double Eagle—the 20 dollar gold piece—is still commonly available, and, at more than $4,000, still reasonably priced. It will not be very long before certain silver coins, moreover, such as Liberty Walking Halves or Morgan dollars, will disappear as well.

In truth, in the coming years, the market can be expected to outgrow the war chests of collectors, and perhaps even the lower echelon of investors as well. It has become difficult for an investor to construct a diversified rare coin portfolio—a reversal of the situation as it stood 25 years ago. At one time, an interested party collected by date, acquiring a single specimen for each year and at each mint that a coin was produced. This is now beyond the means of all but the richest and best connected investors. Most in the current market collect by type; and, even on that basis, a 12-piece set—incorporating one of each 19th century American gold coin in the best available condition—is a struggle to put together, and expensive to secure.

Eventually, as more and more coins are "warehoused," and (with expected changes in the law) funds, partnerships and holding companies center around coins, stock certificates might conceivably replace actual specimens, as they disappear permanently from the market. With each coin numbered and marked for identification, stored in a central clearing house, and represented

CHART 14

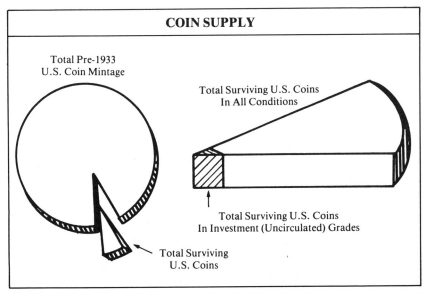

COIN SUPPLY

Total Pre-1933
U.S. Coin Mintage

Total Surviving U.S. Coins
In All Conditions

Total Surviving U.S. Coins
In Investment (Uncirculated) Grades

Total Surviving
U.S. Coins

Of all the Gold and Silver coins minted before 1933, less than five percent have survived in any condition. The large pie on the left represents the entire original mintage.

Of the surviving mintage in all conditions, less than one percent of those have survived in Mint State grades, and only part of that in MS-65. The pie shaped area represents the surviving coins of the original mintage, and the striped area represents the survivors in Mint State grades.

in the world by no more than a sheet of embellished parchment, numismatics will enter the pantheon of entrenched investments personified by the world's stock exchanges.

All this, of course, is informed speculation, and some years in the future. While the current coin market may in ten years be effectively obsolete, it is now open to most investors of means. The point is that coins purchased today will probably be worth fabulous multiples of their purchase prices in the not-too-distant future. And that is perhaps the best advantage of all.

This is why, over the past 30 years, top-quality American rare coins have consistently earned more money for investors than any other commonly traded asset, including stocks, bonds, real estate, collectibles, bullion, and diamonds—to name but a few.

CHART 15

TYPICAL SURVIVAL RATE OF U.S. COINS			
Total Mintage	10,000,000		100%
Total Survivors	500,000*	1 in 20	5.0000%
A. Circulated	475,000	1 in 21	4.7500%
B. Uncirculated	25,000	1 in 400	0.2500%
1. MS-60	16,150	1 in 619	0.1615%
2. MS-63	7,500	1 in 1,333	0.0750%
3. MS-65	1,250	1 in 8,000	0.0125%
4. MS-67	100	1 in 100,000	0.0010%
Total Uncirculated Population	25,000		100%
A. MS-60	16,150	1 in 1.54	64.6%
B. MS-63	7,500	1 in 3.30	30.0%
C. MS-65	1,250	1 in 20.00	5.0%
D. MS-67	100	1 in 250.00	.4%

* This number is a composite. Silver Dollars, for example, have a much higher survival rate. Early Gold (Pre-1834) has a lower survival rate.

Market Cycles

It is important to point out that, like everything else, coin prices experience highs and lows. In fact, the numismatic market moves in cycles, with prices heating up roughly every five years, followed by profit-taking and periods of correction. In the 1960s, before prices really took off, there were price peaks in August of 1964 and the middle of 1968. In the 1970s, when the market began to skyrocket, there were major booms in the summer of 1974 and the winter of 1980. Each was followed by a slowdown, then a bottoming-out of market momentum, then a slow, steady climb back to a new, more lofty peak. It is worth noting that, despite the correction periods—inevitable in a market that periodically builds up frantic heads of steam—rare coin

CHART 16

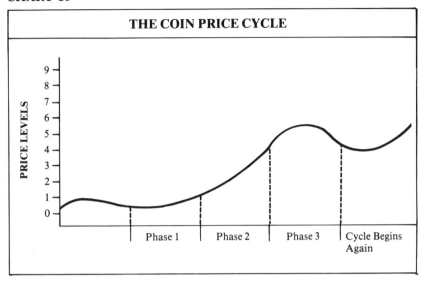

THE COIN PRICE CYCLE

Rare coin prices move in predictable supply and demand cycles. Here, in Phase one, the market is in a plateau, during which dealers lower prices to induce sales. In Phase two, knowledgeable investors and dealers buy at low prices, shrinking the supply and setting prices on an upward trend. Phase three occurs when the upward trend becomes obvious, drawing in many more buyers and finally driving prices to a peak, at which those who bought low sell high. The resulting prohibitively high prices will bring on the next decline causing some dealers to reduce prices during the downward correction process to induce sales. When a market equilibrium is reached and supply and demand are in balance, prices become stable again. In each cycle, the new high is higher than the old high, and the new low is higher than the old low, or in other words, the classic supply and demand cycle.

values never completely collapse. Prices may slip back from their boom period highs, but they always rebuild, and always greatly surpass previous records.

There are a number of explanations for the market's cyclical nature. One is that coins take their cue from the economy, doing well in times of inflation, slowing down when recessions hit. Another ties coins to movement in the bullion market. Both explanations are borne out by the facts and figures, and both are at least partially true. Cycles are also influenced, fairly predictably, by the activities of collectors, investors and speculators. Moreover, because of the lackluster performance of cash assets, even the most cautious investors are now diversifying with rare coins.

Yet the coin market, for better or for worse, has often run contrary to the economy. It posted strong prices and consistent gains when the bullion market was depressed, and saw a variety of market players come and go without changing its fundamental patterns. Essentially, the rare coin market is cyclical because—owing to the economy, metal prices, participant mood, and countless other large and small reasons—no financial asset grows 100 percent of the time. The important thing to keep in mind is that the market's continuing growth stems from a single, unshakable circumstance: a consistently increasing investor base pursuing an ever-diminishing amount of top-quality merchandise.

Foreign and Ancient Coins

Once you have added American rare coins to your portfolio, you may want to consider foreign and ancient coins as well. Though both markets represent an additional diversification, and require greater management, their potential is undeniable. Foreign coins, obviously, are much more numerous than American. Pricing and grading vary from one dealer to the next, often due to a lack of familiarity with the merchandise. Therefore, you must use a numismatist who has a foreign specialist on his staff. Some foreign and ancient coins may lose some of their value following the unanticipated appearance of a newly found hoard (a particular problem in Europe, where people historically amassed coins as a hedge against war and revolution). And, perhaps most important, relatively few Americans collect or invest in foreign coins, and there remains no strong central marketplace in the United States where these coins are traded, as with United States coins.

As for ancient coins, they are bought and sold primarily by a small, select group of people, and few secondary outlets exist in which the larger public can get involved in the United States. There is, however, a very strong European market.

When starting out, stick with rare, top-quality United States coins. They have a proven track record of performance, a solidly established market, and they will make you lots of money. Over the long term, coins have outperformed all other available investments. Nothing else even comes close.

Rare Coins vs. Type Coins

What is the difference between date and type collecting? Collecting dates, or rarity, is entirely different than collecting types. Let us use the example we briefly mentioned in Chapter Two.

A date collector tries to acquire every date and mintmark combination issued for every coin design within a given series. For example, to assemble a complete date set of Buffalo nickels would require a total of 68 coins, including a 1913-P Type I (from Philadelphia), a 1913-D Type I (from Denver), a 1913-S Type I (from San Francisco), and a 1913-P Type II (from Philadelphia) etc. When complete, you would have one of each date made at each mint for every combination manufactured.

Putting together a type set, on the other hand, would require only two Buffalo nickels: one 1913 Type I and one Type II of any date from 1913 to 1938. To build a complete "set" of type coins, you would go on to acquire one Barber dime, one Seated Liberty quarter, one Franklin half dollar, one

Morgan dollar, etc., until you obtained one example of every type (or kind) of coin issued by the United States from the beginning to the present. In date collecting, the emphasis is on rarity, although many date collectors still require gem quality coins. In type collecting, the emphasis is on condition, although some type collectors, albeit not investors, do not require quality.

Since only one representative coin of each design is needed, irrespective of date or mintmark, type collectors seek out the most common or semi-common dates in the series. Fortunately, these common coins also are the least expensive coins in the type. While in date collecting, the emphasis is on acquiring all the dates and mint mark combinations in the series, in type collecting the emphasis is on the quality of a single coin, since rarity is only an incidental consideration.

A Few Words about Quality

Thus far, when speaking about investment-quality rare coins, we have almost always coupled their mention with the words "top quality;" and, indeed, one, as a rule, should *never* think about purchasing any sort of specimen unless it can be characterized as such. There is an old maxim, one that has rung down the corridors of the numismatic world for years, and it has never been more true than it is today. Remember it, believe in it, take it to heart: *Quality is everything.*

We have noted that among the most important elements in calculating the value of a coin are rarity and quality; yet, given what we have seen, does the former not imply the latter? Top-quality rare coins are rare precisely because they are of top quality; as noted, fewer than five percent of all U.S. coins minted have survived in choice uncirculated condition. Something that everyone can get their hands on—namely, worn, scratched, dented and otherwise injured coins—is never going to be worth much, especially in a market in which demand for the very best merchandise is growing daily.

Yet we are not speaking merely of the difference between coins characterized as "mint state" and those in no better condition than pocket change. Degrees of quality within the "mint state" category itself, however small, can mean a difference of thousands of dollars at the moment of sale. Basically, coins are graded on the Sheldon Scale, using a sliding scale of 0, at the bottom, to 70, which is perfect. If a coin is uncirculated or Mint State (new), it will grade at least MS-60. Coins graded MS-60 or MS-63 are the lower grades of new, while coins graded MS-65 or better are considered the finest, and are generally what we would call investment quality. Some people will attempt to convince you that the difference is minimal, a matter of a few small points; and, if you are unfamiliar with the market, this argument will appear to make sense. A close study of the situation, however, reveals a very different truth.

Using as our point of calculation the best, most accurate information, we can assume that the *actual* supply of MS-60 coins is, approximately, at least 20 times greater than that of MS-65 specimens. This figure is further affected, however, by the fact that, as we have discussed, those holding the very best coins remain extremely reluctant to sell them, rendering them, for all practical purposes, "off-the-market," and as if they did not exist. As a rule, investors sell off their finest specimens last, or as a last resort in situations of extreme financial distress. The huge sums brought by major collections at auction have tempted many investors to attempt building their own—a job requiring, ordinarily, several decades of consistent work and good luck. Still others buy coins with no intention other than passing them on to their heirs. The result is that, in real and practical terms, the *available* number of MS-60 coins is roughly 20 to 50 times greater than MS-65 coins. Thus the case for quality becomes that much more evident, and important.

Many dealers specializing in lower-grade coins point out that MS-65 coins are too expensive. This argument is as peculiar as it is wrong. A new Rolls-Royce costs more than a new Toyota. No one wonders why. The reason is quality; quality is the reason people pay more for certain things than others. So it is with coins.

Still others dealing in MS-60 specimens suggest that they are underpriced, and thus a good deal. This argument is undercut by their availability. If they were such a good deal, people would be buying them up by the carload; they'd be scarce. But the fact is that they're readily available. Only one kind of coin becomes scarce in the marketplace: a *top-quality* coin.

It is often argued, too, that many MS-65 specimens are overgraded. The Sheldon Scale, the method by which coins are graded, is highly exact and specific, and leaves little room for conjecture. Though grading is, ultimately, somewhat a matter of opinion, and two numismatists of excellent reputation might disagree about one or another coin, the notion that an entire area of the market—especially the very top—would be overgraded simply doesn't wash. Moreover, anyone who might conceivably overgrade a coin as an MS-65 would also do the same with coins of a lesser grade.

The final arbiter in the matter is, as always, price; and the difference a few points on the grading scale can make can be astonishing.

Obviously, not everyone can afford to buy MS-65 specimens. A good alternative is to always purchase the best quality to be had in your price range. This will insure good value; and it is not unheard of for an investor to trade two or three lesser grade coins for a single, better one.

If you can not afford MS-65 quality, then it is not unreasonable to purchase coins that are graded MS-64 or MS-63. In fact, there are some numismatists who feel that MS-64 or MS-63 coins are undervalued. Of course, no one can know for sure if coins of lesser quality are undervalued, and if, in fact, there are fabulous investments to be had in MS-64 or MS-63 coins. Past experience has shown that the higher the grade, the more likely the investment will perform well. As a rule, we say, buy the *best* quality available, the *best* quality that you can afford.

Of course, when it comes to really rare coins, the rule is to buy the best condition that is available. Some coins are so scarce that they have only survived in lesser conditions and are not always obtainable in uncirculated condition. In these cases, you try to buy the best quality available for that issue. This applies to many of the early coinage issues, such as the copper and silver pieces prior to 1807, and gold coins prior to 1839, which can be purchased in EF-45 (Extremely Fine) condition or better.

It should be noted, however, that in absolute terms, truly rare coins are currently disproportionately undervalued as an investment when compared with lesser rare issues which are bought solely on the basis of quality. For example, an 1881-S silver dollar, which now sells for about $2,000 in MS-67, is one of tens of thousands of such coins. Contrast this with an 1856 "no motto" $10 gold piece (Coronet type), of which only two or three pieces are known to exist in that mint state. This coin is worth about $30,000. It is more than 10,000 times rarer than the 1881-S silver dollar, yet sells for only 15 times as much money. On a strictly "value" basis, this and other rare date coins may be better buys in today's market than some of the coins that are bought solely on the basis of their top-quality condition.

However, not all investors can afford to lay out a huge sum of money for one coin, nor would it be appropriate for their individual market portfolio, which is why we say: *Buy the best quality you can afford.*

Rare coins remain one of the few areas in life in which the pursuit of excellence virtually always yields a tangible reward.

A Few Words about Bullion

We have been consistently advocating the purchase of rare coins over bullion, and this is a philosophy, needless to say, to which we will continue to stick. Rare coins, as we have demonstrated, are a far better investment. Ironically, the reason many supposedly knowledgeable individuals recommend buying bullion is that they don't know anything about coins. We can not, however, ignore economic and market realities. Bullion, especially gold, is popular and, if cautiously bought and sold, a useful investment option. Gold can be a useful medium for short-term speculation, though it must be carefully, consistently monitored. Gold may also function as an excellent long-term inflation hedge. Since a common and popular method of purchasing bullion is via coins, we propose to briefly address the matter, so that, when it comes time for you to make your move into this glittering arena, you will have the facts.

Gold

A look at the history of American gold in this century will reinforce the caution with which it should be approached as an investment, for its purchase and sale has always been affected by government regulation.

In 1933, the ownership of gold bullion was declared illegal, a step taken

POSTMASTER: PLEASE POST IN A CONSPICUOUS PLACE.—JAMES A. FARLEY, Postmaster General

UNDER EXECUTIVE ORDER OF THE PRESIDENT

Issued April 5, 1933

all persons are required to deliver

ON OR BEFORE MAY 1, 1933

all GOLD COIN, GOLD BULLION, AND GOLD CERTIFICATES now owned by them to a Federal Reserve Bank, branch or agency, or to any member bank of the Federal Reserve System.

Executive Order

FORBIDDING THE HOARDING OF GOLD COIN, GOLD BULLION AND GOLD CERTIFICATES.

By virtue of the authority vested in me by Section 5(b) of the Act of October 6, 1917, as amended by Section 2 of the Act of March 9, 1933, entitled "An Act to provide relief in the existing national emergency in banking, and for other purposes", in which amendatory Act Congress declared that a serious emergency exists, I, Franklin D. Roosevelt, President of the United States of America, do declare that said national emergency still continues to exist and pursuant to said section do hereby prohibit the hoarding of gold coin, gold bullion, and gold certificates within the continental United States by individuals, partnerships, associations and corporations and hereby prescribe the following regulations for carrying out the purposes of this order:

Section 1. For the purposes of this regulation, the term "hoarding" means the withdrawal and withholding of gold coin, gold bullion or gold certificates from the recognized and customary channels of trade. The term "person" means any individual, partnership, association or corporation.

Section 2. All persons are hereby required to deliver on or before May 1, 1933, to a Federal reserve bank or a branch or agency thereof or to any member bank of the Federal Reserve System all gold coin, gold bullion and gold certificates now owned by them or coming into their ownership on or before April 28, 1933, except the following:

(a) Such amount of gold as may be required for legitimate and customary use in industry, profession or art within a reasonable time, including gold prior to refining and stocks of gold in reasonable amounts for the usual trade requirements of owners mining and refining such gold.

(b) Gold coin and gold certificates in an amount not exceeding in the aggregate $100.00 belonging to any one person; and gold coins having a recognized special value to collectors of rare and unusual coins.

(c) Gold coin and bullion earmarked or held in trust for a recognized foreign government or foreign central bank or the Bank for International Settlements.

(d) Gold coin and bullion licensed for other proper transactions (not involving hoarding) including gold coin and bullion imported for reexport or held pending action on applications for export licenses.

Section 3. Until otherwise ordered any person becoming the owner of any gold coin, gold bullion, or gold certificates after April 28, 1933, shall, within three days after receipt thereof, deliver the same in the manner prescribed in Section 2; unless such gold coin, gold bullion or gold certificates are held for any of the purposes specified in paragraphs (a), (b) or (c) of Section 2; or unless such gold coin or gold bullion is held for purposes specified in paragraph (d) of Section 2 and the person holding it is, with respect to such gold coin or bullion, a licensee or applicant for license pending action thereon.

Section 4. Upon receipt of gold coin, gold bullion or gold certificates delivered to it in accordance with Sections 2 or 3, the Federal reserve bank or member bank will pay therefor an equivalent amount of any other form of coin or currency coined or issued under the laws of the United States.

Section 5. Member banks shall deliver all gold coin, gold bullion and gold certificates owned or received by them (other than as exempted under the provisions of Section 2) to the Federal reserve banks of their respective districts and receive credit or payment therefor.

Section 6. The Secretary of the Treasury, out of the sum made available to the President by Section 501 of the Act of March 9, 1933, will in all proper cases pay the reasonable costs of transportation of gold coin, gold bullion or gold certificates delivered to a member bank or Federal reserve bank in accordance with Sections 2, 3, or 5 hereof, including the cost of insurance, protection, and such other incidental costs as may be necessary, upon production of satisfactory evidence of such costs. Voucher forms for this purpose may be procured from Federal reserve banks.

Section 7. In cases where the delivery of gold coin, gold bullion or gold certificates by the owners thereof within the time set forth above will involve extraordinary hardship or difficulty, the Secretary of the Treasury may, in his discretion, extend the time within which such delivery must be made. Applications for such extensions must be made in writing under oath, addressed to the Secretary of the Treasury and filed with a Federal reserve bank. Each application must state the date to which the extension is desired, the amount and location of the gold coin, gold bullion and gold certificates in respect of which such application is made and the facts showing extension to be necessary to avoid extraordinary hardship or difficulty.

Section 8. The Secretary of the Treasury is hereby authorized and empowered to issue such further regulations as he may deem necessary to carry out the purposes of this order and to issue licenses thereunder, through such officers or agencies as he may designate, including licenses permitting the Federal reserve banks and member banks of the Federal Reserve System, in return for an equivalent amount of other coin, currency or credit, to deliver, earmark or hold in trust gold coin and bullion to or for persons showing the need for the same for any of the purposes specified in paragraphs (a), (c) and (d) of Section 2 of these regulations.

Section 9. Whoever willfully violates any provision of this Executive Order or of these regulations or of any rule, regulation or license issued thereunder may be fined not more than $10,000, or, if a natural person, may be imprisoned for not more than ten years, or both; and any officer, director, or agent of any corporation who knowingly participates in any such violation may be punished by a like fine, imprisonment, or both.

This order and these regulations may be modified or revoked at any time.

FRANKLIN D ROOSEVELT

For Further Information Consult Your Local Bank

GOLD CERTIFICATES may be identified by the words **"GOLD CERTIFICATE"** appearing thereon. The serial number and the Treasury seal on the face of a **GOLD CERTIFICATE** are printed in YELLOW. Be careful not to confuse **GOLD CERTIFICATES** with other issues which are redeemable in gold but which are <u>not</u> **GOLD CERTIFICATES**. Federal Reserve Notes and United States Notes are "redeemable in gold" but are <u>not</u> "GOLD CERTIFICATES" and are <u>not</u> required to be surrendered

Special attention is directed to the exceptions allowed under Section 2 of the Executive Order

CRIMINAL PENALTIES FOR VIOLATION OF EXECUTIVE ORDER $10,000 fine or 10 years imprisonment, or both, as provided in Section 9 of the order

W. H. Woodin

Secretary of the Treasury.

by President Roosevelt in response to the economic stresses of the time, and one that is still debated. Interestingly, the metal could then only be purchased, legally, in the form of numismatic coins. Through the 1950s, gold bugs contented themselves with the legal (and numismatically appealing) 20 dollar gold piece, or Double Eagle, which was readily available, and traded, through the middle of the following decade. "Twenties" made gold purchase relatively easy, as they contain nearly an ounce of the precious metal, and thus facilitate the incremental aspect of a transaction.

In the 1960s, it became legal to own the Mexican 50 Peso piece, though its importation was still a crime. Once smuggled in, however, the coin, containing 1.2057 Troy ounces of fine gold, quickly found a market, vying with the Double Eagle for popularity. With two options from which to choose, and a rapidly growing market, many new bullion dealers began opening their doors throughout the country, though on a relatively small scale, with some firms importing Twenties from Switzerland to meet the demand. With prices feeling the first stirrings of an exploding market, gold fever began spreading in the early seventies. Two additional bullion coins became legally available in 1974—the Austrian 100 Corona and the Hungarian 100 Korona— and ownership of all gold coins became completely legal at the start of 1975. Over the past decade, the Krugerrand has ruled the bullion coin roost. Its banning by Congress, in response to South Africa's repugnant racial laws, has seen it recently replaced in popularity by the Canadian Maple Leaf, which boasts a full Troy ounce of 24 karat gold. The U.S. Mint is also making bullion pieces.

CHART 17

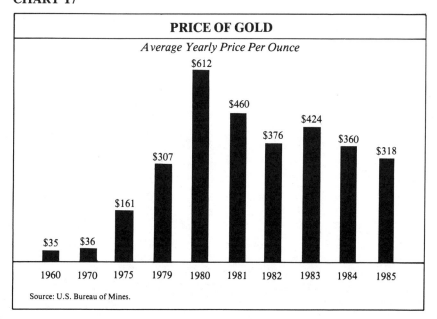

PRICE OF GOLD

Average Yearly Price Per Ounce

1960	1970	1975	1979	1980	1981	1982	1983	1984	1985
$35	$36	$161	$307	$612	$460	$376	$424	$360	$318

Source: U.S. Bureau of Mines.

CHART 18

RARE GOLD COINS VS. BULLION AND BULLION-RELATED COINS 1980–1985				
Date	Spot Price Gold Bullion Per oz.	Kruggerrand (from 1/84 Maple Leaf)	U.S. $20 St. Gaudens Grade XF	U.S. $20 St. Gaudens MS-65
Jan. 18, 1980	$708.50	$743.60	$940.00	$1,205.00
April 4, 1980	505.00	540.00	715.00	1,205.00
July 11, 1980	673.50	699.00	821.00	1,550.00
Oct. 3, 1980	660.50	687.00	831.00	1,610.00
Jan. 2, 1981	585.50	610.00	747.00	1,665.00
April 3, 1981	513.00	528.00	723.00	1,780.00
July 3, 1981	427.50	445.75	632.00	1,780.00
Oct. 2, 1981	431.30	450.25	629.00	1,665.00
Jan. 15, 1982	386.20	404.00	502.00	1,725.00
April 2, 1982	323.30	339.75	521.00	1,610.00
July 2, 1982	310.70	326.25	447.35	1,552.50
Oct. 1, 1982	404.50	424.12	603.75	1,667.50
Nov. 26, 1982	405.00	424.00	586.50	1,667.50
Feb. 4, 1983	508.50	529.75	746.35	1,725.00
May 6, 1983	429.10	448.50	704.40	1,980.00
Sept. 16, 1983	415.75	435.25	825.60	2,190.00
July 27, 1984	339.75	356.50	676.00	2,190.00
Dec. 17, 1984	316.85	325.50	635.95	2,000.00
April 3, 1985	317.00	333.00	623.80	2,500.00
July 22, 1985	321.80	339.00	645.00	3,000.00
Nov. 21, 1985	326.00	344.00	690.00	3,200.00
Percentage Change (1980–85):	−54%	−53.7%	−26.6%	+165.5%

Reference Source: *The Coin Dealer Newsletter,* N.Y. Comex.

The activity of the past ten years has led to the development of gold markets throughout the world, with trading especially strong in such places as London, Zurich and Hong Kong. The New York market seems to be dominant at present, though how long this will last is anyone's guess.

There are a number of things to keep in mind when making gold purchases. If you are not personally very familiar with them, stay away from gold bars. While bars are a perfectly legitimate and psychologically attractive investment, unless you have a reliable broker to handle the transaction, without an assay for purity they may not always be as easy to resell as one might think. Amateurs should stick to bullion coins, which at least have the guarantee of a government behind them and are assay-free and easy to

CHART 19

CHOICE GOLD COINS VS. GOLD BULLION			
Past Performance Comparisons			
	8/27/76 Low	11/21/80 High	1/4/86 Current
Gold Bullion	$103	$850	$338
Gold Coins (MS–65):			
$1 Type I	450	7,000	7,300
$1 Type II	2,200	22,500	25,000
$1 Type III	400	6,000	5,500
$2.50 Liberty	165	2,650	4,250
$2.50 Indian	220	2,850	4,250
$3	1,600	15,000	14,000
$5 Liberty WM	160	3,200	6,100
$5 Indian	475	4,800	7,300
$10 Liberty WM	250	4,000	6,400
$10 Indian WM	250	4,500	6,700
$20 Liberty Type III	205	1,900	5,000
$20 St. Gaudens WM	215	1,350	3,200
Total:	6,590	75,750	95,000

	Gold Bullion	Gem Gold Coins
8/27/76 Low to 11/21/80 High	+825.2%	+1149.4%
11/21/80 High to 1/4/86	− 60.2%	+ 25.4%
8/27/76 Low to 1/4/86	+ 228%	+1341.5%
$10,000 invested 8/27/76 Low, sold 11/21/80 High	+$82,510	+$114,940
$10,000 invested 8/27/76 Low, sold 1/4/86	+$32,810	+$144,150

Reference Source: *The Coin Dealer Newsletter,* N.Y. Comex.

recognize. Avoid the commodity markets as well—they are risky, expensive, and time-consuming, unless you are a professional or trade like one. Buy bullion coins, and *always* take physical possession of your bullion at the time of purchase. It will also be worth your while to do a little comparison shopping; this can make a difference, not just on the front end, but when it comes time to sell, too.

The figures in Chart 19, above, show the price performance of gold bullion compared to the 12 major U.S. gold coins during the climb from the last major bottom (1976) to the last major peak (1980) and the present. The results show that *Choice Quality* rare gold coins dramatically outperformed gold bullion on the way up and then declined a lot less on the way down!

The conclusion: If you bought *Choice rare gold coins* in August of 1976 and still had them today, you would have made more money than a person who bought *gold bullion* at the very bottom and sold at the very top!

Silver

The principal demand for silver is industrial. It is one of the world's most versatile, useful metals and, as such, remains constantly in demand. The metal which adorns our belts, fingers, lapels and dinner tables is also among the finest known conductor of electricity, used for circuitry of all sorts. Silver's reflective qualities are also unequalled, making it of use for everything from mirrors to solar energy cells. Medical uses stem from the metal's ability to naturally kill certain germs. And it remains an important ingredient in many photographic processes. It is difficult to imagine a world without a strong, consistent demand for silver; thus, it has long remained a steady and reliable investment.

Silver may be purchased via buying United States "90 percent" silver coins (of no numismatic quality) which sell in bags of $1,000 face value, at the price of the silver plus a slight premium over melt. Bars are less bulky, but be sure to purchase bars only from nationally recognized refiners that are acceptable on at least two commodity exchanges. As with gold, all the rules of purchase—and caveats about the market—apply, principal among them:

Proceed with caution.

CHART 20

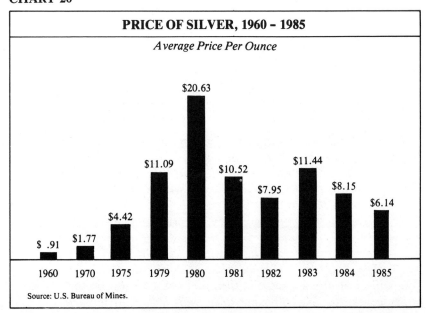

PRICE OF SILVER, 1960 – 1985

Average Price Per Ounce

Year	Price
1960	$ .91
1970	$1.77
1975	$4.42
1979	$11.09
1980	$20.63
1981	$10.52
1982	$7.95
1983	$11.44
1984	$8.15
1985	$6.14

Source: U.S. Bureau of Mines.

CHART 21

	SILVER COINS VS. SILVER BULLION 1980–1985			
Date	Spot Price Silver Bullion Per oz.	Common Date 1881-S Morgan MS-65	Better Date 1921-S Morgan MS-65	Rare Date 1883-S Morgan MS-65
Jan. 18, 1980	$46.75	$ 56.00	$ 745.00	$2,500.00
April 4, 1980	14.20	60.00	805.00	3,075.00
July 11, 1980	16.70	65.00	930.00	3,250.00
Oct. 13, 1980	20.35	75.00	965.00	3,510.00
Jan. 2, 1981	15.75	86.00	1,065.00	3,735.00
April 3, 1981	12.15	92.50	1,090.00	3,850.00
July 3, 1981	8.58	93.75	1,090.00	3,850.00
Oct. 2, 1981	8.84	112.00	1,200.00	3,850.00
Jan. 15, 1982	8.08	115.00	1,190.00	3,450.00
April 2, 1982	7.09	120.00	1,220.00	3,450.00
July 2, 1982	5.35	112.12	1,092.50	2,760.00
Oct. 1, 1982	8.22	138.00	1,035.00	2,185.00
Nov. 26, 1982	9.28	138.00	1,035.00	2,185.00
Feb. 4, 1983	14.25	143.75	1,063.75	2,185.00
May 6, 1983	12.06	162.00	1,110.00	2,280.00
July 29, 1983	12.44	162.00	1,140.00	2,640.00
Sept. 16, 1983	12.28	169.80	1,140.00	1,880.00
July 27, 1984	7.26	264.00	1,140.00	3,960.00
Dec. 17, 1984	6.56	294.00	1,140.00	3,840.00
April 3, 1985	6.44	380.00	1,140.00	4,345.00
July 22, 1985	6.16	525.00	1,540.00	5,225.00
Nov. 21, 1985	6.17	570.00	1,540.00	5,640.00
Percentage Change 1980–85:	−86.8%	+1,017.8%	+206.7%	+225.6%

Reference Source: *The Coin Dealer Newsletter,* N.Y. Comex.

The intent of the chart is to compare bullion prices with prices of three categories of Morgan dollars—the more common dates of 1881-S and 1921-S and the rare date of 1883-S. Note that the investor lost money on the price of bullion, and made money on the coins. The more common the coin, the better the investment performed!

Now that you have become familiar with the "Why?," the next question is, "How?" Though we never recommend that the novice rare coin investor get involved in the market without the assistance of a numismatist, there are some basic rules of investment that will help you on your way. These simple guidelines are outlined in Chapter Four; and, whether you are investing $1,000 or $100,000, they will form the bedrock of all your movements and decisions.

Early Colonial Coins

MARYLAND (LORD BALTIMORE) SIXPENCE

To alleviate a shortage of coins in the colonies, Cecil Calvert, Lord Baltimore, the "Lord Proprietor of Maryland," had coins struck in 1658 in London for use in Maryland. The coins were issued in the following denominations: shilling, sixpence and fourpence (groat) in silver; and a copper penny (denarium).

The silver coins are identical in design, with the bust of Lord Baltimore on the obverse and the Baltimore family Arms and the legend, Crescite et Multiplicamini (Increase and multiply) on the reverse.

PINE TREE SHILLING

This is one of the most romantic issues among early American coinage. The Massachusetts Bay Colony issued various "tree" coins (Oak Tree, Pine Tree and Willow Tree) until 1682, although all bore the same date, 1652.

During this period, witch hunts spread throughout New England and many colonists wore the Pine Tree Shilling around their necks as a charm to ward off witches. As a result many of the surviving shillings are holed.

Chapter Four
BASIC RULES OF RARE COIN INVESTMENT

There are a number of factors to keep in mind when investing in rare coins: the type of coins to buy, grading, prices to pay, the structure of the market, and so forth, as well as different avenues of purchase and sale. If, at first, this all sounds complicated, do not get discouraged. It is not as difficult as it might seem. Once you have become familiar with some basic principals, the path of a rare coin investment is no more difficult to follow than that of any other investment.

Since market emphasis has shifted from the collector to the investor, the methods of acquisition—indeed, the nature and size of collections themselves—have changed dramatically. In the old days—by which we mean prior to 1950—purchasers built their collections slowly, year after year, through sources as varied as professional numismatists, U.S. Mint sales, hobby shops and mail order houses.

Amon Carter Sr., founder and publisher of the Fort Worth Star-Telegram, began collecting in the 1940s. His son, Amon Jr., assumed both his father's publishing and numismatic mantles in 1955, and, by the time of his death in 1982, had built the family coin collection into one of the world's finest. One of the collection's prizes, a 1794 mint state silver dollar, was snapped up by the old man in 1947, in a mail bid sale, for $1,200. When this extreme rarity—a famous and well-known specimen of the Mint's first silver dollar— sold at auction in January of 1984, the price paid was $264,000, a gain in value of some 22,000 percent. Nor was this unique:

The Bareford Collection, assembled in the 1950s for a total of $16,000, sold at auction in the late seventies for $1.2 million.

One of the few surviving examples of the privately made Brasher Doubloon, America's most valuable coin, was purchased at auction for $3,000 in 1922 by Virgil M. Brand, the Chicago brewery tycoon, who compiled the biggest coin collection of all time. His Brasher Doubloon was auctioned 57 years later for $430,000.

Even this pales beside the price brought by the Garrett specimen of the Brasher Doubloon. T. Harrison Garrett began collecting in 1860; his sons, Robert and John Work, continued adding specimens through the early 1940s.

At the Garrett auction, in November, 1979, their uncirculated Brasher Doubloon sold for $725,000—an all-time record of astonishing proportions.

As you can plainly see, there is money to be made—if you follow a few simple rules of investment.

The Ten Basic Rules Of Rare Coin Investment

1. Buy the best quality you can afford. The truth is, you can never stress quality too much. So we will say it again: *Quality is everything.* An MS-60 coin is not a bargain basement version of an MS-65. *Buy the best quality available.* The best brings the best price at sale. And that, after all, is the point.

2. Diversify. Not just within your overall portfolio, but among your rare coins as well. This, when you get right down to it, is nothing more than good common sense. Spreading your investment across the numismatic board insures that your coins will support each other when different market areas are strong or weak, and keeps you flexible, with different specimens peaking at different times.

We, and many Financial Planners, recommend that no more than 10 to 15 percent of the average investment portfolio be devoted to numismatics. As has been repeatedly noted, no single option can fulfill all your investment needs; and successful individuals pursue as much diversity as is reasonable and prudent. This percentage affords the liquidity, stability, diversification and, above all, high returns that all investors seek.

3. Buy coins that you can sell. This is not as obvious a statement as it sounds. If you have, for example, $10,000 set aside for rare coin investments, some dealers might advise you to spend it all on one coin. While, in some cases, this may make sense, such a course may limit your liquidity.

Stay away from esoterica, also. In a market full of available and popular merchandise, why bother with gambles and longshots? The average rare coin investor should restrict purchases to those areas of the market that have proven performance records and solid opportunity for growth.

These are:

a) gold coins of numismatic (as opposed to bullion) value. For example, the most affordable St. Gaudens Double Eagles (1907–32);
b) Nineteenth century type coins, such as Barber Dimes, Quarters and Halves, Liberty and Shield Nickels, etc;
c) Silver dollars of the Morgan (1878–1921) and Peace (1921–1935) types; and
d) what have come to be known as "modern singles"—Jefferson and Buffalo Nickels, Mercury Dimes, Washington Quarters, Franklin and Kennedy Halves, and the like, dated (with some obvious exceptions) through mid-20th century.

We suggest, as an effective portfolio mix in today's market, the following apportionment of your investment dollars:

—30 percent gold coins
—30 percent type coins
—20 percent silver dollars
—20 percent modern singles

Choice and gem quality gold coins remain among the rarest and most desirable of U.S. coins, thereby all but guaranteeing their continued upward growth. Type coins have considerable aesthetic and historical appeal, and are in relatively short supply in Choice Uncirculated condition (the lower grades are readily found). Silver dollars have remained in the very forefront of the market since it took off in the early 1970s and continue to post strong, steady gains. The least expensive group, with the largest base of collectors, modern singles represent a strong, and still developing, market sector, with enormous future potential.

4. Seek professional help. Work with a professional numismatist if you are making your first venture into the rare coin market. Just as you would never buy stocks without a broker, do not try to buy coins on your own. Though you may, after some years of dedicated study and consistent hands-on involvement, have enough knowledge to do some of your own trading, reading any book—as thorough and comprehensive as it may be— will not give you all you need to know.

5. Make your purchases from a reputable dealer. This industry, like every other investment industry, has plenty of incompetents. You would not buy stocks from a stranger on the street. Be just as careful picking your numismatist. Friends already active in numismatic investment might be able to help you in this regard.

6. Do not overpay. This, too, seems obvious. But think about it. How is a novice to gauge real worth? How can someone making an initial foray into numismatics distinguish between a good value and a flagrant rip-off? It can be difficult, and tricky. Most numismatic investment firms mark up their purchases approximately 30 percent over wholesale. However, markups of up to 200 percent are not unheard of; and these, obviously, can wreak havoc upon your potential profits.

The best way to avoid overpaying—apart from dealing with a reputable coin broker—is to familiarize yourself with prices. Comparison shop. Study the bid/ask prices in the *Coin Dealer Newsletter,* or the weekly newspapers, *Coin World* and *Numismatic News.* Try to get some consensus of where prices are for a coin or a particular group of coins. Once you can reasonably ball-park the merchandise of your choice, you will be able to question dealers with a certain amount of knowledge—and, thus, power. Always beware of prices that are too low—such coins may have been tampered with or mis-graded.

7. Become as knowledgeable as you can about all your investments. You should know at least enough to avoid suspect deals and apparent hustles.

8. Take delivery of your investment. The whole purpose of owning a hard asset, from historical times to the present, is to hold onto it. Do not let *anyone,* even your trusted dealer of proven reputation, keep your coins for you if you can avoid it.

9. Carefully store and insure your portfolio. This is so easy and inexpensive that you might forget, or do it carelessly. But remember: your coins will only be of value, when the time comes to sell, if they are in the same pristine condition as when you bought them. So find a suitable safe deposit box, and tuck them in for the long haul. And be sure the insurance policy you select contains a provision covering bank theft.

For coin dealers, theft and robbery are ever present possibilities, and elaborate protective measures are necessary. Costly insurance policies—requiring intricate alarms and detection devices, the service of guards, and all but impregnable safes—must be maintained to safeguard inventory not kept in bank vaults. When transporting his stock, perhaps from one coin show to another, the dealer is an ideal target. Portable, easily concealed, highly liquid, rare coins are simple to steal and fence.

Fortunately, the investor is spared these concerns, and may protect his portfolio much more simply. The most important rule to remember, of course, is: *never* store coins at home. Do not be tempted by your investment's attractiveness, or that handsome display holder with which you may have been provided, to set it on the piano beside the family portrait. A common burglar will have less trouble unloading your Barber Dime than your clock radio. Nor is a home safe entirely reliable (especially if you are requested, at gunpoint, to open it).

Remember: What a safe deposit box takes from you in aesthetic pleasure it returns in peace of mind.

10. Buy and hold. We have characterized rare coins as a long-term investment, giving five years as the minimum length of holding time. Do not invest funds that can not be tied up for this period of time. It is also true that money can be made after 18 months or less. But the fact is, truly legendary profits have been made over the past 30 years, and not by people who were seeking merely to outpace inflation, or even to ride the cycles which characterize the market. The really big scores were realized by those who, after following the rules of investment delineated above, were willing to sit back for up to a decade or more, and let values escalate. Their patience was rewarded with gains, not untypically, on the order of 1,000 percent. Now, it is difficult to let profits of 30, 40, and 50 percent or more go by without itching to sell—especially when the market flattens out and prices begin to drop. It is hard not to lose your nerve. But if you can manage to buy and hold—and hold, and hold—your fortitude will be grandly, expensively rewarded.

On the other hand—and there always is another hand, it seems—do not get greedy. Set a target, know when the time has come to sell, and sell.

Taxes

It is also of benefit to the investor to keep abreast of the tax laws pertaining to rare coins. At present, transactions remain anonymous, but this could change. Rare coins were disallowed in self-directed pension plans, such as Individual Retirement Accounts (IRAs) and Keoghs, several seasons back; again, this situation may well reverse itself. Knowing where you stand at all times will better enable you to make decisions regarding what to buy, what to sell, and when.

For general tax purposes, two sets of rules apply: the first pertains to the collector for whom coins are a hobby, the second to the investor interested in financial gain. Both may turn a profit, but it is the collector who will be taxed at the higher rate: capital gains reductions are currently available only to the investor. Further, the investor may deduct related expenses, including those stemming from income production (professional fees, insurance, and the like) and property management (such as a safe deposit box), as well as any financial losses incurred.

The question is: how does the Internal Revenue Service decide whether or not someone is an investor? This has at times proven difficult, and numerous court cases have been devoted to determining whether or not a collection has been accumulated for pleasure or profit. There are some federal guidelines; these include whether or not the activity has been carried out with a degree of expertise, the amount of time consumed, and proof of the expectation of gain. The profit motive is also presumed present if the income from an activity is greater than the accumulated deductions for two out of five years, measured consecutively. Investors must also avoid the hallmarks of coin collecting—display cases, home storage, and so forth; and hobbyist's materials, when purchased, should not be deducted as business expenses. Good records must be kept, including the date, mint, denomination and grade of each coin, dates and prices of purchases and sales and commission fees incurred.

Buying

When you go to a contemporary coin dealer to make a purchase, you are not limited, as you once were, to those specimens he or she has in stock. For over 20 years, approximately 500 of the nation's most prominent numismatists have been linked by teletype, offering a highly automated, up-to-the-minute, instant-access information system. The teletype enables dealers to immediately communicate with one another, and exchange data relating to, among other things, available merchandise. The sophistication of the system streamlines the process for those seeking to start investing quickly.

Because the extraordinary demand for rare coins has created something of a shortage of top-quality merchandise, some numismatic houses have begun to put together limited and/or general partnerships, enabling investors (usually for a minimum of between $5,000 and $10,000) to get involved with portfolios worth $250,000 or more. Such partnerships simplify the investment process, leaving the purchasing and management to the experts, and eliminating the problems inherent in searching out desirable specimens, as well as substantially diversifying the overall risk.

With or without professional help, there are a variety of ways to buy coins. One of the most common methods is through the mail. Many publications directed toward those interested in numismatics feature lists of coins for sale. These publications function as clearing houses for the world's coin collecting community; through them, you may locate interesting coins, or advertise those you wish to sell. Any resulting transactions may then be completed through the post. Mail-order coins may require an advance deposit, but they are always sold on an approval basis; when dealing with a reputable house, the buyer may reject them without fear of monetary loss. This technique is an old and honored one in the trade, dating from the 18th century; and the collector who chooses to act alone will find this method convenient.

The coin show is another important forum for trade, and conventions are held continuously in various places around the country. Each show, organized by an individual or association, occupies a date on a full calendar of shows, and, frequently, will be repeated annually. This provides a steady stream of shows at which to trade—a circumstance which is, of course, of benefit to investors. If, for example, after consulting with a client a coin broker does not have in stock those specimens best suited to the client's investment strategy and budget, the broker may dispatch a staff member to a show to make the purchase, or alert other dealers as to his needs.

Almost as important as the coin show, and often held in conjunction with it, is the coin auction. This is perhaps the most exciting forum for the trading of rare coins, though not for the novice or investor lacking professional advice. The outcome is always uncertain. A particular "lot" may sell for a song, or set a record. It all depends upon the bidders. The auction is in many ways a place of negotiation, one at which interested parties conduct business publicly, signaling interest, opinion—even, perhaps, the start of a trend—with the mere raise of a bid.

Bids may be submitted in two ways: via the mail, to the auction house beforehand; or, conventionally, given verbally at time of auction. Often both methods are used, with the lot going to whomever has, in the end, the highest bid. This is particularly useful for auctions that are also events, as may be the case when large collections or estates reach the block. When the auction is of nationwide interest, mail bids enable those who cannot attend to participate.

When buying at auction, it is a good idea to follow a few basic rules. Do not bid on a specimen you have not thoroughly examined. Determine what a coin is worth to you, based on your means, and a realistic estimate of what it will bring at sale. Do not rely solely on the advice of the auction house as regards what you should bid. And never go after a coin simply because a known numismatist is doing so. It might be his own coin that he is bidding on.

Selling

When it comes to leaving the market, rare coins offer complete liquidity. The industry—comprised of dealers linked together by teletype, computer inventory terminals, widely circulated coin publications, direct mail catalogues, and weekly national coin shows and auctions—responds rapidly to changing market trends, providing innumerable outlets for the investor ready to sell, whether he is divesting himself of a single coin or an entire portfolio.

The market's backbone is, of course, comprised of investors and collectors, of whom there are some 15 million in the United States alone. These individuals, who are also tied in to retailers, numismatic organizations, and coin publications, offer a steady, stable market for quality coins. This is particularly reassuring in a world in which the fate of so many investments is determined by uncertain political climates and questionable international financial policies.

If you decide to sell your coins at auction, be sure that you have an exact written determination of grade (prior to consignment). Better coins should be sold separately, rather than by lot. Comparison shopping, again, can be of use, as certain auction houses will offer better terms, particularly on commissions. The dealer who sold you the coins originally may be of help in arranging the resale. Do not ask too little for your higher-grade coins, or too much for lower-grades—a typical seller error.

We have discussed a variety of ways to purchase and invest in rare coins. Though some of these have not required the services of a professional, the novice rare coin investor would be well advised to seek out, and avail himself of, the talents of an experienced numismatist. A quality coin broker brings to the job a knowledge of history, the market, and the market's future, as well as being able to grade and authenticate accurately. Moreover, most numismatists will guarantee their expertise—a substantial psychological boon.

If, as previously noted, quality is indeed everything, then the ability to determine quality—accurately and consistently—is perhaps the most important skill a numismatist may possess. Within the profession, the skill is known as grading; and, in the following chapter, we will examine in detail the methods behind this exacting and critical endeavor.

The World's Most Valuable Coin

THE BRASHER DOUBLOON, 1787

The most valuable coin in the world, the 1787 Brasher Doubloon, a Spanish-style gold doubloon, was produced prior to the establishment of the mint by New York City gold- and silversmith Ephraim Brasher, a next-door neighbor of George Washington in New York. Few specimens exist; those that do rarely appear on the auction block; and when they do, they invariably bring record prices at sale. A Brasher Doubloon sold for $725,000 in 1979—an all-time record for a numismatic coin.

Chapter Five

GRADING AND AUTHENTICITY, RARITY AND THE ESTABLISHMENT OF VALUE

Grading

We have consistently stressed the critical importance of quality when investing in rare coins, and illustrated the vast price differentials generated by even the slightest incremental changes in a coin's grade, defined as condition or state of wear. Grading remains the single most important element impacting on numismatics—and few skills are more difficult to learn.

While grading is not an exact science, neither is it strictly a matter of opinion. It is governed by exacting standards and rules that insure a relative uniformity of appraisal from dealer to dealer. At one time, a collector was forced to depend almost entirely upon his knowledge, intuition and "eyeballing" abilities—all of which were, of course, uncertain. Over the last 20 years, however, owing in large part to the Sheldon Scale, the rigorous application of clearly defined specifications has made grading more objective and, thus, uniform. Minor disagreements still occur; but the investor will not receive radically different estimates from competent numismatists.

Until the rare coin market became primarily investor-based, and the need for greater degrees of accuracy and consistency arose, grading was a relatively subjective business, based on the knowledge and experience of whoever happened to be grading a coin. The result was a lack of standardization.

In 1948, Dr. William Sheldon, in his book about Large Cents, *Early American Coppers,* introduced a grading scale that, in a modified form, has become the standard for the industry today. Other significant landmarks included Martin R. Brown and John W. Dunn's, *A Guide to the Grading of Rare Coins* (1958) and James F. Ruddy's *Photograde* (1970), both of which contributed substantially to the evolution and standardization of grading.

In 1977, *The Official American Numismatic Association Grading Standards for U.S. Coins* expanded the Sheldon Scale to include all coins, thus further legitimizing this most comprehensive and effective of methods. That same year, *Grading Coins: A Collection of Readings,* edited by Dr. Richard Bagg, drew together in summary form almost everything written on the subject since the 1890s, thus providing a valuable guide to the evolution of numismatics' most critical science.

A variety of factors affect a coin's grade. Marks may be inflicted by the die during the minting process, or result from the condition of the planchet (the metal disc from which a coin is struck). Irregularities and imperfections found on the die may stem from the engraver's errors, or something so simple as wear and tear. Substandard manufacturing often resulted in coins that seemed to be in worse condition than they really were. This is particularly true of early American issues, most of which were produced under primitive conditions. Coins minted with poorly made or overused dies sometimes seem more worn then they really are—a condition known as apparent wear. Worn dies were often polished and reused, resulting in the removal of fine design details found in the original design or the addition of a new date or mint mark. This produced what are called "varieties" of the original coins.

But while die marks in general have the least bearing on a coin's worth, planchet irregularities can be more serious. These have various causes. For example, planchets for gold coins were weighed before striking, to insure the presence of the proper amount of gold; those found in excess were filed down to the appropriate weight. This left file grooves on the planchet, called adjustment marks, that often remained visible after the coin was struck. If present, they will be taken into consideration when the coin is graded. Other planchet marks result from irregular blanks and some numismatists specialize in collecting such coins.

By far the most common marks that appear on coins are inflicted after minting. So-called "bag marks" result from the banging together of coins after they have been bagged for shipment or storage, and the number of marks, and their placement, makes a difference. Coins are also subject to the effects of daily use—dents, scratches, bends, rim damage, and the like. Or they may have been damaged intentionally, as is the case with coins worn as jewelry, and marred in the mounting process. Such insults will significantly diminish a coin's worth.

Toning or coloration is also a consideration. Metals often react to their environments by changing color; and numismatists must learn how coins of differing alloys can be expected to color after years of use—or, for that matter, disuse. This knowledge is necessary and invaluable. If a coin is shiny and bright, just as if it left the mint, but its surface is scratched and marred, a competent numismatist should suspect polishing or chemical treatment at the hand of an unscrupulous vendor.

Of all the metals used in the creation of American coins, copper is the most susceptible to changes in color. A copper coin, when minted, will have the familiar brilliant pale red color we associate with new pennies; this mellows first to a reddish brown, and finally a glossy brown color. When an expert grades a copper coin, its color will be taken seriously into consideration: those that retain their original mint brilliance are considerably more valuable than those having a darker tone. Additionally, the surfaces of some copper coins may become spotted with corrosion, and investors living in humid locations should be particularly careful to store them in dry environments.

Like copper, silver is a highly active metal, and may darken from its initial brightness into various colors or hues. The value of a silver coin can be greatly increased by attractive original toning.

Nickel's silvery brilliance pales with time into a dull grey color. Nickel is very susceptible to corrosion.

And gold, the least reactive of coin metals, exchanges its alluring bright yellow-orange for a deeper, more full-bodied tone, sometimes containing brown streaks produced by the alloying material. A handsomely-toned gold coin will be especially prized by investors.

Natural or original toning is caused by the surface of a coin coming in contact with the atmosphere for years and oxidizing. The toning process is accelerated when a coin is housed in one of the old type paper envelopes, due to the sulfuric content in the paper. Coins stored in these paper envelopes tend to tone evenly because the obverse and reverse are in full contact with the paper surfaces. On the other hand, when coins are kept in coin albums, toning first occurs by the rim or edge and progresses toward the center of the coin. Coins are often taken out of these paper albums before the toning process is complete, resulting in a ring of peripheral toning.

Coins may tone in almost any hue of the rainbow, or a combination of colors. A choice coin may often bring a tremendous premium because of its gorgeous toning, which is derived from the amount of "flash" or eye appeal a coin offers. This is part of the subjective value of a rare coin. Some uninformed buyers consider toned coins "dirty." Others prefer to buy toned coins rather than brilliant specimens. In the end it is a matter of personal taste.

In the grading process, coins are divided into two broad categories: circulated (used) and uncirculated (new). Uncirculated or Mint State coins (UNC or MS) have never been used, and appear virtually as minted, without signs of wear. Uncirculated coins are not necessarily perfect in every respect: they are struck without special care, and packed en masse in bags. Marks are thus to be expected. The larger the coin, the more marks are likely. To accommodate imperfections, uncirculated coins are graded with Mint State designations, from MS-60 (Uncirculated) through MS-65 (Choice Uncirculated) to MS-70 (Perfect Uncirculated), with grading dependent upon the degree of imperfection.

MS-70   Perfect Uncirculated

> A flawless coin, exactly as it was minted, with no trace of wear or injury. The coin must have full mint luster, and brilliance, or original toning. For all intents and purposes, this grade is theoretical. Only a specialist can grade this coin.

MS-67   Gem Uncirculated

> Minutely disturbed surfaces, well struck, superior luster, and incredible eye appeal.

MS-65   Choice Uncirculated
A coin that is far above average uncirculated; a coin that possesses a superior strike, exceptional luster or desirable original toning with only some minor marks which do not detract from the overall pleasing appearance of the coin.

MS-63   Select Uncirculated
A mid-range uncirculated coin which may exhibit numerous but non-severe marks. It may have a weak but not a poor strike, and it may not be fully brilliant, although it will not have a dull finish.

MS-60   Uncirculated
A coin that will have no trace of wear but may show numerous contact or bag marks, nicks or spots. It may lack luster and/or have a weak strike. This is the lowest grade a coin can be and still be new.

Circulated coins, as their designation suggests, have been used to some degree. The grading scale for such specimens stems from 3, applicable to an example so worn its features are barely visible, to 59, which denotes a nearly uncirculated appearance. It is virtually impossible to make distinctions between coins adjacent on the grading scale—for example, a 30 and a 31; as a result, the scale has been divided into groups:

AU-58   Choice About Uncirculated 58
This is virtually a new coin, with luster and the basic appearance of a new coin, but has slight wear. It is sometimes called a "slider."

AU-55   Choice About Uncirculated 55
The wear is bearly distinguishable but is visible on the highest points.

AU-50   About Uncirculated 50
Nearly all of the detail and most of the luster are still present, but there is light wear on the high points.

EF-45 (or XF-45)   Choice Extremely Fine 45
There is visible wear on the highest points and most of the luster is still present.

EF-40 (or XF-40)   Extremely Fine 40
Most of the detail and some of the luster are still present.

VF   Very Fine 20, 25, 30 or 35
Light to moderate wear with most of the design still visible and the high points rubbed smooth.

F   Fine 12 or 15
Moderate to heavy wear with up to half of the design rubbed smooth.

VG   Very Good 8 or 10
Some of the design still visible but still having full rims.

G   Good 4 or 6
Some of the design still visible but will be weak and may not have full rims.

AG   About Good-3
                       Most of the design will be gone.

Fair   Design will be bearly distinguishable but still recognizable.

It is recommended that you consult an expert to grade all coins that are AU-50 (about uncirculated) or better. A circulated coin's grade is usually straightforward, though there is just as much overgrading among circulated coins as uncirculated. Nonetheless, when one side of a coin has worn at a different rate than the other, the numismatist must resort to a so-called "split grade": two grades for one coin. A coin with an obverse (head) grade of EF-40 and a reverse (tail) of EF-45 would be graded at EF-40/EF-45 (or, commonly, 40/45). It is by the lower of the two grades by which the coin is traded.

Precision Grading

Due to changing market conditions, such as the increased importance of mint state coins (the most commonly traded investment material), near mint state coins, and the demand for gem or perfect specimens, discrepancies have developed between the various grades and their pricing structure. Because of the geometric climb in value of quality coins, a circumstance which is characteristic in the real world of investing in and collecting objects of art, Precision Grading was developed by a group of coin dealers to overcome discrepancies in the pricing of middle grade uncirculated coins. The following two tables illustrate what Precision Grading is and how it works. Example 1:

	AU-50	MS-60	MS-63	MS-65
Large Cent (common date)	$100	$ 200	$ 500	$ 2,000
Indian $5 Gold (common date)	300	1,000	2,500	6,750
1886 Liberty Seated Quarter (better date)	350	1,250	3,500	14,000

This example illustrates the dramatic rise in price toward the higher grades. When choice material falls between these grades, it causes general confusion as to what these coins should be worth. Thus, Precision Grading came about to develop slots into which middle grade coins could fit, not perfectly, but much more precisely. The following table illustrates how middle grade uncirculated coins would be priced on the Precision Grading scale. Example 2:

	MS-60	MS-61	MS-62	MS-63	MS-64	MS-65
Large Cent	$ 200	$ 300	$ 400	$ 500	$ 900	$ 2,000
Liberty Seated Quarter	1,250	2,000	2,750	3,500	5,900	14,000
Bust Half Dollar	640	800	1,100	1,450	3,500	7,500

Not all dealers use Precision Grading. However, a dealer using this system would use a chart much like the one we have just seen, with the addition of the middle grade uncirculated coins.

MS-70   Perfect Uncirculated
A flawless coin, exactly as it was minted, with no trace of wear or injury. The coin must have full mint luster, and brilliance, or original toning. For all intents and purposes, this grade is theoretical. Only a specialist can grade this coin.

MS-69   Superb Gem Uncirculated
A coin that is exactly as it was minted, with virtually undetectable flaws and only a few minor marks that keep it from being nearly perfect. The coin must be brilliant or have original toning. You need a specialist on this grade, also.

MS-68   Gem Uncirculated
One or two barely noticeable, minor marks or abrasions, well struck, blazing luster and spectacular eye appeal.

MS-67   Gem Uncirculated
Minutely disturbed surfaces, well struck, superior luster, and incredible eye appeal.

MS-66   Choice Uncirculated
This grade coin is basically a premium quality MS-65 specimen; an MS-65 which possesses extra special appeal that adds to the overall beauty of the coin.

MS-65   Choice Uncirculated
A coin that is far above average uncirculated; a coin that possesses a superior strike, exceptional luster or desirable original toning with only some minor marks which do not detract from the overall pleasing appearance of the coin.

MS-64   Select Uncirculated
A nearly MS-65 coin; a coin that may slightly lack in one of the key areas. It possesses either slightly more marks, slightly less luster or a weaker strike.

MS-63   Select Uncirculated
A mid-range uncirculated coin which may exhibit numerous but non-severe marks. It may have a weak but not a poor strike, and it may not be fully brilliant, although it will not have a dull finish.

MS-62   Uncirculated
A coin that is nearly MS-63; a piece that may have one excessive mark, or reasonably weak strike.

MS-61   Uncirculated
A high-end range MS-60 coin. It may have excessive marks and possess a weak strike, but it is not in the worst mint state grade available.

MS-60   Uncirculated
A coin that will have no trace of wear but may show numerous contact or bag marks, nicks or spots. It may lack luster and/or have a weak strike. This is the lowest grade a coin can be and still be new.

Originally, proof coins were made exclusively for presentation to visiting dignitaries and heads of state; today, they are readily available to investors from the U.S. Mint. These coins are minted from carefully selected blanks which are hand-fed into the minting press. The proof dies are specially cared for, and highly polished, and the coin itself is struck repeatedly, to heighten and enhance all the engraver's details. Most proof coins have a reflective, mirror-like appearance; some proof coins dating from 1909 through 1917, however, show a variety of matte finishes. The finished product is then carefully packaged, thus preventing even the most negligible marks found in top-grade uncirculated coins. The result is a memorable work of art. Proof coins are graded the same way business strikes (coins made for use in circulation) are although "Proof" is not a grade; it is a method of manufacture.

Several other types of coins, never intended for circulation, are of interest to more advanced investors. One of these is known as a "pattern," or an experimental coin design which, for one reason or another, was never manufactured for circulation. Another is the die "trial piece," usually struck from other than a circulating metal to test a die, or determine the correct pressure for achieving the proper level of relief.

Any discussion of coin grading must include a caveat: in the world of numismatics, like the world of all investments, the buyer must indeed beware. While traders in stocks, bonds, commodities, foreign exchange, and real estate are strictly licensed by federal and state authorities, coin dealers are not monitored. It is relatively easy for an incompetent or unscrupulous merchant to call himself a numismatist, open an office, and sell overgraded coins for exorbitant sums to unsuspecting buyers. Overgrading may be avoided by dealing with an established and reliable coin broker.

Investors often locate trustworthy dealers via word of mouth, or through familiar coin organizations; but investors unfamiliar with the terrain would do well to find a broker who has been around awhile. Most reputable coin dealers guarantee their grades. A few offer grading insurance, which guarantees that, if the firm goes out of business, and the coins they sold you prove to be overgraded, you can, within a prescribed time period, get back what you paid for them, plus a 15 percent per year premium. This is an excellent deal; moreover, any numismatist making such an offer obviously has confidence in his grading abilities.

Finally, there is one last changing market factor. The personal tastes of the people who buy coins. At one time, toning on a coin commanded a large premium. Today, it only commands a premium if it is a top-quality coin. Once, collectors preferred proof-like Silver Dollars to uncirculated, bag-mark-free ones, but that is no longer the case. From time to time these personal standards change, and this affects the market.

Lastly, it is very important to remember that grading is the subjective description of an opinion of a particular numismatist as to the state of preservation of a particular coin. No warranty, whether it is expressed or implied, even when made in good faith, can be made with respect to these adjectival or numerical descriptions, which can and do vary among experts. Grading standards have changed in the past, and they might do so again in the future.

Authenticity

Throughout history, whenever an article of value has been produced, an attempt has been made to duplicate it at a far lesser cost or with inferior materials. Every major, and many minor, tangible asset has been counterfeited. Rare United States coins, fortunately, remain under the scrutiny of the U.S. Secret Service. It is against federal law to sell, transport, trade or own counterfeit coins of U.S. or foreign origin. Because of this law, and also due to the technical difficulties inherent in the production of coinage, the determination of genuine coins has become a science. Coins, and United States coins especially, are the only collectibles that can make this claim.

The term "counterfeiter" usually brings to mind a mild-mannered chiseler, sitting in his basement, patiently carving plates for $1,000 bills. We, however, are concerned with the criminal producing coins for the investor market; and the dishonest or ignorant dealer who sells them. Counterfeit rare coins are more common than might be expected, and many investors, some of them quite experienced, have been taken. Dealing with a savvy numismatist is ultimately your best protection, and will save you considerable pain.

The matter of authentication is complicated by the fact that rare coins were not always finely fashioned and minted. Early American issues were often crude, resembling nothing so much as amateur attempts at coining— which, in fact, they were. Thus it can be difficult to distinguish a bad replica from a bad original. In the 1850's, for example, a gentleman named Mr. Getchell faked several examples of the famed Pine Tree Shilling issued in Massachusetts in 1652. Not satisfied with capitalizing on its already considerable numismatic popularity, Getchell produced dated shillings which preceded all other known specimens by two years. These were quickly snapped up in a mail order deal by a prominent Boston collector, and no one was the wiser until the decade's end, when the diary of John Hull, the coin's designer, was published. The document made it apparent that this rare date was so rare as to be nonexistent. The ruse was discovered—but only through luck. Getchell's fakes were no more primitive-looking than the originals, and his implausible dates might have been convincingly explained as Hull's first pattern attempts. Fortunately, the science and study of numismatics have progressed considerably since then. A contemporary expert would not be so easily fooled.

Today's counterfeiters tend to be less imaginative than Getchell, often content to skillfully alter existing coins using a variety of common techniques. A counterfeiter may remove the mint mark, or part of the date, from an otherwise authentic specimen; conversely, he may add a mint mark, either with solder or glue, or by stamping it into the coin. In the latter case, the surrounding area is carefully buffed so as to make the phony mark appear raised. A more recent method involves drilling a hole in the side of a coin and inserting a tool, to raise a mint mark from within. Another rather crude technique involves joining together halves of different coins; this is effected by hollowing out one half of a coin, leaving the edge intact, after which a second half, with its edge shaved off, is fitted into the "shell." Perhaps the simplest and most common altering technique, called "whizzing," involves the polishing of coins with a wire brush to make them appear uncirculated.

Much of the counterfeiter's craft is obvious, and there are different things a purchaser may look for to avoid victimization. Nearly all American coins were struck and not cast; and cast coins, regularly counterfeited from rubber or sand molds, have recognizable characteristics. They lack crisp details, may be inaccurate in size or weight, and often exhibit surface bubbles or air holes. Made of joined halves, such fakes may show seams on their rims; and often are soft and greasy to the touch. Nor will cast coins ring when tapped against a hard surface, producing instead a dull thud.

A coin's edges, known as reeding, may also give away the game: counterfeits often show irregular, poorly fashioned lines. And evidence of polishing will show, under magnification, telling light parallel scratches.

Having read these pages, however, you are not now armed with sufficient knowledge to authenticate even an obvious fake. It ordinarily takes a professional years to acquire the skills and learn the nuances of authentication. The novice should no more attempt his own authentication than his own brain surgery.

Rarity and the Establishment of Value

Factors other than a coin's grade contribute to the establishment of value—most notably rarity. If a coin is not well-preserved, but is in scarce supply due to a low original or surviving mintage, its value may be higher than a similar grade coin much of whose mintage was saved, and is therefore more common. The following example demonstrates this point:

Type	Condition	Scarcity	Value
1849-C Gold Dollar Closed Wreath	XF	11,634 minted	$3,000
1849-C Gold Dollar Open Wreath	XF	4 known	90,000*
			* Auction 1979

Lower mintage, however, does not in itself guarantee scarcity or value, or necessarily make for a good investment, as the following chart shows:

Date	Condition	Mintage	Value
1877 Indian Cent	Unc.	571,990	$1,500
1909-S Indian Cent	Unc.	309,000	400

Although there were more 1877 cents minted, there are far fewer survivors and greater demand, and the price differential reflects this.

Comparing two silver dollars with the same mintage again illustrates the unreliability of mintage figures in determining scarcity and value:

Year	Condition	Mintage	Value
1893-S Morgan Dollar	Unc.	100,000	$65,000
1894 Morgan Dollar	Unc.	110,000	7,500

Relatively few 1893-S dollars have survived, and, of those, even fewer in uncirculated condition, as compared with 1894 dollars. Thus the discrepancy in value.

There are actually two principal forms of rarity numismatists consider when establishing value—*absolute* and *condition*. An absolute rarity is a coin, the entire population of which is extremely small. A good example is the 1822 Half Eagle, of which there are only three in existence. Obviously, under such circumstances, grade is of virtually no significance.

A condition rarity, on the other hand, is a coin that may be widely available in one condition, but remains extremely rare in the top grades. The 1878-S Morgan Dollar, for example, in MS-65, sells for approximately $1,000, because there are quite a few; the finest known, however, one of very few in nearly perfect condition, sold for $34,700 in February, 1986.

As is evident, mintage figures are not always a reliable determinant of value. This is why, once again, quality is of such extreme importance in numismatic investing.

Market Demand

The overall state of market demand is also of considerable importance. Although condition and rarity may be the same, the market demand for a particular coin may drive values up. For example, the Three Dollar gold piece is generally more in demand than a Liberty Seated dime:

Type	Condition	Scarcity	Value
1879 Liberty Dime	Choice Unc.	15,100 minted	$ 650
1859 $3 Gold	Choice Unc.	15,638 minted	$3,800

There are more collectors of Three Dollar gold pieces, both by type, and by date and mint, than collectors of Liberty Seated Dimes, and, again, the price differential reflects this difference in demand.

There are three influences on the value of a coin: Rarity, condition and market demand. The greater the combination of these factors, the more valuable the coin will be. Theoretically, you would want to invest in a rare, high grade coin that is in great demand.

As always, diversification is the key—not just within your overall investment portfolio, but within that portion of your portfolio devoted to rare coins. In Chapter Six, we will discuss some important things to keep in mind when planning your investment strategy; and look, as well, at six sample coin portfolios, based on different levels of income.

The First Commemorative

1848 CAL. QUARTER EAGLE

The 1848 Cal. Quarter Eagle, or $2.50 gold piece, was struck from the first deposit of California ore, signalling the start of the great western gold rush. The military governor of California sent 228 ounces of ore, averaging .894 fine gold, to Washington, D.C., where it greatly excited eastern imaginations. Secretary of War W. L. Marcy forwarded it to the Philadelphia Mint, suggesting, "As many desire to procure specimens of coin made of the California gold . . . I would suggest that it be made into quarter eagles with a distinguishing mark on each."

The result was the unusual $2.50 gold piece shown above, which bears the lettering CAL. punched above the eagle on the reverse. Only 1,389 pieces were struck and today, the coin, in top-quality condition, remains a beautiful rarity of signal historical significance.

A Gold Rarity, the 1819 Half Eagle

1819 HALF EAGLE

The Half Eagle, or five dollar gold piece, bears several interesting distinctions that set it apart from other U.S. coins. It stands as the very first American gold coin struck for general circulation by the mint, and it also is the only coin that was produced at all eight of the branches of the mint.

Early Half Eagles also are characterized by extreme rarity; and among the rarest is the 1819 issue, featuring a so-called "blundered" reverse ("5D." stamped over "50"), of which there are only five known specimens.

Among Half Eagle rarities, this particular variety runs a close third behind the 1822, in first place, and the 1815, in second.

Chapter Six
PLANNING YOUR RARE COIN PORTFOLIO

As with all other assets in your portfolio, your U.S. coins should represent one facet of a larger, comprehensive plan—a plan for your future. Before investing in anything, it is important to consider the various, often changing factors that will impact upon your circumstances. While you can not do much about what is to come (at least in the larger sense), you can react to it ahead of time; and a thoughtful, sober look at a few choice specifics should precede any actions you take.

Planning Your Portfolio

To begin, you would be well served by deciding for what length of time you propose to remain in the investment market. Though we expend a great deal of energy considering what we are going to put our money into, it is easy to lose sight of the fact that, sooner or later, we are going to pull it out. The question is, when? After a decade? Two? Where do we want to be, socially and economically, when the time comes? How will we apply the fruits of our investment after the harvest? All these are useful, not to say critical, questions to consider before getting started.

Next, you should consider the projected economic picture across the life span of your investments. Which trends appear short-lived? Which are likely to stay put? If you can work up a vision of the future, however necessarily imperfect, based on economic forecasts, political projections, and simple market truths, you can look at the performance records of potential investment options, and choose the best ones for the place in the world you anticipate. Of course, you could be wrong; and flexibility—a willingness to adapt yourself to a changing, often volatile world—may prove one of your best weapons in the battle. If you are expecting—as seems likely—an inflation at some point, based on federal deficits, an eroding dollar, and a growing money supply, it makes eminent sense to plan for it, with investments that perform well under such circumstances. Considering that, by the century's end, you may well need to make better than a quarter of a million dollars a year to live as well as you can on $25,000 today, this seems a wise course to follow.

Six Sample Rare Coin Portfolios

Now that you have got the basics down, it is time to start buying coins. The question is, where to begin? With that in mind, we have put together six sample rare coin portfolios, each geared to a different financial level, to give you some idea of what to expect for your money. The coins listed below are good, solid, proven gainers; they are drawn from market areas we believe in and recommend; and they stand to reap high profits in the years to come. As always, let us repeat it again; never buy any of these coins in anything less than choice uncirculated condition.

These are *sample* portfolios and although you might want to get involved with them, they are not the only coins available to you in your price range. While they all represent excellent investments, they may not be the best investment for you. *It is important to note that the following portfolios are examples of what can be obtained at each price level, and that other coins can be substituted according to your individual preferences.* Before taking the time and trouble of searching out the coins listed below, or any other coins, talk to your Financial Planner and/or a reputable and experienced rare coin dealer. They will make sure you are pointed in the right direction.

$2,500. This is a basic and "introductory" investment portfolio that is, nonetheless, solid and diverse with regard to selection. Experience has shown us that high quality and highly popular, yet affordably priced, issues have consistently performed remarkably well over the years and fit into any size portfolio. One of each of the following is included.

1) 1881-S Morgan Silver Dollar, MS-65.
2) 1941-P Liberty Walking Half Dollar, MS-65.
3) 1942-P Liberty Walking Half Dollar, MS-65.
4) 1941-D Washington Quarter Dollar, MS-65.
5) 1942 Washington Quarter Dollar, Proof-65.
6) 1944-D Mercury Dime with Full Split Bands, MS-65.
7) 1937-P Buffalo Nickel, MS-65.
8) 1909 VDB Lincoln Cent, MS-65.

$5,000. This particular investment category might include some of the basic material mentioned previously, but with a slightly stronger emphasis on the more difficult to locate dates and mints. Additionally, this investment figure often sees the introduction of a 19th century "type" coin, for example, an Indian Cent. Once again, *quality,* not quantity, is strictly adhered to. One of each of the following is included.

1) 1880-S Morgan Silver Dollar, MS-65.
2) 1882-S Morgan Silver Dollar, MS-65.
3) 1942-P Liberty Walking Half Dollar, MS-65.
4) 1943-P Liberty Walking Half Dollar, MS-65.
5) 1946-D Liberty Walking Half Dollar, MS-65.

6) 1938 Washington Quarter Dollar, Proof-65.
7) 1937-P Washington Quarter Dollar, MS-65.
8) 1935-P Mercury Dime with Full Split Bands, MS-65.
9) 1944-D Mercury Dime with Full Split Bands, MS-65.
10) 1938 Jefferson Nickel, Proof-65.
11) 1883 Indian Cent, MS-65.

$10,000. A noticeably broader degree of diversification becomes possible at this level. The same selection of silver, nickel and copper coins previously included is maintained, but also included is an investment grade example of the highly popular and sought-after Saint Gaudens Double Eagle ($20 Gold). A portfolio at this level may find an example of a Proof-65 Three Cent Nickel, Liberty Nickel or Buffalo Nickel. Then again, an MS-65 Liberty Standing Quarter might be included instead. One of each of the following is included.

1) 1924-P Saint Gaudens Double Eagle, MS-65.
2) 1881-S Morgan Silver Dollar, MS-65.
3) 1922-P Peace Silver Dollar, MS-65.
4) 1943-P Liberty Walking Half Dollar, MS-65.
5) 1944-P Liberty Walking Half Dollar, MS-65.
6) 1950-P Franklin Half Dollar with Full Bell Lines, MS-65.
7) 1940-P Washington Quarter Dollar, MS-65.
8) 1941 Washington Quarter Dollar, Proof-65.
9) 1941-P Mercury Dime with Full Split Bands, MS-65.
10) 1941-D Mercury Dime with Full Split Bands, MS-65.
11) 1884 Three Cent Nickel, Proof-65.
12) 1919-S Lincoln Cent, MS-65.

$25,000. At this level, the investor achieves broad depth and fine diversification. A variety of U.S. Gold coins begin to make their appearance here. In addition to a Saint Gaudens Double Eagle ($20), either a Liberty Quarter Eagle ($2.50), Indian Quarter Eagle, or Liberty Double Eagle, Type III, may be included. Or, perhaps, one each of both Quarter Eagles, or one each of the Double Eagles instead.

A portfolio of this size allows for the inclusion of proof or uncirculated examples of the Barber series (dime, quarter or half dollar) to represent 19th century type coins. Then again, an example in the Liberty Seated series (dime, quarter or half dollar) might just as easily be found instead. In addition, U.S. Commemoratives and a Liberty Standing Quarter may make their appearance. One of each of the following is included.

1) 1926-P Saint Gaudens Double Eagle, MS-65.
2) 1928-P Indian Quarter Eagle, MS-65.
3) 1880-S Morgan Silver Dollar, MS-65.
4) 1881-P Morgan Silver Dollar, MS-65.
5) 1883-CC Morgan Silver Dollar, MS-65.

6) 1885-O Morgan Silver Dollar, MS-65.
7) 1923-P Peace Silver Dollar, MS-65.
8) 1936-D San Diego Commemorative Half Dollar, MS-65.
9) 1942-S Liberty Walking Half Dollar, MS-65.
10) 1944-P Liberty Walking Half Dollar, MS-65.
11) 1945-P Liberty Walking Half Dollar, MS-65.
12) 1947-P Liberty Walking Half Dollar, MS-65.
13) 1928-P Liberty Standing Quarter Dollar, MS-65.
14) 1934-P Washington Quarter Dollar, MS-65.
15) 1941-S Washington Quarter Dollar, MS-65.
16) 1941-P Washington Quarter Dollar, Proof-65.
17) 1892-P Barber Dime, MS-65.
18) 1916-P Mercury Dime with Full Split Bands, MS-65.
19) 1938-S Mercury Dime with Full Split Bands, MS-65.
20) 1891 Liberty Nickel, Proof-65.

$50,000. A stronger commitment to the portfolio is evidenced by further intensification in the series previously mentioned as well as new areas not mentioned. The U.S. gold section at this level may include one or more of the universally popular St. Gaudens Double Eagles as well one or more specimens from the following group: Gold Dollar Type I or III, Liberty Quarter Eagle, Indian Quarter Eagle, Liberty Half Eagle, Indian Half Eagle, Liberty Eagle, Indian Eagle, Liberty Double Eagle Type II or III. Better date and rare date gold coins are possible here, but, once again, we emphasize quality and diversification.

The silver section is well represented with the inclusion, once again, of better and rare date Morgan Dollars, Liberty Walking Halves, Liberty Standing Quarters, Washington Quarters and Mercury Dimes. Indian Cents, Large Cents or, possibly, Flying Eagle Cents representing copper may be included in either uncirculated or proof condition, too.

Type material should, if possible, include one example of the Liberty Seated series, in either "with motto" or "no motto" varieties, in proof or uncirculated condition. Barber material, too, can be included in place of or in association with the Seated coins. Another nice addition, if possible, is either an uncirculated or proof specimen of the elusive Liberty Seated Half Dime. One of each of the following is included.

1) 1927-P Saint Gaudens Double Eagle, MS-65.
2) 1901-S Liberty Eagle, MS-65.
3) 1903-P Liberty Quarter Eagle, MS-65.
4) 1879-S Morgan Silver Dollar, MS-65.
5) 1880-S Morgan Silver Dollar, MS-65.
6) 1881-S Morgan Silver Dollar, MS-65.
7) 1882-P Morgan Silver Dollar, MS-65.
8) 1887-P Morgan Silver Dollar, MS-65.
9) 1884-CC Morgan Silver Dollar, MS-65.
10) 1922-P Peace Silver Dollar, MS-65.

11) 1923-P Peace Silver Dollar, MS-65.
12) 1937 Roanoke Commemorative Half Dollar, MS-65.
13) 1939-P Liberty Walking Half Dollar, MS-65.
14) 1939-D Liberty Walking Half Dollar, MS-65.
15) 1939-S Liberty Walking Half Dollar, MS-65.
16) 1940 Liberty Walking Half Dollar, Proof-65.
17) 1941-P Liberty Walking Half Dollar, MS-65.
18) 1942-P Liberty Walking Half Dollar, MS-65.
19) 1943-P Liberty Walking Half Dollar, MS-65.
20) 1944-P Liberty Walking Half Dollar, MS-65.
21) 1883-P Liberty Seated Quarter Dollar With Motto, MS-65.
22) 1898-P Barber Quarter Dollar, MS-65.
23) 1917-P Liberty Standing Quarter Dollar with Full Head, MS-65.
24) 1940 Washington Quarter Dollar, Proof-65.
25) 1932-P Washington Quarter Dollar, MS-65.
26) 1939-P Washington Quarter Dollar, MS-65.
27) 1938-P Mercury Dime with Full Split Bands, MS-65.
28) 1938-D Mercury Dime with Full Split Bands, MS-65.
29) 1938-S Mercury Dime with Full Split Bands, MS-65.
30) 1940 Mercury Dime, Proof-65.
31) 1944-D Mercury Dime, MS-65.
32) 1885 Three Cent Nickel, Proof-65.
33) 1898 Indian Cent, Proof-65.

$100,000. Numismatic portfolios of this size achieve a magnitude of scope that can be fascinating. The possibilities that lie within such a portfolio are myriad and would truly approach a most thorough degree of what is termed diversification.

The U.S. Gold section is strongly emphasized with the inclusion of Liberty and Indian Gold of various types and denominations with the addition of better date material. There is even room for examples of proof Gold Dollars (Type III) and Liberty or Indian Quarter Eagles.

This size portfolio allows for the inclusion of sets, such as original early proof sets, type sets of nineteenth century coins, and the choices are limited only by availability in the market.

A Twenty-cent piece would have a place within a portfolio of this magnitude (either proof or uncirculated) as would much rarer date or Proof Morgan Dollars.

A concentrated effort should be made to provide better date material within the series and include "branch mint" coins; i.e., San Francisco "S," Denver "D," Carson City "CC," etc., wherever and whenever possible, since larger portfolios allow for greater flexibility and growth. One of each of the following is included.

1) 1904-P Liberty Double Eagle, Type III, MS-65.
2) 1923-D Saint Gaudens Double Eagle, MS-65.
3) 1932-P Indian Eagle, MS-65.

4) 1909-D Indian Half Eagle, MS-65.
5) 1925-D Indian Quarter Eagle, MS-65.
6) 1878-CC Morgan Silver Dollar, MS-65.
7) 1878-S Morgan Silver Dollar, MS-65.
8) 1879-S Morgan Silver Dollar, MS-65.
9) 1880-P Morgan Silver Dollar, MS-65.
10) 1880-S Morgan Silver Dollar, MS-65.
11) 1881-CC Morgan Silver Dollar, MS-65.
12) 1881-O Morgan Silver Dollar, MS-65.
13) 1881-S Morgan Silver Dollar, MS-65.
14) 1882-CC Morgan Silver Dollar, MS-65.
15) 1883-O Morgan Silver Dollar, MS-65.
16) 1884-O Morgan Silver Dollar, MS-65.
17) 1885-O Morgan Silver Dollar, MS-65.
18) 1886-P Morgan Silver Dollar, MS-65.
19) 1887-P Morgan Silver Dollar, MS-65.
20) 1888-P Morgan Silver Dollar, MS-65.
21) 1897-S Morgan Silver Dollar, MS-65.
22) 1898-O Morgan Silver Dollar, MS-65.
23) 1904-O Morgan Silver Dollar, MS-65.
24) 1923-P Peace Silver Dollar, MS-65.
25) 1925-P Peace Silver Dollar, MS-65.
26) 1895 Barber Half Dollar, Proof-65.
27) 1936 Gettysburg Commemorative Half Dollar, MS-65.
28) 1936-P Liberty Walking Half Dollar, MS-65.
29) 1936-D Liberty Walking Half Dollar, MS-65.
30) 1936-S Liberty Walking Half Dollar, MS-65.
31) 1937-P Liberty Walking Half Dollar, MS-65.
32) 1940-P Liberty Walking Half Dollar, MS-65.
33) 1941-P Liberty Walking Half Dollar, MS-65.
34) 1941-D Liberty Walking Half Dollar, MS-65.
35) 1941-S Liberty Walking Half Dollar, MS-65.
36) 1942-P Liberty Walking Half Dollar, MS-65.
37) 1942-D Liberty Walking Half Dollar, MS-65.
38) 1942-S Liberty Walking Half Dollar, MS-65.
39) 1943-P Liberty Walking Half Dollar, MS-65.
40) 1944-P Liberty Walking Half Dollar, MS-65.
41) 1944-S Liberty Walking Half Dollar, MS-65.
42) 1945-P Liberty Walking Half Dollar, MS-65.
43) 1946-P Liberty Walking Half Dollar, MS-65.
44) 1947-D Liberty Walking Half Dollar, MS-65.
45) 1895 Barber Quarter Dollar, Proof-65.
46) 1920-P Liberty Standing Quarter Dollar with Full Head, MS-65.
47) 1939-D Washington Quarter Dollar, MS-65.
48) 1940-D Washington Quarter Dollar, MS-65.
49) 1887-S Liberty Seated Dime, Legend Obverse, MS-65.
50) 1895 Barber Dime, Proof-65.
51) 1930-S Mercury Dime with Full Split Bands, MS-65.
52) 1931-S Mercury Dime with Full split Bands, MS-65.

53) 1895 Liberty Nickel, Proof-65.
54) 1865 Two-Cent Piece, MS-65.
55) 1895 Indian Cent, Proof-65.

There you have six ways to profit handsomely in the rare coin investment market. Whether you choose one of these simple portfolios or, working with your Financial Planner or coin broker, devise another one of your own, consider that the laws of supply and demand dictate that the best quality merchandise will not always be there for the asking, and, with the market poised for yet another explosion, you will want to maximize your profits. Remember to purchase the best quality available, the best quality that you can afford.

Though we have sketched out general areas of investment for different economic groups, the specifics—namely, which coins to buy, and when to sell them—are for you, your Financial Planner, and your Coin Dealer to decide. The trip from the general to the specific can be a tricky one; but, armed with the above information, and the expertise of your savvy professionals, the results should be eminently satisfactory.

The Financial Planner

What is a Financial Planner? Too many people assume that a Financial Planner is someone to whom you can turn over your entire financial life. In fact, that is not—and should not be—the case. The job of a financial planner is to aid you in the structuring of the different elements of your personal economic picture into a workable and productive strategy, one that takes into account all your needs, interests and habits, and offers enough flexibility to accommodate change. Given these requirements, a skilled Financial Planner should have a working knowledge of a variety of financial areas, including, not just family money management, but investing, taxes, insurance, and retirement and estate planning.

In practical terms, this translates into an ability to total up your net worth, break down your cash flow situation, come up with a budget you can live with, and devise a solid long term and short term plan of investment. A Financial Planner must also be a good coordinator, capable of drawing together your accountant, insurance agent, investment broker, and attorney when their services are required.

The most important qualifications to look for, whether your Financial Planner is an accountant, lawyer, broker, or all three, are reliability and experience. Look for solid credentials, ones that require compliance with regulations: certain professionals can lose their licenses for mishandling a client's assets. Some Financial Planners are registered with the National Association of Securities Dealers (NASD) or the Securities and Exchange Commission (SEC). This insures that you will receive, in writing, an accounting of your planner's experience, education and form of payment, as well as the sort of work done by his or her firm. Professional affiliations can also prove instructive. The Institute of Certified Financial Planners and the International Association for Financial Planners both offer referrals. The latter features a subgroup, the Registry of Financial Planning Practitioners, that requires members to have a minimum of three years' full-time experience on the job, and a related degree or certification.

The profession itself is rather a recent one; thus, most Financial Planners were previously engaged in other activities, notably law, accounting or finance. Such prior affiliations generally indicate strengths and preferences.

And what of the plan itself? Fundamentally, it should be simple, direct, and specifically tailored to your needs. The plan must be in writing, and fully explain each and every decision; and it should take into account inflation rates, rates of return on investments, and your tax bracket. A sound financial plan usually comes in two parts, the first dealing with your present financial situation, and its strengths and weaknesses, the second pointing you in the right direction, with different alternatives and solutions. Above all, the plan should be directed at *your* goals, and deal nonjudgementally with your wants and needs, whatever they may be.

The Financial Planner and the Numismatist

We have dealt with the subject of financial planners because, while we can readily recommend a balanced rare coin portfolio, there are very different kinds of investments to be found among rare coins, and some may not be suitable to your needs. If you are unsure of how to proceed on your own, a professional overview may be in order, one that takes into account the big picture as well as the specifics. In this regard, a financial planner, armed with a knowledge of your personal needs, can be as worthwhile an asset as the investments themselves.

Just as a financial planner must possess a wide range of skills, a numismatist (rare coin dealer) brings a number of complex abilities to the task. The numismatist must, of course, understand the overall market and be able to estimate changes and trends. He must be familiar with the vital facts of a specimen's history. He must be able to establish the authenticity of a coin and detect even the subtlest tampering, including bogus toning and cleaning. The numismatist must be able to determine if a coin is well struck and its grade. And he must also keep abreast of the laws governing the purchase and sale of his product.

Working together, a financial planner and a rare coin dealer comprise a formidable team. Reviewing a client's portfolio, they determine its strengths and weaknesses, whether or not rare coins will be suitable, what percentage of a client's overall investment package should be devoted to coins, and which coins to buy. Thus an investor capable of investing a large sum may be advised to invest in a small number of expensive, top-quality rare coins. At the same time, someone requiring a greater degree of liquidity than expensive coins can provide may opt for a larger number of less costly specimens.

Whatever the case, this pair of professionals affords you a superb opportunity to maximimze profit potential, no matter your financial situation.

Nine Strategic Rules of Investment

Finally, we would like to suggest nine principles that will be of use to you when you are investing. They also happen to be the nine classic principles governing the prosecution of war as set forth in the U.S. Army field service regulations. If this strikes you as strange, remember that the terminology of economics and war are strikingly similar: the government, for example, is always "declaring war" on inflation, "battling" unemployment, and "devising new strategies" to deal with the federal deficit. So it is no surprise that these basic military concepts can be so easily applied to your personal financial affairs:

1. Objective. Like any competent field commander, you should not commit your resources to engagement without a clear idea of what you expect to gain. A solid working knowledge of the market—and your place in it—is essential. U.S. coins are long-term investments, and a variety of different alternatives are available within the overall market, each of which requires a specific sort of management, and returns a different level of gain. Unless all of these factors (and others as well) are considered before determining your investment strategy, heavy losses will be unnecessarily incurred, diminishing your strength and weakening your position.

2. Offensive. This one is simple, and paramount. Its essence can be summarized in three words: *Go for it.* Invest wisely, even cautiously, but never half-heartedly or with fear; the failure to act can prove as detrimental as rash action. While you should never invest more than you can afford to lose, neither should you commit so little capital that a profit will be of negligible concern.

3. Simplicity. An uncomplicated, lucid plan of action is essential, and only possible with a clear understanding of the market. Investors are often defeated by the terminology or specifics of an investment option, getting involved without an overall picture of the field or a sufficient awareness of the results of their actions. Do not let this happen to you.

4. Unity of Command. Avoid discord among the strategists. Do not try to make short-term profits when your accountant is lobbying for capital gains.

5. Mass. Mass is described as "maximum available power applied at the point of decision." Do not spread yourself too thin. Concentrate on a single deal at a time, and undertake each as if it were the most important of all.

6. Economy. Resources must not be unnecessarily expended. Make your mistakes and learn from them. The more we do, the more mistakes we make. Further wisdom at the same cost is intolerable. Develop a pattern of operation that works for you, apply it, and do not try to reinvent the wheel every time you buy a coin—or anything else.

7. *Maneuver.* While you should have a fair picture of the sort of market that would prompt you to buy or sell, always be ready to reverse your position if the situation warrants. You never have to be in a particular market or deal. This flexibility is healthy and wise, and is in fact one of the prime virtues of a secure plan of action.

8. *Surprise.* "Optimum exploitation of the situation." When the moment to buy or sell arrives, seize it. Luck, as has often been said, is nothing more than preparation meeting opportunity.

9. *Security.* No army ever retires for the night without positioning sentries along the perimeter. Every measure must be taken to avoid the unforeseeable, and preserve freedom of action. Be aware of the market's strong points, and the ways in which they and the pitfalls relate to your own investments, and do not accept advice or statements of fact without good arguments or proof to back them up.

In the preceding chapters, we have talked a lot about what makes a rare coin valuable. Now, let us talk about history, beauty, art, and a variety of other intriguing and, yes, romantic things. Now we will take a look at that past in greater depth. There are not many investments earning equally high marks on the scales of profit and history. Since rare coins are the foremost, we would like you to have both pleasures.

Chapter Seven

THE HISTORY OF COINS

Regardless of their size, shape, or value, regardless of the society, culture or era which spawned them, coins maintain an importance beyond their primary function. They may be collected as fine art, or struck to commemorate special events and occasions. As popular objects of intrinsic worth, coins have been hoarded in times of economic or political instability. Most significantly, quality coins have always increased in value: from virtually their inception to the present—with true historical monotonousness—coins have remained a good investment. History, we have learned, repeats itself; and the history of coins does not disprove this maxim.

To cover thousands of years of history very briefly: coins were devised to fill the need for an unwavering scale of value. Prior to their existence, men were compelled to decide an exchange rate for each new trade. How much food for a pitcher of water? How many slaves for a wife? It was necessary, if cumbersome, for a trader to *carry* everything he might conceivably want to swap.

Such was life under the barter economy. Life changed dramatically, however, with the appearance of money: a standard item of trade, against which everything of value might be measured. Initially, this did not mean coins. Shells, animals, slaves, beads, grain—all served as standards of exchange at different times and places. Certain commodities, among them cattle, and such useful implements as axes and knives, derived part of their value from the prestige associated with their ownership. Alaskan Native Americans employed fish hooks as their medium of exchange, while Northwest Pacific Indians were known to favor woodpecker scalps. The Pacific islands yield a variety of examples, among them whale and dog teeth. On one such island, Yap, huge round stones with holes in their centers—often weighing in excess of 100 pounds each—were popular. The size of these "coins" made moving them quite impossible; so, while ownership might be transferred from person to person, the stone itself remained fixed in a public place, usually beside a road.

Another, perhaps more sophisticated, standard of value was the Anglo-Saxon Wegeld, or "worth of a man," which referred to the value paid in compensation for someone's death (the amount being based on the status of the deceased). Over time, the concept of the Wegeld came to include injuries of a lesser nature, and, later, losses in property as well. Eventually, our ancestors extended it to a diversity of goods and services—thus establishing an early money economy.

As man progressed—and more areas of commerce developed between peoples—the need for a universally acceptable medium of exchange must certainly have been felt. Such standard commodities as silver and iron, upon whose value most were in agreement, began to emerge; and, although they did not apppear until much later in man's history, coins seem to have evolved as an antidote to the inevitable and time-consuming problems of weighing and measuring. Each was meant to represent an exact unit of a desirable metal commodity, marked for easy identification by an established authority for all tradesmen.

Although it is not, and perhaps never will be, known which peoples first created coins, it is likely that the Chinese were among them. Evidence of Chinese coinage extends back as far as 1,000 B.C., to the Emperor Ch'eng Wang, though it was not used exclusively (tea and hard cheese also being popularly traded commodities).

In the west, coins surface in the writings of the Greek traveller and historian, Herodotus. He speaks of their use in Lydia, the area known today as Turkey. This region was rich in gold and silver alloys and according to the Greek historian, the residents tired of endless measuring and developed a system of coinage in about the 7th century B.C. The coins were emblazoned with the lion, symbol of the Lydian kings.

From Lydia, the use of coins spread across the Aegean lands into the empires of the Mediterranean, greatly aiding in the extension and increase of trade. The Persians, conquering the Lydians in the 6th century B.C., adopted their monetary system, and promoted it throughout their farflung domain. The great seafaring traders of the time, the Phoenicians, immediately recognized the worth of this now broadly accepted medium, and further extended its use.

Thus, what had begun as an innovation meant to facilitate trade became the fundamental unit of all commerce.

American Coinage

Although the specie of all nations is of potential numismatic value, the bulk of the investment-quality coins we deal with are of American origin, and were struck both before and after the U.S. became an independent nation.

The first colonial coins developed from direct necessity. Among the many problems the earliest American settlers faced was the lack of an indigenous coinage. In a sense, our forefathers found themselves thrust back into the ancient world, compelled to barter and establish value standards each time they traded. This problem, initially minor in the face of the greater, more basic challenge of survival, became significant as the colonists grew more secure in their new land.

When trading with the indigenous Indian population, the 17th century settlers employed the Indians' form of money as an exchange medium. Wampum—beads fashioned from polished and punctured sea shells—was frequently used. This "money" also served as a form of adornment, to be worn around the neck, waist, or wrist; and, to the Indian, it was a sign of status. When trading with each other, however, the colonists dealt in less exotic commodities. Tobacco was very popular in Virginia and Maryland, as a heavy European demand insured its value. In the northeastern settlements, and other places where tobacco was of less importance, such items as musket balls and nails were exchanged.

Our forefathers, of course, had the skill and foresight to establish their own monetary system. But England refused them permission to mint their own coins, intending thereby to compel the colonies to trade solely with the Mother Country. The settlers were "encouraged" to exchange their raw materials only for the yield of Britain's industries. With England refusing also to mint special coins for the colonies, early Americans were forced to make do with a paltry trickle of British and other foreign currency.

A variety of coins found favor. In use as early as 1630 was the Bermuda Hogge (or "Hog," as it was called), which derived its name from the hog design that appeared on the obverse. Spanish Doubloons and the Pesos were also common in the colonies. The silver Peso was stamped with an 8, denoting its equivalence to eight Spanish Reales (or Royals)—thus the famous pieces of eight. This coin was frequently broken up into "bits," two being equal to a quarter of a piece of eight, four to a half; and it is from these that our quarters derive their slang name. Also to be found in colonial pockets were the Dutch Ducat, the French Louis d'Or, and the Italian Seguin.

The supply of foreign coins was at best uncertain, creating a constant shortage, and trade was often needlessly slowed. It was inevitable that men would become willing to risk England's displeasure to meet this need; and in 1652, John Hull established the first mint, in the colony of Massachusetts, at Saugus. Here the first coins manufactured on U.S. soil were produced, beginning an era of colonial coinage that would last until 1792. The Saugus issue included the famous Pine Tree Shilling, and other coins featuring the oak and the willow tree.

Other Americans soon took their cue from Hull. By 1658, the second Lord Baltimore was minting coins in Maryland. In 1785, Vermont contracted with private individuals to mint copper coins, the first of which depicted a rising sun on the obverse. Beginning in the same year, Connecticut minted no less than 300 varieties of cents, the majority of which bore the legend "Auctori Connec" ("by the authority of Connecticut").

Money was also issued by the provisional Continental Congress to support the Revolutionary War effort. As often happens during wartime, hard money had become scarce; hoarding was commonplace, and the interruption of trade with foreign nations exacerbated the shortage. The Continental Congress responded by issuing paper money. This soon proved worthless, however, and patterns for Continental Dollars followed. These were designed to replace the war-scarce pieces of eight and featured a chain with thirteen links on the obverse—signifying the newly created states. They were never, however, produced in large numbers.

Although individual colonies and private citizens created numerous coins, it was not until 1787 that the fledgling U.S. government produced a coin of its own: the Fugio Cent, minted in New Haven, Connecticut. The motto, "Fugio," was supplied by Benjamin Franklin; it means "I fly," and refers to time. The coin was also adorned by a sundial, and bore the admonition, "Mind Your Own Business."

That same year, the government finally sought to bring order to the nation's chaotic monetary affairs. Attempts were made to redeem the worthless paper issued by the Continental Congress, which helped to establish credibility with the new country's prospective trading partners. And the individual states were enjoined from coining their own money. This right was eventually rendered exclusively to the federal government.

In March of 1791, Congress authorized that a mint be established in Philadelphia, and a decimal system of coinage, featuring ten standard coins, quickly followed. On April 2, 1792, American coinage was officially authorized by law.

The mint became a popular tourist attraction, and visitors were, of course, always under escort; a night watchman was retained; and an arms chest, containing "a musket and bayonet, two pistols and a sword . . . to be kept in perfect order and to be inspected . . . once a month" was kept at hand. These extensive security measures, however, failed to keep out Peter, an American eagle said to have inhabited the building for six years. His image, perhaps in honor of his guile, is emblazoned on the 1836, '38 and '39 Pattern Silver Dollars. The bird came and went as it pleased, invariably returning from tours of the city well in advance of closing time. Unfortunately, Peter met an untimely end in the flywheel of a large machine, and could thereafter be viewed, stuffed, in a large glass case.

One of the more interesting features of the young U.S. mint was the Cabinet. Organized by Mint Director R. M. Patterson in 1838, the Cabinet was a room set aside for the development and display of a coin collection—initially American, then, over time, foreign coins were added. Private citizens donated coins to the cabinet, prompting noted author George Evans to note that the collection grew to admirable proportions with only 300 dollars worth of federal support; and drew a lesson from this that still speaks to investors and collectors.

"The economic principal upon which the collection has been gathered," Evans wrote, "is a lesson to all governmental departments in frugality, as well as restraint upon the natural tendency to extravagance which has heretofore distinguished those who have a passion for old coins. There are thousands of coin collectors in the United States and fortunes have been accumulated in this strange way. More than one authenticated instance has been known in this country where a man has lived in penury, and died from want, yet was possessed of affluence in time-defaced coins." It is worth nothing that these thoughts were recorded in 1888.

Among the new coins issued in Philadelphia were the copper cent, the silver dollar and the five and ten dollar gold pieces. The dollar, comprised of 100 parts, or cents, became the standard monetary unit. Yet the government's considerable corrective actions did not immediately solve the hard currency problem. Due to the inefficiency and inadequacy of minting procedures and machinery, the coin supply continued to lag far behind demand for a number of years.

Interestingly, the mint's first gold coin issue, the half eagle, contained an amount of gold equal to its face value. The government went so far as to place a silver insert, or plug, into the 1792 copper penny—for, to hold a penny's worth of copper, it would have had to have been impracticably large. Over the years, the U.S. government has abandoned the practice of minting true intrinsic value into its coins, in part because wholesale melting occurred whenever metal prices increased. As a result of this, certain U.S. coin issues became especially rare (about which more later).

After the Philadelphia mint's 1792 founding, other mints were established in different regions. In 1834, gold was revalued, but the demand for coins had become so great—as a result of continued melting—that branch mints became necessary. These sprang up in Charlotte, North Carolina; Dahlonega, Georgia and New Orleans, Louisiana—all established in 1838. Initially, to meet the rush, these mints were equipped with primitive screw presses, and leftover equipment from Philadelphia. This quite naturally resulted in inferior coinage—the reason that, today, high-quality coins from the first years at these mints are extremely rare. Coins originating at these mints bear the marks "C," "D," and "O" respectively.

The Charlotte and Dahlonega mints struck gold coins only, from 1838 to 1861. The New Orleans mint functioned until 1909. Although dormant during the Civil War and for a time thereafter (1861–1879), New Orleans produced a variety of gold and silver coins.

In response to the extraordinary silver lodes unearthed in the region, the Carson City, Nevada mint was authorized in 1861 and opened in 1870. It produced gold and silver coins until 1893. By 1878, pressure on the government from silver interests was so great that the Bland-Allison Act was passed. This required the Treasury to purchase between two and four million dollars worth of silver monthly, to be made into coins. In 1890, The Bland-Allison Act was replaced by the Sherman Act, which was nothing more than an out-and-out government subsidy for the silver miners, allowing the Treasury to purchase 4.5 million ounces of silver per month. Bland-Allison and the

Sherman Act account for the hundreds of millions of top-quality silver dollars from the period to be found today. They were never needed, never issued, and never used.

The San Francisco mint ("S") began production in 1854 and continues today (with a long inactive period between 1955 and 1968), producing proof sets for collectors as well as standard currency. A mint has been productive in Denver since 1906 (mint mark "D"). Most of the Philadelphia mint's coins carry no mint mark. However, during World War II, nickels carried the mint mark "P." Susan B. Anthony dollars also carried the mint mark and, since 1980, all of Philadelphia's issue have borne the mint mark "P." A submint of Philadelphia was established at West Point in 1974. Since 1984 it has been independent, and its issue is characterized by the mint mark "W."

United States coins are produced to a .900 fine standard: for every 900 parts of silver, for example, there are 100 parts of an alloy which give the coin its strength and durability. Gold, silver, copper, nickel, and even aluminum have been used. And the 1943 Lincoln cent bore a zinc coating, in order to preserve the bronze needed for the war effort.

Rarity

Though we have noted that investment-quality coins remain extremely rare, we have yet to discuss the reasons for that reality. In fact, a number of circumstances have combined over the years to produce the situation that exists today.

The problems began, in effect, at the beginning. The mint's earliest efforts to economize met with poor results. In 1795, the mint purchased 1,000 pounds of used copper tokens, which were then restruck into Half Cents. The results, from a quality standpoint, were less than satisfactory. Two years later, 15 tons of second-rate copper planchets were purchased from England; and these further contributed to the poor condition and rarity of early copper coins—a situation that directly affects the current investment market.

The value of bullion at the time also affected the future of hard metal currency. Upon the establishment of the mint, Treasury Secretary Alexander Hamilton set the value of gold at 15 times that of silver; by 1799, it had climbed to 16 to one. At this point, the metal content of a gold coin became greater than its face value, and wholesale melting and exporting began, a practice that continued, off and on, through 1834. It is for this reason that, today, pre-1834 gold coins are rare.

Bullion values also had an effect on the production of coins. Certain periods of American history boast more varieties of the coins than others; and one reason for this is the periodic change in bullion weights. In 1853, the weight of silver coins was reduced; 20 years later, the weight went back up again. The coins were marked with arrows each time.

The Civil War further contributed to the rarity that certain coins enjoy today. At the outset, both the Union and Confederate governments shipped most of their hard money abroad in exchange for weapons; what remained was hoarded by individuals—a typical occurrence in time of war. Today, coins produced by Southern mints—when they can be found—show extreme wear. As for the Union, they began printing greenbacks in 1861, to pay bills; and, during the war years, and for some time after, only a very few gold coins were minted.

Following the repeal of the Sherman Act, which subsidized silver production, the country was placed on a single standard by the Gold Standard Act of 1900. Then, in the depths of the Depression, President Roosevelt issued his now-famous order prohibiting banks from redeeming gold certificates with gold and also prohibiting private citizens from owning gold bullion. These restrictions were removed in 1975 and all gold coins may now be collected and saved legally.

On July 23, 1965, President Johnson signed the Coinage Act of 1965. This eliminated all silver in nickels, dimes and quarters, and lowered the content in halves to 40 percent. For all practical purposes, with the exception of commemoratives, this ended the minting of collectible coins in America.

Denominations

Today, the denominations of circulating U.S. coins are relatively few, including only the cent, nickel, dime, quarter, half dollar, and dollar coins; yet there have been many others manufactured at one time or another:

Half cent	1793–1857
One cent	1793–present
Two cent	1864–1873
Three cent (nickel)	1865–1889
Three cent (silver)	1851–1873
Half dime (silver)	1792–1873
Five cent (nickel)	1866–present
Dime	1796–present
Twenty cent	1875–1878
Quarter dollar	1796–present
Half dollar	1794–present
Silver dollar	1794–present
Trade dollar	1873–1885
Gold dollar	1849–1889
Two and one-half dollar gold	1796–1929
Three dollar gold	1854–1889
Four dollar gold	1879–1880
Five dollar gold	1795–1929
Ten dollar gold	1795–1933
Twenty dollar gold	1849–1933
Fifty dollar gold	1851–1852, 1915

It must be noted, in connection with these various issues, that not all were minted for every inclusive date. The cent comes closest, missing only the year 1815.

The Making of a Coin

Today, coins are created via a technique which, at its most basic level, has not been significantly altered for thousands of years: a punch or die is driven into a piece of unmarked metal, thereby imprinting upon the blank a mirror image of the die's design. The methods by which the die is propelled have changed with the development of technology, but the fundamental process remains intact.

The Lydians made their coins in this fashion, placing a piece of metal on an anvil and striking it with a distinctively marked punch. The anvil is thought to have been grooved, to provide a pattern for the coin's reverse side.

The Greeks typically introduced a certain sophistication into the process. Molten metal was poured into carved rock molds, which produced blanks, or planchets, which were then splashed with water to speed their cooling. The blank would next be removed with tongs and heated on burning coals. Following this, the hot blank was placed on an anvil marked with a pattern of the coin's reverse; and a second worker would then strike it with a die, to produce a coin marked on both sides. To insure that the coins and dies would hold firm, the anvil, blank and upper die were enclosed in a box before striking, providing the finished coin with a clearer impression.

Unlike the Lydians and early Greeks, who carved designs on the surface of their dies so that the design would be incused into the coin, later Greek coin makers cut designs *into* their dies, which created a high relief on the surface of the coin, rather than an impression *into* the planchet. This process is known as intaglio, and is today the standard method of coin production.

The Greeks also introduced master dies into the coining process. A master die, cut in the old relief fashion, would be used to create secondary intaglio dies for the actual stamping process. If a die broke, as frequently happened, a new one could be made from the master.

The Middle Ages produced few changes in the coining process. The natural course of events that followed, however, was to have a dramatic effect on both world history and the history of coinage. In the 14th century, Europe was horribly cursed with bubonic plague. Perhaps as much as half the population died during this period. When the wreckage of the "black death" was finally cleared, it became apparent that the balance of economic power had been dramatically altered. Death had consolidated much of the wealth in fewer, now more affluent, hands; and a demand for consumer goods, created in part by this unprecedented financial strength, created an acute shortage of coins.

This sudden demand for hard currency gave rise to a prospecting frenzy in the Hartz mountain range (located today in Czechoslovakia), which, between 1515 and 1540, yielded three million ounces of silver. It was left for technology to catch up with need; and it did, by way of the first mechanical stamping machines. These were used to mint the famous Joachimsthaler, or Thaler, from which the word dollar is derived.

At the same time, the wide-ranging effects of the Renaissance were finding their way into the coining process. Although not himself responsible for the first stamping machines, Leonardo Da Vinci produced the first known drawings for a prototype coin planchet cutting machine. By the end of the 16th century, the face of coin production had been considerably altered. Metal was rolled into sheets for the new punching machines; and the innovative screw press stamped the blanks. In this process, the blanks and dies were pressed together through the action of a heavily weighted screw.

Today, coining begins with the rolling of metal into slabs; the process is repeated until the proper thickness and hardness is achieved. Following this, metal strips designed to become "clad," or "sandwich," coins undergo extensive cleaning, and then bonding to other metals. For example, two strips of

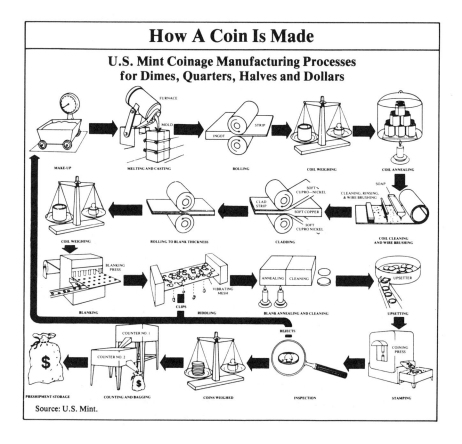

How A Coin Is Made

U.S. Mint Coinage Manufacturing Processes for Dimes, Quarters, Halves and Dollars

MAKE-UP | MELTING AND CASTING | ROLLING | COIL WEIGHING | COIL ANNEALING

COIL WEIGHING | ROLLING TO BLANK THICKNESS | CLADDING | COIL CLEANING AND WIRE BRUSHING

BLANKING | RIDDLING | BLANK ANNEALING AND CLEANING | UPSETTING

PRESHIPMENT STORAGE | COUNTING AND BAGGING | COINS WEIGHED | INSPECTION | STAMPING

Source: U.S. Mint.

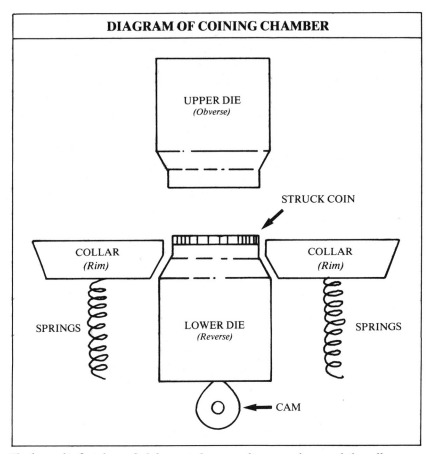

The lower die first drops slightly, next the upper die comes down and the collar moves sideways toward the planchet, which is then struck into a coin.

copper nickel alloy are bonded to one of nickel to form an American quarter. This achieved, the strips are placed in a blanking press, in which planchets slightly larger than finished coins are punched out of strips. Planchets are then annealed, or softened, so as to prolong the life of the dies that strike them with the coin's design. After a cleaning process, a machine called an upsetting mill presses the raised rims we find on both edges of our coins. This accomplished, the blanks then move on to the coining press for minting (stamping), followed by inspection, weighing, counting, bagging, and shipment.

Coins and the Coin Collector

Strictly speaking, numismatics refers to the collection of coins, paper money, tokens, and medals of various kinds; and the numismatist is someone schooled in this endeavor. However, early numismatists concerned themselves with all manner of collectibles. Their 19th century organization was known as the American Numismatic and Archaeological Society, and its members were interested in all manner of historical materials, including Indian artifacts (arrowheads), autographs and rare books. In the numismatic publications of the day, one finds reports of such disparate events as Egypt's gift to New York City of Cleopatra's Needle for placement in Central Park, and the sale of the Guttenberg Bible. This multiplicity of concern derives from the early coin collector's often parallel interest in history. Coins are connections to the past, and it is not unusual to hear avid collectors express the feeling that through coins they touch past individuals and times.

Coin Collecting

Though in this volume, we have been primarily concerned with their investment value, the collecting of coins is also both popular and important.

At first blush, there may seem little, if any, connection between collecting and investing. Do not be deceived. Many wonderful collections that have been assembled through the years have turned out to be some of the most prestigious and important investments ever made. Though profit motive was not the initial reason for a number of great collections, a spectacular investment was in the making. Simply because something is beautiful and enjoyable to own does not preclude it from also being a money-making investment.

Indeed, with almost 15 million collectors in the United States, it has become the nation's premier hobby. This is not surprising, as the pursuit is fascinating, rewarding (in ways other than the strictly monetary), and suited to almost any set of financial circumstances. Coin collecting is fun. It is challenging, it can be adventurous, and there are a number of ways to do it. What's more, a collection, no matter how large, takes up little space, is easily catalogued, and relatively durable. Small wonder that coin collecting has achieved such widespread popularity.

This was not always the case, however. As far as we can tell, coin collecting barely existed in Colonial America, and developed only slowly until the Civil War years, during and after which it enjoyed something of a boom. In 18th century America, as we have seen, there was barely even coinage, let alone hobby shops or the traditional numismatic outlets Europeans enjoyed. The earliest recorded mention of a coin collection on these shores appears in the late 1700s, when a Swiss named Pierre duSimitiere arrived in New York with 135 specimens, a lot he used as a security pledge. Prior to that, in 1752, coins were actually donated to the Library Company of Philadelphia, the first such institutional grant.

After the Revolution, institutions continued to acquire coins, usually through donations, but occasionally via direct purchases as well. New York's Museum of the American Tammany purchased an unspecified number of ancient coins in 1793; by 1811 the museum boasted in excess of 300 ancients, perhaps the greatest such collection of its day.

Privately, James Hall, a native of Allentown, Pennsylvania, is surely among the first collectors, having begun at 15 years of age, in 1788. Hall compensated for the limited number of available indigenous types by corresponding with his opposite numbers overseas. He was also a co-founder in 1858 of the first American collectors' club, the Numismatic and Antiquarian Society of Philadelphia. That same year saw the beginning of the American Numismatic Society (originally the New York A.N.A.), and later entitled the American Numismatic and Archaeological Society, reflecting the varied tastes of most early collectors.

Perhaps the most notable aspect of American coin collecting, from its origins to the present—and into the future—that has important echoes in the current investment market—was its focus on domestic coinage. While the emphasis in Europe and elsewhere remained on the worldwide, U.S. collectors realized that, by limiting themselves to the readily available and affordable issue of their native land, they could conceivably build collections that would, ultimately, be complete. This was something, obviously, that foreign collectors could not do; and it is the principal reason, today, that the investment market is made up primarily of American rare coins.

The rules of thumb governing coin collecting are relatively simple. Needless to say, it is best to decide what kinds of coins you want to collect, and how you plan to go about it, before beginning. For example, you may seek to put together a set, by date (one example from each year of a coin's mintage), variety (mintmarks as well as dates), or, more commonly, by type (one specimen, regardless of date or mintmark, of each design). Though not as important as when investing, condition—*quality*—should never be overlooked. Do not be temped to rummage through your pocket change merely to complete a set, even if it is only of Lincoln Cents. Preserve the quality of your collection by keeping it in albums, either the printed sort (usually for one specific type) or those comprised of clear vinyl pages with individual windows for each specimen. You will need a magnifying glass as well, especially after you have become more exacting, but this need not be expensive.

Finally, most serious hobbyists find it worthwhile to join a local coin club, no matter how small the membership. Apart from being excellent places for the exchange of both information and actual specimens, such clubs are invariably peopled by collectors with enormous amounts of knowledge, men and women long steeped in numismatic lore. You can learn a lot at a coin club and you will hear a lot of good stories, too. And you will doubtless have a lot of fun—which is, after all, the ultimate aim of any hobby, and the principal dividend of them all.

Chapter Eight

CURRENT ECONOMIC CLIMATE

Before putting together your investment portfolio, take into account the world in which your investments will have to sink or swim. As of this writing, the American economy is on an upswing, with reasonable interest rates, low inflation, and a booming stock market. Yet a closer look reveals a number of deeply disturbing time bombs, particularly as regards the banking system and the federal deficit. Both will severely affect your personal financial picture in the not-too-distant future, when today's "prosperity" has melted away.

Banks

When we think of bank failures it is usually in the past tense—the bleak years of the Great Depression. Yet, today, even after more than half a century of protective measures, bank failures are numerous and on the rise. The figures to date are astonishing and alarming. As of July 12, 1985, no fewer than 987 of the country's 14,700 commercial banks could be found on the government's official "problem" list—a figure growing at a rate of 22 banks per month, and 120 failures in 1985, as compared with seventy nine in 1984, itself a post-Depression record. On May 30, 1985, seven banks in four states went belly-up, a record for a single day's failures since the Depression. Moreover, in the past four years, bank failures involved losses exceeding four billion dollars, compared with 500 million dollars total for the period between 1933–1981.

What's more, even if your money is insured, there is no guarantee you will be able to get your hands on it. "Insurance," whether offered by the Federal Deposit Insurance Corporation (FDIC) or Federal Savings and Loan Insurance Corporation (FSLIC), is not the true insurance system most depositors have been led to believe. Banks and thrifts advertise this guarantee, with the subtle implication that the public is dealing with a "safe" institution. But neither the bank nor Savings and Loan is "insured." The government only guarantees that as a last resort, in the event that the bank fails and all other means of rescuing the bank have failed, it will make good on deposits; a process that can take months, if not years, while depositors wait for their money. At least 300 S&Ls still doing business are insolvent because their debts are greater than their assets. They should have been closed by the government long ago, but they've been allowed to stay alive because the FSLIC doesn't have enough cash available to make good on its insurance commitment to the depositors involved.

Currently, the FDIC has 17 billion dollars in assets. But it has guaranteed $1.4 trillion in member banks across the nation. In other words, the FDIC does not have enough money to cover every deposit. In fact, it only has resources to cover about 1.2% of the deposits it insures. In 1985, for instance, to ease the pressure on the state's privately insured thrift institutions, Maryland levied a $1,000-per-month withdrawal limit on its 102 savings and loan associations. While depositors eventually got some of their money out, they had to wait to do it. Meanwhile, more than one billion dollars are still tied up over a year later, and the Governor of Maryland estimates his state's losses at over 50 million dollars, and concedes it could go much higher.

Thus far, mostly smaller banks have succumbed. The headlines, however, have not wanted for bigger fish, the most obvious being Continental Illinois National Bank & Trust Company, the nation's eighth largest bank. In 1984, Continental Illinois required a $7.5 billion federal bailout to keep from closing its doors—a circumstance, it was widely assumed, that would have triggered an epidemic of bank runs, wounding America's financial system, and perhaps creating an international depression. This bailout cost the FDIC $1.3 billion in outright losses.

Bank of America's future was clouded by a triple whammy. The nation's number two bank was fined a staggering $4.75 million for failing to report large cash transactions. The same day its parent, BankAmerica, reported a $337 million loss. Then, having reduced its dividend last August, the big West Coast bank eliminated it entirely for the last quarter. The loss came largely from its troubled portfolio of bad loans. The outlook for banks, where your money is stored, continues to be overcast. Many of the big banks are stuck with foreign loans that will never be repaid yet are still carried on the books at full value.

Such problems impact variously on the life of the nation. To cite a few examples: Farm Belt banks constitute a fourth of the troubled institutions. There are about 4,000 banks that have more than 25 percent of their portfolios in farms, and of these some 1,300 are in need of "special supervision" by the Comptroller of Currency.

Soft commodity prices and high interest rates, in tandem with the depreciating value of agricultural equipment and farmland itself, have left approximately ten percent of all farm loans in jeopardy. In Texas, Oklahoma and Louisiana, in which most banks have approximately 20 percent of their loans in oil and gas ventures, it is feared that, if oil prices drop low enough, bank failures could be triggered in all three states.

Savings and loan institutions have fared no better, and too often worse, with roughly 850 having merged or vanished entirely since 1981. The Federal

Savings and Loan Insurance Corporation, which insures 3,150 thrifts, used to keep a problem list of S&Ls with a net worth of less than two percent. But when the number got up to 265 in 1981, the FSLIC quit publishing the total. The FSLIC says there are 216 institutions with assets of $80 billion that require FSLIC assistance, and the FSLIC will need to spend between 16 and $22.5 billion in the next five years on problem cases.

Meanwhile, as a result of a major policy change in March, 1986, Federal bank regulators now will allow problem banks to use a more "liberal" accounting method on problem loans, and the methods by which they are reported. Currently, regulators require that banks keep six percent of their assets in capital, but this will be modified on a "case-by-case" basis, with no official uniform floor on capital reserves. This will allow banks to carry troubled loans without having to take large write-offs. If the banks can't stay solvent, it seems the FDIC just changes the definition of solvent.

The lesson? Do not take it for granted that, just because your life savings is tucked away in a federally insured savings bank, it will still be there when you need it. You must diversify your investments to truly insure their solidity and safety.

CHART 22

U.S.-INSURED INSOLVENT THRIFTS			
Period	Total number of institutions	Number of insolvent institutions	Net worth of insolvent institutions*
1980 1st half	4,021	16	0.0
2nd half	3,993	16	0.0
1981 1st half	3,916	21	0.0
2nd half	3,743	53	−0.3
1982 1st half	3,533	156	−1.0
2nd half	3,287	219	−2.0
1983 1st half	3,206	243	−2.3
2nd half	3,146	279	−2.1
1984 1st Q	3,139	321	−2.3
2nd Q	3,148	370	−2.9
3rd Q	3,137	417	−3.0
4th Q	3,135	434	−3.3
1985 1st Q	3.160	455	−3.6
2nd Q	3,180	461	−3.4

* Using generally accepted accounting principles. Rounded to nearest tenth of $1 billion.
Source: *The Washington Post.* Federal Home Loan Bank Board.

Business

While on the surface the economy seems to be improving, there are still a number of unsettling areas on the horizon.

CHART 23

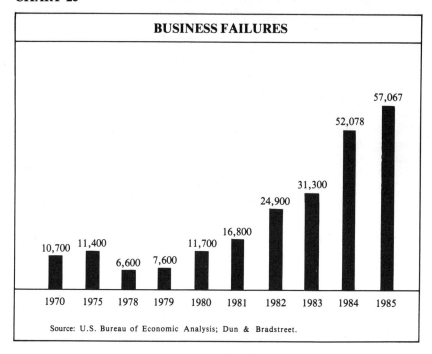

BUSINESS FAILURES

1970	1975	1978	1979	1980	1981	1982	1983	1984	1985
10,700	11,400	6,600	7,600	11,700	16,800	24,900	31,300	52,078	57,067

Source: U.S. Bureau of Economic Analysis; Dun & Bradstreet.

In 1985, no fewer than 57,067 businesses of all kinds collapsed, a figure exceeding those tallied during the 1980–82 recession—exceeding, indeed, every year since the Depression peaked in 1932. This represents an 81 percent increase since 1970. And small business failures could reach crisis proportions in 1986, particularly in the Midwest. The lesson here is that investing in business may not always be as safe as you think. Time to diversify.

The prices of junk bonds (bonds originally rated BB or lower) issued by many oil producers and oil-service companies are falling almost as fast as the price of oil itself, saddling investors with big losses. Four companies in the oil sector were unable to make debt payments due in 1985, as junk-bond defaults soared above one billion dollars for the first time.

So far, issuers have now defaulted on about $2.3 billion of the high-yield debt brought to market from 1977 to 1983. During this period, 16 billion dollars in new junk bonds were sold. A precise figure for convertible junk bonds is not available but is thought to be about five billion dollars. That works out to a default rate of about *11 percent*. This junk debt is a mountain of high risk, highly vulnerable debt that is resting like a time bomb underneath America's financial institutions and placing them in great jeopardy.

The junk-bond market's oil-patch nightmare demonstrates anew two fundamental tenets of investing. The first is the value of diversification: Sharehold-

CHART 24

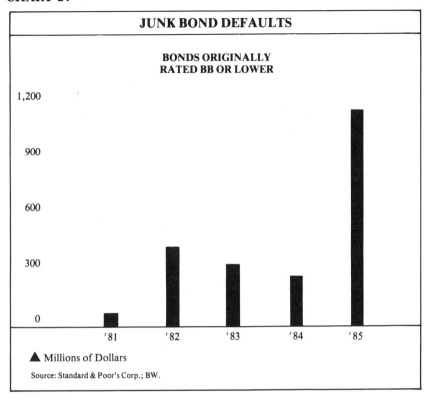

JUNK BOND DEFAULTS

BONDS ORIGINALLY
RATED BB OR LOWER

▲ Millions of Dollars

Source: Standard & Poor's Corp.; BW.

ers of junk-bond mutual funds with only a smattering of oil issues can count themselves smart—or at least lucky. But the leap of junk-bond defaults illustrates the even more basic notion that there is no free lunch. To earn higher yields, you must take higher risks. Most professionals urge investors to focus on quality: Government and the highest-rated corporate securities in the fixed-income sector; large-capitalized, high-quality companies among the equities.

In the quest for the investment dollar, the financial markets are offering an increasing number of exotic instruments, such as junk bonds, index futures, bundled mortgages, etc. and few participants understand fully what they are buying and selling. One can easily imagine a default, say in the junk bond market, that would bring the saleability and hence liquidity of these instruments to an abrupt halt. Yet everyone—consumers, businesses, Government—continues to go into debt at record rates. If the market stays strong, your diversified position is just a little safer. And if it sinks, the diversified position may just save your investment position.

Real Estate

There is almost a unanimous opinion that investments in real estate will show only modest gains, or even decline, for the rest of the decade, just as they did in the 1920s. Then, as now, farm prices were the first to show declines. But by 1926, residential properties were also beginning to fall in value. Of late, we have seen considerable weakening in the price of California real estate, some resort condominiums, and farm-land, and a decline in big city cooperative and condominium prices may also be ahead of us.

Foreign Debt

Most of the aforementioned problems stem from within. From without, Third World debt, and potential default, looms as a frightening threat, not just to the American banking system, but to the entire international economy.

CHART 25

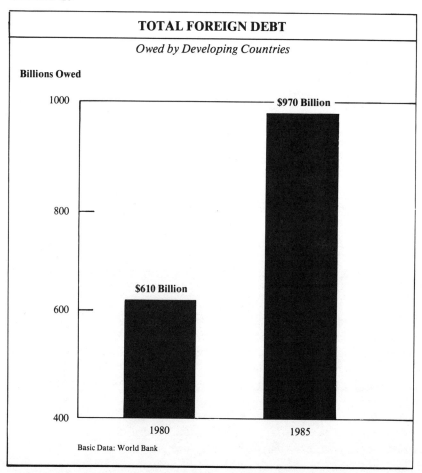

TOTAL FOREIGN DEBT

Owed by Developing Countries

Billions Owed

1000 — $970 Billion

800

$610 Billion

600

400

1980   1985

Basic Data: World Bank

Third world nations will have debts totalling one trillion dollars in 1986, according to the World Bank. That is almost the size of the whole United States budget. And the total is expected to soar even further by 1990, with interest charges alone coming to 60 billion dollars annually.

It has been estimated that if even one country such as Argentina, Brazil, Mexico or Venezuela defaults on its loan, hundreds of banks in the U.S. might be forced to close their doors. Precisely why supposedly intelligent bankers would set themselves up for such a colossal and apparent fall remains a mystery. Numerous African nations, caught in the grip of devastating economic turmoil, cannot repay their debts. Latin nations owe so much that Fidel Castro has publicly urged them just to forget the whole thing. And, of course, let us not leave out the Soviets, Poland and the rest of the Eastern Bloc. For all intents and purposes, that debt money is gone for good, too, and the aftermath is almost too terrible to contemplate. If we are correct about the potential disaster inherent in this debt problem, then a diversified investment position is a must for survival.

The Federal Deficit

The current budget deficit—now estimated at over 200 billion dollars—can be truthfully attributed to three principal causes: record defense spending

CHART 26

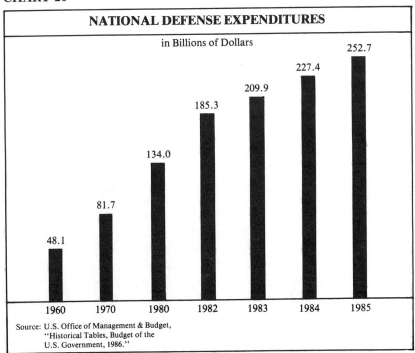

NATIONAL DEFENSE EXPENDITURES

in Billions of Dollars

48.1	81.7	134.0	185.3	209.9	227.4	252.7
1960	1970	1980	1982	1983	1984	1985

Source: U.S. Office of Management & Budget,
"Historical Tables, Budget of the
U.S. Government, 1986."

(with the Pentagon now shelling out more daily than the total tax-take in the late 1940s), the President's popular but dangerous 1981 tax cuts, and, ironically, escalating interest payments of the debt itself. Translated into numbers, this one-two-three punch becomes even more staggering. By 1990, the Congressional Budget Office (CBO) projects that the annual budget will be in excess of $1.3 *trillion.* The interest payments alone on this kind of money are virtually unimaginable. This year, they'll come to roughly $134 billion in interest alone. That's enough to wipe out poverty in the United States or to bolster United States defenses. Instead, the full $134 billion will go merely to pay the finance charges. Within six years, the CBO reported, interest payments will have reached $185 million per annum. What does it all add up to?

Essentially, apart from cutting every single federal expense to the bone and beyond, there is only one way to pay off such a debt—a method to which the government is uniquely entitled: print the money. And that translates, of course, into massive and crushing inflation—an inflation on the order of which the world has perhaps never seen.

CHART 27

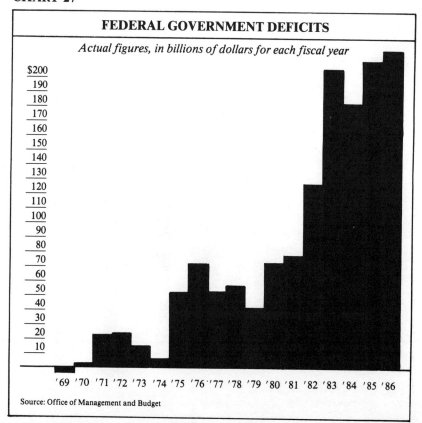

Another reason long-term investment in coins is necessary today is because of the shrinking dollar. According to United States government figures, the official value of the dollar has fallen 68.2% in the past 17 years. But, in reality, the dollar has fallen 76 percent in value during this period. As long as the government runs up deficits each year, inflation will be an eventuality and the value of your money will continue to evaporate. As an investor, you can't afford to ignore the dwindling value of the dollar. It is the major consideration in creating any long-term investment strategy. Long-term planning is crucial.

CHART 28

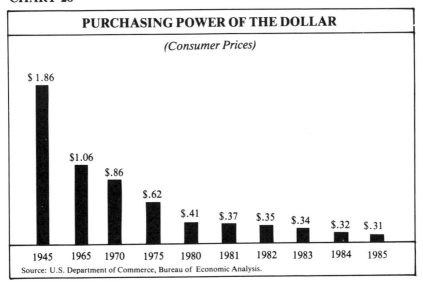

For the last few years, the U.S. has been a magnet for a one-way flow of capital from global money markets. This is draining the world economy of money. Fortunately, thanks to a relatively free world trade, this is balanced by U.S. exports. Unfortunately, this situation translates into a merchandise Trade Balance deficit, or better known as the Trade Deficit. The Trade Deficit has increased 386% since 1980, and 1,205% since 1975, our last year without a deficit.

This year, according to Commerce Sec. Malcolm Baldridge, the trade deficit is likely to soar above 140 billion dollars and could reach 150 billion dollars, compared with last year's record 124 billion dollars. With such trade deficits piling up, the United States may soon become the world's biggest debtor. The big budget deficits are helping to create America's two-tier economy, with strong growth in service sectors and slow growth or recession in the manufacturing sector.

CHART 29

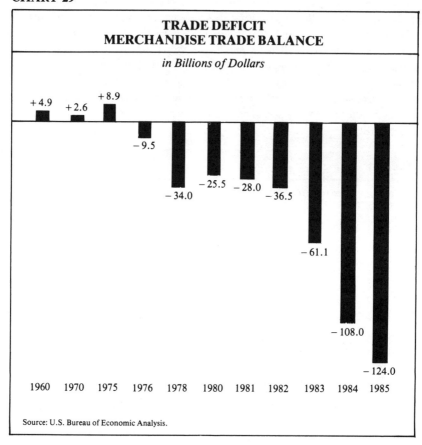

TRADE DEFICIT
MERCHANDISE TRADE BALANCE

in Billions of Dollars

+4.9   +2.6   +8.9

−9.5

−25.5   −28.0
−34.0   −36.5

−61.1

−108.0

−124.0

1960   1970   1975   1976   1978   1980   1981   1982   1983   1984   1985

Source: U.S. Bureau of Economic Analysis.

Does anyone really know how the economy is doing? "Recovery" and "prosperity" aren't as certain as some people would have you believe. The problem is *nobody* knows the facts!

A case in point:

On June 13, 1984, the Wall Street Journal reported that two of the world's leading economists, Nobel Prize-winner Milton Friedman and the widely respected, multi-named John Kenneth Galbraith, had come to the same economic conclusion: inflation was imminent, and prices would rise, said the article, "at nearly a ten percent annual rate by year's end." Of course, being "long-term ideological enemies," they arrived at the same point via totally different means. Friedman studied growth patterns in the money supply. Galbraith looked at the budget deficit. Each poo-pooed the other's methods. Both, curiously, were "completely at odds with most private economic forecasters."

And both were also completely wrong.

CHART 30

HOW YOUR PURCHASING POWER HAS DECLINED:			
	1967 Price	1985 Price	# times 1967 price
Monthly Housing Expense	$114.31	$ 678.40	5.9
Monthly Automobile Expense	$ 82.69	$ 369.82	4.5
Loaf of Bread	$ .22	$ .99	4.5
Gallon of Milk	$ 1.15	$ 2.02	1.8
Sugar—5 lb. bag	$ .10	$ .32	3.2
Pound of Hamburger	$ .39	$ 1.25	3.2
Coffee—2 lbs.	$ .49	$ 2.59	5.3
Candy Bar	$ .10	$ .35	3.5
6 Oz. Frozen Orange Juice	$ .11	$ .39	3.5
Steak	$ .98	$ 2.49	2.5
Natural Gas	$153.00	$ 770.00	5.0
Gasoline (per gallon)	$ .23	$ 1.21	5.4
Electricity	$128.02	$ 430.00	3.4
Men's Dress Shirt	$ 5.00	$ 28.00	5.6
Postage	$ .05	$ .22	4.4
Resident College Tuition	$294.00	$1,581.00	5.4

1985 Prices Are An Average Of 4.2 Times As High As 1967 Prices.
Basic Data: Departments of Commerce, Labor, Energy, and others.

Nor are government forecasts reliable. Scores of statistics, from the index of leading economic indicators to the gross national product, are becoming increasingly more unreliable. The economic figures of a given administration, moreover, are subject to the usual effects of politics, namely juggling, withholding and extreme selectivity. And, sometimes, they are simply, wildly, wrong. In 1982, to cite a recent and glaring example, the Reagan Administration's first budget deficit forecast came to a (mere) figure of 45 billion dollars. Later in the year, the figure was revised to more than *twice* the original. As Lawrence Kudlow, at the time the Office of Management and Budget's chief economist, said, "If that figure had been made public ten months earlier, Reagan's fiscal program wouldn't have gotten through."

Perhaps the most trenchant assessment of the government's figures and forecasts appeared in the June 3, 1985 issue of Forbes: ". . . sophisticated business people and economists regard the figures with amusement. They are still taken seriously only by newspaper editors, TV commentators, politicians with an axe to grind and market players with a phone in their hands."

CHART 31

RISING COST OF LIVING		
Prices in the Year 2000 Will Be Over Nine Times Higher Than 1985 Prices.		
	1985 Price	2000 price (with 16% average annual inflation)
Monthly Housing Expense	$ 678.40	$ 6,288.77
Monthly Automobile Expense	$ 369.82	$ 3,428.23
Loaf of Bread	$ .99	$ 9.18
Gallon of Milk	$ 2.02	$ 18.73
Sugar—5 lb. bag	$ .32	$ 2.95
Pound of Hamburger	$ 1.25	$ 11.59
Coffee—2 lbs.	$ 2.59	$ 24.01
Candy Bar	$ .35	$ 3.24
6 Oz. Frozen Orange Juice	$ .39	$ 3.62
Steak	$ 2.49	$ 23.08
Natural Gas	$ 770.00	$ 7,137.90
Gasoline (per gallon)	$ 1.21	$ 11.22
Electricity	$ 430.00	$ 3,986.10
Men's Dress Shirt	$ 28.00	$ 259.56
Postage	$ .22	$ 2.04
Resident College Tuition	$1,581.00	$14,655.87

Basic Data: Departments of Labor, Energy, Commerce.
The Grace Commission.

The question remains: Where are we headed? The possibilities are not very pleasant. Stephen Marris, an analyst with the Institute for International Economics, believes that, unless a policy change of the first order is effected—both here and abroad—the uncertain dollar could take a severe nose dive, perhaps by as much as 40 percent or better over the next several years. The resulting financial market crunch could conceivably raise interest rates by as much as five points.

The view in Europe is that things are already so unstable that a recession or inflation are virtual certainties. Inflation, in turn, devalues the dollar and, by extension, your savings. Current events also loom. The uncertain Middle Eastern and Latin American situations have already had disastrous—and tragic—results for the United States, and show little, if any, signs of improvement. The Social Security system, on uncertain ground, has the potential

CHART 32

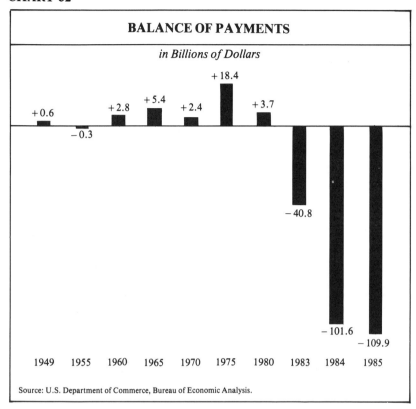

BALANCE OF PAYMENTS

in Billions of Dollars

+0.6 −0.3 +2.8 +5.4 +2.4 +18.4 +3.7 −40.8 −101.6 −109.9

1949 1955 1960 1965 1970 1975 1980 1983 1984 1985

Source: U.S. Department of Commerce, Bureau of Economic Analysis.

to generate yet another budget-related crisis.

In a lengthy, and rather disturbing, article published in July of 1985, the New York Times asked the question, "Is the U.S. Headed for a 1920s-Style Inflation?" There are a number of "disturbing parallels" between the two, the article stated, adding that while few, if any professionals expect the 1980s to end with another Great Depression, "some of them do expect a financial retrenchment of serious dimensions in the 1990s." The similarities cited are numerous, and include the fact that both decades followed periods of extremely high inflation. And both periods witnessed high real interest rates and low inflation; a very strong dollar; slow economic growth; proliferating bank failures; and a real estate boom, followed by "a crack" in prices.

Though few of the safeguards in place now existed then, "the risks are there [today], including the calls for protection, high Federal deficits, the third world debt and the increasing use of margin, or credit, in the financial market." The article went on to quote the executive vice-president of an

CHART 33

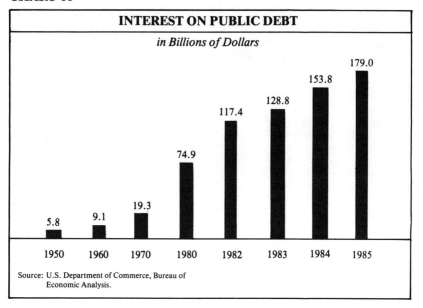

INTEREST ON PUBLIC DEBT

in Billions of Dollars

5.8	9.1	19.3	74.9	117.4	128.8	153.8	179.0
1950	1960	1970	1980	1982	1983	1984	1985

Source: U.S. Department of Commerce, Bureau of
Economic Analysis.

CHART 34

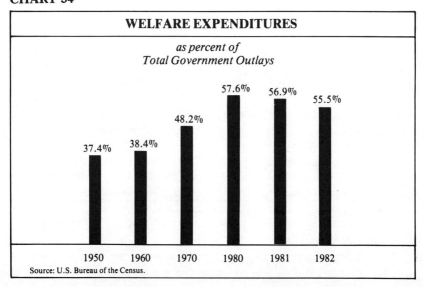

WELFARE EXPENDITURES

*as percent of
Total Government Outlays*

37.4%	38.4%	48.2%	57.6%	56.9%	55.5%
1950	1960	1970	1980	1981	1982

Source: U.S. Bureau of the Census.

CHART 35

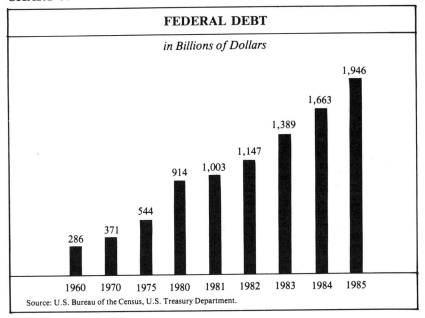

FEDERAL DEBT

in Billions of Dollars

Source: U.S. Bureau of the Census, U.S. Treasury Department.

investment counseling firm as saying that "the late 1980s and early 1990s will be a 'delicate period.' " And an influential economist: "The bad news is that in the late 80s or 90s we have a depression."

All of which echoed Federal Reserve Board Chairman Paul Volcker's ominous remark to Congress early in 1985: "We are in a real sense living on borrowed time and money."

Given all this, it seems eminently reasonable to assume that your investment portfolio will have to return profits on the order of 20 percent to keep you ahead of the economy. Thus we can expect typical "loan" investments—T-bills, CDs, bonds of all sorts, and so forth—to lose out. Presently, about the best an investor can do is seven or eight percent (insured), and that's not good enough. The future requires "owned" investments—stocks, bonds, commodities, bullion, and the like—for a portfolio to have real meaning. And, as we have seen, far and away the most successful performer of the lot remains rare coins. Only coins have the history, the track record and the future to confront and best the coming economic situation.

Classic Numismatic Rarities

1894-S BARBER DIME

The 1894-S Barber Dime, of which only 12 specimens are known, is one of the most sought-after rarities in U.S. numismatics—perhaps because its origins and history are somewhat shrouded in mystery. Only 24 of the coins were minted, all in proof. According to Hallie Dagget, daughter of the 1894 San Francisco mint superintendent, they were divided equally among eight persons, herself included. A youngster at the time, she promptly spent one for a dish of ice cream.

As the identities of the other seven recipients of the coins remain unknown, we can never be entirely sure of the actual number of 1894-S dimes that are still available. In 1980, a specimen was auctioned for $145,000.

1885 TRADE DOLLAR

U.S. Trade Dollars were minted from 1873 to 1885. Slightly heavier th
dard silver dollars, they were made for circulation in the Orient, where they competed with similar-sized foreign coins.

Although no record of their having been made appears in mint records, five proof 1885 Trade Dollars were struck—and their existence, in a collection of proof sets owned by the famed collector, William Idler, was not known of until Idler's death in 1908. The coin is, as such, one of the great American rarities, and specimens usually appear for auction no more than once in a generation—and, of course, always bring top dollar.

CONCLUSION

"What do you know about this business?" the King said to Alice.
"Nothing," said Alice.
"Nothing whatever?" persisted the King.
"Nothing whatever," said Alice.
"That's very important," the King said.

—*Alice In Wonderland*

This extract seems not irrelevant to the lack of comprehension encountered by many who are anxious to invest in rare coins. This is a new area for many in the rapidly changing investment arena.

In the introduction to this book, we noted that the single greatest obstacle standing between rare coins and the investor is a lack of information. This should no longer be the case. Having read the preceding eight chapters, you are now armed with a thoroughgoing and comprehensive working knowledge of the world of numismatic investments.

You have seen the dramatic increases in value over the last three decades—and, in the Salomon Brothers survey, seen coins outperform virtually all other, better-known investment options. You have learned what gives rare coins their value, and the significant dos and don'ts of their purchase and sale. The development and use of a uniform, reliable system of grading has been explored and detailed. We have considered coins as part of an overall investment portfolio, set against a background of future economic uncertainty, and developed with your individual wants and needs in mind. And you have learned something of the history of coins as well, with an emphasis on the actions and events which contributed to their current status as investments.

If we have succeeded in taking the mystery out of investing in rare coins, and make it possible for you to approach a coin dealer or broker with confidence, this book will have succeeded in its mission.

Like all books about individual assets, we have done some drumbeating. But we think it is justified. We stand by and believe in what we have repeatedly proclaimed: that quality rare coins are one of the very best investments to be found in the world today—perhaps *the* best.

Yet our final word on the subject has less to do with coins than with the *true* subject of this or any book about investing: protect your hard-earned dollars, no matter the financial weather. And the truth of it is, no single investment, no matter how strong, will do the trick. The most important thing to remember—to live by—as a participant in the marketplace is:

Experienced and successful investors diversify their portfolios. And one of the best means of diversification to be found today is in quality rare American coins.

GLOSSARY

ADJUSTMENT MARKS   File marks, put on a planchet by the Mint before striking, to decrease the weight of an overweight planchet to mint standards.

ALTERED DATE (OR MINT MARK)   The illegal practice of modifying a date or mint mark on a common coin to make it appear to be a rarer coin.

ANNEALING   The softening of planchets by heat followed by slow cooling. Annealing makes the planchets more easily struck.

APPARENT WEAR   A coin may appear to have more wear then it actually has due to poorly made dies or the prolonged use of worn dies.

BAGMARKS   The abrasions which coins receive through contact with one another. Most coins were thrown into bags soon after minting, and shipped everywhere in the country. The coins banged one another and usually received a considerable number of abrasions. The presence of abrasions does not mean that a coin has been circulated as all business strikes have some bagmarks. Bagmarks are a very important consideration in the grading of coins.

BASINING (OF DIES)   The process of polishing the field of the die before its use in the coining process. Most prooflike dollars are the result of this process, which is done infrequently and, as a result, are more valuable.

BLANK   The metal disc on which a coin is struck. (See planchet.)

BORDER   Within the raised rim of a coin was formerly a protective ornamentation either of radial lines or beads (see denticles).

BRANCH MINT   Subordinate mints in locales other than Philadelphia. Branch mints are presently operating in Denver, San Francisco, and West Point. They formerly operated in New Orleans, Los Angeles, Carson City, Nevada, and the two "gold mints" at Charlotte, North Carolina, and Dahlonega, Georgia.

BRILLIANT UNCIRCULATED (or BU)   Literally, not circulated, with mint luster. A coin which is still in mint state condition. (See Uncirculated, Mint State.)

BULLION   Coins that have little numismatic value but are purchased for their precious metal content. The Canadian Maple Leaf and the Mexican Fifty Peso are two examples.

BUSINESS STRIKE   A coin intended for commercial use which has been struck with no special care.

CARBON SPOT   A dark discoloration upon the surface of a coin which was in the planchet prior to annealing. Reference is usually made to copper coins.

CENT U.S. copper coin (1793–present). The 1/100 of a dollar. First coin struck under the authority of the U.S. Government. (See Indian Cent, Large Cent, Lincoln Cent.)

CIRCULATED A coin passed from hand to hand in commerce and, therefore, shows signs of wear. A used coin. There are various degrees of wear. See text for the specifics of grading.

CLAD U.S. coinage issued since 1965 made of cupro-nickel, and for all practical purposes, having no interest to investors.

CLASH MARKS Impressions on a die from another die caused when the two dies impact without a planchet between them.

COLONIALS Any coin made for circulation in or by the various colonies before the adoption of the Constitution.

COMMEMORATIVES Coins that are issued by the U.S. Government to celebrate important events in our nation's history. They are extremely popular with collectors.

COMMON DATE Coins with dates that are easy to acquire, usually because they have high mintages.

CONDITION The diagnostic features that describe a coin's state of preservation.

COPY A forgery. (See reproduction).

COUNTERFEIT A forgery intended to deceive.

DATE The year that appears on a coin, which is usually and legally the year of manufacture, although there are some exceptions to this rule.

DENTICLE Small, tooth-like or radial-line unit of border ornamentation.

DEVICES The principal design elements of a coin, such as the head of Liberty on the obverse of a silver dollar and the Eagle on the reverse, for example.

DIE The engraved punch used to strike coins.

DIE VARIETY A coin which evidences different characteristics from all other pieces struck from different dies of the same year. Usually refers to those die varieties which exhibit unusual characteristics which set them apart from their counterparts.

DIME, DISME U.S. silver coin (1796–1964). The 1/10 part of a dollar. Disme was the term used in 1792. Dimes are now struck in cupro-nickel.

DOLLAR U.S. silver coin (1794–1934). Monetary unit weighing about 26.73 grams intended as equal to the Spanish Eight Reales. Dollars were formerly also coined in gold (1849–89). (See Thaler).

DOUBLE EAGLE U.S. gold coin (1849–1933). Value of twenty dollars.

EAGLE U.S. gold coin (1795–1933). Value of ten dollars. The basic standard from which all other gold coins derive their value, either in fractions or multiples of an eagle.

FIELD The flat, undetailed part of the surface of a coin surrounding and between the portrait, symbol, legend and other raised portions of the design including the date. Visually important to most numismatists as an aid to determining grade.

FIRST STRIKE Early impression from working dies retaining their initial polishing. (See prooflike).

GRADE The condition, or state of preservation of a coin. One of the main determining factors of value.

HAIRLINES   Tiny scratches on a coin caused by cleaning or mishandling. When appearing on proofs, the coin may be called impaired.

HALF CENT   U.S. copper coin (1793–1857).

HALF DIME   U.S. silver coin, 1794–1873 = 1/20 dollar or five cents.

HALF DOLLAR   U.S. silver coin (1794–1964). (50 cents). Half dollars are now made of cupro-nickel.

HALF EAGLE   U.S. gold coin (1795–1929) with a value of five dollars. The most difficult series of gold coins to collect.

HIGH RELIEF   The designing of a die so as to create a deep concave field upon the surface of a coin for maximum contrast with the devices or raised parts of the coin such as the head of Liberty or the Eagle. The 1907 St. Gaudens double eagle was designed with a high relief which required the use of increased pressure for striking, thus lessening die life, and making the coins harder to stack. (See Low Relief.)

HUB   A type of die used for imparting designs to working dies. Later hubs included lettering; still later ones included dates. Not used for actually striking coins. (See master coins.)

IMPAIRED PROOF   A proof which has hairlines, or has been mishandled or used. (See Hairlines.)

INCUSE(D)   Sunk below neighboring surfaces (intaglio). Design only used in Indian Quarter Eagles and Half Eagles (1908–1929) in the U.S. gold series.

INDIAN HEAD CENT   U.S. copper coin (1859–1909). Common name for the Longacre design of cent.

KEY DATE   The opposite of common date. Coins with low mintages or with mintages having few survivors. (See Rare, Scarce.)

LARGE CENT   U.S. copper coin (1793–1857).

LEGEND   The main inscription on a coin.

LINCOLN CENT   U.S. copper coin (1909–present). 1/100 of a dollar or one cent.

LOW RELIEF   The designing of a die so as to create a shallow relatively flat field upon the surface of a coin in order to improve die life. Most of the aesthetic deficiencies of the 1908 St. Gaudens double eagle are due to the change from a high relief design (1907) to a low relief design (1907–1933). (See High Relief.)

LUSTER   The brightness or brilliance of the coin's metal, the luster of a coin can vary considerably due to factors such as wear, polishing of dies or planchets, exposure to chemicals, humidity or temperature extremes.

MATTE PROOF   A proof given a uniformly granular or dull surface at the mint. The process used at the Philadelphia Mint from 1908–1917. (See Proof.)

MASTER DIE   The die which is used to produce several hubs, which in turn are used to make many working dies. The master die is never used to strike coins. (See Hub.)

MINT MARK   Usually a small letter, which indicates at which mint the coin was manufactured.

MINT STATE   A term denoting the condition of a coin which is free from any trace of wear. A mint state silver dollar may exhibit surface abrasions, be poorly struck, or exhibit varying degrees of toning. (See Brilliant Uncirculated, Uncirculated.)

NICKEL   U.S. nickel coin (1866–present). 1/20 of a dollar or five cents.

NUMISMATICS   The study of coins, and sometimes related items such as currency, tokens and medals.

NUMISMATIST   Technically, a student of numismatics, but more usually a professional coin dealer.

OBVERSE   The front or face of a coin; the side which portrays the principal design or device. Usually, the side which bears the bust of Liberty or a personage or the date.

ORIGINAL BAG   Descriptive of a sack of uncirculated coins, all of the same date, which were assembled at time of manufacture at a mint. There are twenty silver dollars to a roll and 1,000 to a bag.

OVERDATE   A coin whose date has been punched first with one date, and then with another, with the bottom date showing under the top one.

OVERGRADE   To assign the wrong grade to a coin, either by error, lack of knowledge, maliciousness, or with criminal intent.

OVERSTRIKE   A struck coin which is passed through the dies and has been struck again.

PATTERN   Proposed coin design which may or may not have been adopted. An experimental striking of a proposed design.

PLANCHET   The blank disc of metal upon which the dies are struck to produce a coin. (See Blank.)

PRESENTATION PIECES   Coins minted with unusual care from new dies on carefully selected blanks intended as gifts for VIPs on visits to the mint.

PROOF   A coin made from carefully selected coin blanks that have been highly polished, and dies that are also highly polished. The coins are hand-fed into a slow-moving press. This assures a well-struck, more even impression and makes the design more distinct. Each coin is struck twice or more. The finished coins have an almost mirror surface. (See Matte Proof.)

PROOF, BRANCH MINT   A proof coin which has been struck at a mint other than Philadelphia. For example, branch mint proofs are known to exist of the following dates of Morgan Dollars: 1879-O, 1883-O, 1893-CC, etc. . . .

PROOFLIKE   A coin which has been struck from a new die which leaves a mirror-like reflective surface upon the field and occasionally the devices of a coin. Prooflike coins are business strikes and therefore usually have abrasions. (See First Strike.)

PROOFLIKE, CAMEO   A prooflike coin in which the reflective mirror finish is confined to the fields of the coin. The devices will evidence the natural frost of silver thus producing a very striking contrast of the device from the field.

QUARTER DOLLAR   U.S. silver coin (1796–1964). 1/25 of a dollar or 25 cents. They are now made of cupro-nickel.

QUARTER EAGLE   U.S. gold coin (1796–1929). The $2.50 gold piece.

RARE   A coin of which only a small number exist. (See Scarce.)

RARITY SCALE   Estimate of the surviving population of a coin.

UNIQUE	One known
R-8	Estimated 2 or 3 known (Excessively Rare)

R-7 (High)	Estimated 4 to 6 known (Extremely Rare)
R-7 (Low)	Estimated 6 to 12 known (Very Rare)
R-6	Estimated 13 to 30 known (Rare)
R-5	Estimated 31 to 75 known
R-4	Estimated 76 to 200 known
R-3	Estimated 201 to 500 known
R-2	Estimated 501 to 1,250 known
R-1	Estimated over 1,250 known

RELIEF   Any part of a coin's design which is raised. (See High Relief, Low Relief.)

REPAIR   An area of a coin which has been worked on to fix a defect. Repairs must be mentioned in the description of the coin. (See Altered Date.)

REVERSE   The back of a coin. The side usually opposite from the portrait or date.

REPRODUCTION   A copy so marked as required by law with an "R" or "C." (See Copy.)

RIM NICK   Refers to an abrasion or cut into the rim or edge of a coin, usually through contact with another coin or coins (as in a bag of coins.)

ROLL   Original coins, assembled at the time of manufacture, usually by a bank and then placed into a paper tube. There are, for example, twenty Dollars in a roll.

SCARCE   A coin of which only a small number exist, but more common than rare. (See Rare.)

STELLA   Pattern Gold coin (1879–80). Four Dollar denomination.

STRIKE   The sharpness or lack of sharpness of design in a coin. A sharp strike, for example, is one in which all the detail shows on a coin.

THALER   Common name for various European dollar-sized silver coins, predecessors to the Dollar.

THREE-CENT NICKEL   U.S. nickel and silver coin (1865–89). Issued to retire three-cent fractional notes.

THREE-DOLLAR GOLD PIECE   U.S. gold coin (1854–1889).

TONING (PATINA)   Refers to the mellowed appearance upon the surface of a coin. Caused by the chemical combination of the metal in the coin with other elements over a long period of time due to place of storage or the sulphur from a paper envelope.

TWO-CENT PIECE   U.S. copper coin (1864–73).

TYPE   Major subdivision of a design within a particular denomination. A design change.

TYPE SET   A type set incorporates all coins sharing single specific characteristics. For example, an American gold type set features one example of each type of all gold coins issued by the U.S. Mint from 1795–1933.

UNCIRCULATED   A coin with no trace of wear. (See Brilliant Uncirculated, Mint State.)

VARIETY   See Die Variety.

WEAR   The removal of metal from a coin by its use in commerce.

WHIZZING   Any artificial process which removes metal from the surface of a coin to make it appear to be in better condition than it actually is. Most whizzed coins have an unnaturally shiny appearance due to abrasive action. Coins are also whizzed to remove or reduce unsightly abrasions or to mask the effects of adding or removing a mintmark or altering a date. A deception. Whizzing is now illegal.

WORKING DIE   Any die which is actually used to strike coins.

BASIC BIBLIOGRAPHY

AHWASH, Kamal, *Encyclopedia of United States Liberty Seated Dimes, 1837–1891.* Kaman Press, 1977.

AKERS, David W., *United States Gold Coins: An Analysis of Auction Records, One Dollar Gold through Double Eagles* (6 Vols.). Englewood, Ohio: Paramount Publications, 1975–1981.

AKERS, David W., *United States Gold Patterns.* Englewood, Ohio: Paramount Publications, 1975.

BAGG, Richard A. and J. J. Jelinski, *Grading Coins: A Collection of Readings.* Portsmouth, N.H.: Essex Publications, 1977.

BEISTLE, M. L., *A Register of Half Dollar Die Varieties and Subvarieties.* Shippensburg, PA.: The Beistle Company, 1929.

BOLENDER, M. H., *The U.S. Early Silver Dollars.* Omaha, Nebraska: Bebee's Inc., 1950.

BOWERS, David Q., *The History of United States Coinage: As Illustrated by The Garrett Collection.* Los Angeles, California: Bowers & Ruddy Galleries, Inc., 1979.

BOWERS, David Q., *U.S. Gold Coins: An Illustrated History.* Los Angeles, California: Bowers & Ruddy Galleries, Inc., 1982.

BOWERS, David Q., *Virgil Brand, The Man and His Era.* Wolfeboro, N.H.: Bowers and Merena, 1984.

BREEN, Walter and A. Swiatek, *Encyclopedia of Silver and Gold Commemorative Coins.* New York, N.Y.: F.C.I. Press, Inc./Arco Publishing, Inc., 1981.

BREEN, Walter, *Major Varieties of U.S. Gold Dollars Through Eagles.* (5 Vols.) Chicago, Illinois: Hewitt Bros., 1964.

BREEN, Walter, *Walter Breen's Encyclopedia of United States and Colonial Proof Coins.* Albertson, N.Y.: F.C.I. Press, Inc., 1977.

BREEN, Walter, *Walter Breen's Encyclopedia of United States Half Cents, 1793–1857.* South Gate, California: American Institute of Numismatic Research, 1984.

BROWNING, A. W., *Early Quarter Dollars of the United States, 1796–1838,* New York, N.Y., 1925. Reprinted 1962.

CLAIN-STEFANELLI, E., *Select Numismatic Bibliography.* New York, N.Y.: Stack's, 1965.

CROSBY, Sylvester S., *The Early Coins of America.* New York, N.Y.: Quarterman Publications, 1983. (Copy of 1875 Edition.)

CROSBY, Sylvester S., *United States Coinage of 1793, Cents and Half Cents.* 1897. Reprinted 1962.

DOTY, Richard. *The Macmillian Encyclopedic Dictionary of Numismatics.* New York, N.Y.: Macmillian Publishing Co., 1976.

FRIEDBERG, R., *Gold Coins of the World,* various editions. New York, N.Y.: The Coin and Currency Institute, Inc., 1958 to date.

FRIEDBERG, R. *Paper Money of the United States,* various editions. New York, N.Y.: The Coin and Currency Institute, Inc. 1953 to date.

GANZ, D. L., *The World of Coins and Coin Collecting.* New York, N.Y.: Charles Scribner & Sons, 1980.

GILBERT, Ebenezer, *The U.S. Half Cents from 1793 to 1857.* New York, N.Y.: The Elder Numismatic Press, 1916.

HARRIS, Robert F., *Gold Coins of the Americas.* Iola, Wisconsin: Anco Publications, 1971.

HASELTINE, John W., *Type Table of United States Dollars, Half Dollars, and Quarters.* Philadelphia, 1881. Reprint: by B. Max Mehl, Ft. Worth, Texas, 1927.

JUDD, J. Hewitt, *United States Pattern, Experimental and Trial Pieces,* 7th Ed. Racine, Wisconsin: Western Publishing Company, Inc., 1982.

KAGIN, Donald, *Private Gold Coins and Patterns of the United States.* New York, N.Y.: Arco Publishing, 1981.

MILLER, Wayne, *Analysis of Morgan and Peace Dollars.* Helena, Montana: Adam Smith Publishing Co., 1976.

NEWCOMB, Howard, *U.S. Copper Cents, 1816–1857.* New York, N.Y.: Stack's, 1944.

NEWMAN, Eric P. and K. Bressett, *The Fantastic 1804 Silver Dollar.* Racine, Wisconsin: Whitman Publishing Co., 1962.

OVERTON, Al C., *Early Half Dollar Varieties.* Colorado Springs, Colorado: Al C. Overton, 1964, reprinted 1980.

RAYMOND, Wayte, *Standard Catalogue of United States Coins.* New York, N.Y.: Wayte Raymond, Inc., 1936–1957.

SCHILKE, Oscar and R. Solomon, *America's Foreign Coins.* New York, N.Y.: The Coin and Currency Institute, Inc., 1964.

SHELDON, William H., *Penny Whimsy.* New York, N.Y.: Harper Bros., 1958.

STACK, Norman, *United States Type Coins.* New York, N.Y.: Stack's 1977.

TAXAY, Don, *The U.S. Mint and Coinage.* New York, N.Y.: Arco Publishing Co., 1966, reprinted 1983.

TAXAY, Don, *Counterfeit, Mis-struck and Unofficial U.S. Coins.* New York, N.Y.: Arco Publishing Co., 1963.

TAXAY, Don, *The Catalogue and Encyclopedia of U.S. Coins.* New York, N.Y.: Scott Publishing Co., 1976.

VALENTINE, Daniel W., *United States Half Dimes.* Lawrence, Massachusetts: Quarterman Publications, 1975 (reprint of 1931 edition).

YEOMAN, R. S., *A Guide Book of United States Coins.* Racine, Wisconsin: Western Publishing Company, Inc., published annually, 1948 to date.